Dear Dad,

Thanks for all of the love & support.

Love Tom xxx

Making Miracles in Medieval England

The cult of the saints was central to medieval Christianity largely due to the miraculous. Saints were members of the elect of heaven and could intercede with God on behalf of supplicants. Whilst people visited shrines and prayed to the saints for many reasons, it was the hope of intercession and the praise of miracles past which drove the cult of the saints.

This book examines how a person solicited aid from a saint, how they might give thanks and the ways in which post-mortem miracles structured the cult of the saints. A huge number of miracle stories survive from medieval England, in dedicated collections as well as in saints' lives and other source material. This corpus is full of stories of human relationships, vulnerability and deliverance of people from all parts of society. These stories reveal all manner of details about ordinary people in extraordinary circumstances. They also show us how people navigated the world with the aid of the saints. Saints could help with wayward livestock, lost property or lawsuits as well as fire, plague and injury. They could also protect members of their communities, correct lapses by their custodians and even kill those who mistreated them. A respectful relationship with a saint could be proof against any problem.

Making Miracles in Medieval England will appeal to all those interested in religious practices in medieval England, medieval English culture and medieval perceptions of miracles.

Tom Lynch studied at University College London, Royal Holloway and the University of Cambridge. He now works at the British Library and is interested in the interdisciplinary study of societies past and present.

Studies in Medieval History and Culture

Recent Titles Include

People, Power and Identity in the Late Middle Ages
Essays in Memory of W. Mark Ormrod
Edited by Gwilym Dodd, Helen Lacey and Anthony Musson

The Experience of Neighbourhood in Medieval and Early Modern Europe
Edited by Bronach C. Kane and Simon Sandall

The Myths and Realities of the Viking *berserkr*
Roderick Dale

The Others, Identity, and Memory in Early Medieval Italy
Luigi Andrea Berto

Women and Violence in the Late Medieval Mediterranean, ca. 1100–1500
Edited by Lidia L. Zanetti Domingues, Lorenzo Caravaggi, and Giulia M. Paoletti

Albertino Mussato: The Making of a Poet Laureate
A Political and Intellectual Portrait
Aislinn McCabe

Authorship, Worldview, and Identity in Medieval Europe
Edited by Christian Raffensperger

Marian Devotion in the Late Middle Ages
Image and Performance
Edited by Gerhard Jaritz and Andrea-Bianka Znorovszky

Food Consumption in Medieval Iberia
A Socio-economic Analysis, 13th–15th Centuries
Juan Vicente García Marsilla

Fragmented Nature: Conceptions of the Natural Order in the European Middle Ages
Edited by Mattia Cipriani and Nicola Polloni

Adam of Bremen's Gesta Hammaburgensis Ecclesiae Pontificum
Origins, Reception and Significance
Edited by Grzegorz Bartusik, Radosław Biskup and Jakub Morawiec

Making Miracles in Medieval England
Tom Lynch

For more information about this series, please visit: www.routledge.com/Studies-in-Medieval-History-and-Culture/book-series/SMHC

Making Miracles in Medieval England

Tom Lynch

Taylor & Francis Group

LONDON AND NEW YORK

First published 2023
by Routledge
4 Park Square, Milton Park, Abingdon, Oxon OX14 4RN

and by Routledge
605 Third Avenue, New York, NY 10158

Routledge is an imprint of the Taylor & Francis Group, an informa business

© 2023 Tom Lynch

The right of Tom Lynch to be identified as author of this work has been asserted in accordance with sections 77 and 78 of the Copyright, Designs and Patents Act 1988.

All rights reserved. No part of this book may be reprinted or reproduced or utilised in any form or by any electronic, mechanical, or other means, now known or hereafter invented, including photocopying and recording, or in any information storage or retrieval system, without permission in writing from the publishers.

Trademark notice: Product or corporate names may be trademarks or registered trademarks, and are used only for identification and explanation without intent to infringe.

British Library Cataloguing-in-Publication Data
A catalogue record for this book is available from the British Library

Library of Congress Cataloging-in-Publication Data
A catalog record has been requested for this book

ISBN: 978-1-032-07161-9 (hbk)
ISBN: 978-1-032-07162-6 (pbk)
ISBN: 978-1-003-20569-2 (ebk)

DOI: 10.4324/9781003205692

Typeset in Times New Roman
by Apex CoVantage, LLC

Contents

Acknowledgements vi
List of Abbreviations vii

Introduction 1
1   Writing Miracles 15
2   Making Shrines 35
3   Petitioning the Saints 65
4   Retribution and Reconciliation 86
5   Giving Thanks for Miracles 110
6   Conclusions 123

Appendix I Saints in the Liturgy 131
Bibliography 139
Index 152

Acknowledgements

Thanks to everyone who has ever spoken with me about the saints.

Tom Lynch
St Valentine's Day
2022

Abbreviations

Liber Eliensis = *Liber Eliensis*, ed. by E. O. Blake, Camden Third Series, 92 (London: Royal Historical Society, 1962)

Miracula S. Ætheldrethe = Anonymous *Miracula S. Ætheldrethe*, in Goscelin of Saint-Bertin, *The Hagiography of the Female Saints of Ely*, ed. and trans. by Rosalind C. Love (Oxford: Clarendon, 2004), pp. 95–131

Miracula S. Bege = Anonymous *Vita et miracula S. Bege*, in James Wilson, ed., *The Register of the Priory of St Bees*, Publications of the Surtees Society, 126 (Durham: Surtees Society, 1915), pp. 497–520

Miracula S. Guthlaci = Anonymous *Translatio et miracula S. Guthlaci*, in *Acta Sanctorum*, Aprilis, II, 54–60

Miracula S. Ithamari = Anonymous *Miracula S. Ithamari*, in D. Bethell, ed., 'The Miracles of St Ithamar', *Analecta Bollandiana*, 89 (1971), 421–37

Miracula S. Mylburge = Anonymous *Miracula Inventionis Beate Mylburge Virginis*, in Paul Antony Hayward, ed., 'The *Miracula Inventionis Beate Mylburge Virginis* Attributed to the Lord Ato, Cardinal Bishop of Ostia', *English Historical Review*, 114 (1999), 543–73

Miracula S. Oswini = Anonymous *Vita, inventio et miracula S. Oswini, regis Deirorum*, in James Raine, ed., *Miscellanea Biographica: Oswinus, Rex Northumbriae, Cuthbertus, Episcopus Lindisfariensis, Eata, Episcopus Haugustaldensis*, Publications of the Surtees Society, 8 (London: Nichols, 1838), pp. 1–59

Miracula S. Swithuni = Anonymous *Miracula S. Swithuni*, in Michael Lapidge, ed. and trans., *The Cult of St Swithun*, Winchester Studies, 4.II (Oxford: Clarendon, 2003), pp. 647–97

Miracula S. Yuonis = Anonymous *Miracula S. Yuonis*, in W. D. Macray, ed., *Chronicon Abbatiae Rameseiensis*, Rolls Series, 83 (London: Longman, 1886), pp. lxxv–lxxxiv

Passio S. Edwardi = Anonymous *Passio S. Edwardi regis et martyris*, in Christine E. Fell, ed., *Edward, King and Martyr* (Leeds: University of Leeds, 1971)

Vita S. Birini = Anonymous *Vita S. Birini*, in Rosalind C. Love, ed. and trans., *Three Eleventh-Century Saints' Lives: Vita S. Birini, Vita et Miracula S. Kenelmi, and Vita S. Rumwoldi* (Oxford: Clarendon, 1996), pp. 2–47

Vita S. Rumwoldi = Anonymous *Vita S. Rumwoldi*, in Rosalind C. Love, ed. and trans., *Three Eleventh-Century Saints' Lives: Vita S. Birini, Vita et Miracula S. Kenelmi, and Vita S. Rumwoldi* (Oxford: Clarendon, 1996), pp. 92–114.

Vita Sexburge = Anonymous *Vita Beate Sexburge Regine*, in Goscelin of Saint-Bertin, *The Hagiography of the Female Saints of Ely*, ed. and trans. by Rosalind C. Love (Oxford: Clarendon, 2004), pp. 133–89

Abbo, *Passio S. Eadmundi* = *Passio S. Eadmundi*, in Michael Winterbottom, ed., *Three Lives of English Saints* (Toronto: Pontifical Institute of Mediaeval Studies for the Centre for Medieval Studies, 1972), pp. 67–87

Aelred, *De sanctis Hagustaldensis* = *De sanctis ecclesiae Hagustaldensis*, in James Raine, ed., *The Priory of Hexham*, Publications of the Surtees Society, 44 & 46, 2 vols (Durham: Andrews, 1864–1865), I, 173–203

Arcoid, *Miracula S. Erkenwaldi* = *Miracula S. Erkenwaldi*, in E. Gordon Whatley, ed. and trans., *The Saint of London: The Life and Miracles of St Erkenwald*, Medieval & Renaissance Texts & Studies, 58 (Binghamton, NY: Medieval & Renaissance Texts & Studies, 1989), pp. 100–65

Bede, *HE* = *Bede's Ecclesiastical History of the English People*, ed. and trans. by Bertram Colgrave and R. A. B. Mynors (Oxford: Oxford University Press, 1969)

Byrhtferth, *Vita S. Ecgwini* = *Vita S. Ecgwini*, in Byrhtferth of Ramsey, *The Lives of St Oswald and St Ecgwine*, ed. and trans. by Michael Lapidge (Oxford: Clarendon, 2009), pp. 205–303

Byrhtferth, *Vita S. Oswaldi* = *Vita S. Oswaldi*, in Byrhtferth of Ramsey, *The Lives of St Oswald and St Ecgwine*, ed. and trans. by Michael Lapidge (Oxford: Clarendon, 2009), pp. 1–203

Dominic, *Miracula S. Ecgwini* = *Miracula S. Ecgwini*, in Thomas of Marlborough, *History of the Abbey of Evesham*, ed. and trans. by Jane Sayers and Leslie Watkiss (Oxford: Clarendon, 2003), pp. 84–125

Eadmer, *Miracula S. Dunstani* = *Vita et miracula S. Dunstani*, in Eadmer of Canterbury, *Lives and Miracles of Saints Oda, Dunstan, and Oswald*, ed. and trans. by Andrew J. Turner and Bernard J. Muir (Oxford: Clarendon, 2006), pp. 41–212

Eadmer, *Miracula S. Oswaldi* = *Vita et miracula S. Oswaldi archiepiscopi*, in Eadmer of Canterbury, *Lives and Miracles of Saints Oda, Dunstan, and Oswald*, ed. and trans. by Andrew J. Turner and Bernard J. Muir (Oxford: Clarendon, 2006), pp. 213–323

Eadmer, *Vita S. Anselmi* = *Vita S. Anselmi*, in Eadmer of Canterbury, *The Life of St Anselm*, ed. and trans. by R. W. Southern (Oxford: Clarendon, 1962)

Geoffrey, *Miracula S. Modwenne* = *Vita et miracula S. Modwenne*, in Geoffrey of Burton, *Life and Miracles of St Modwenna*, ed. and trans by Robert Bartlett (Oxford: Clarendon, 2002)

Goscelin, *Miracula S. Edmundi* = *Miracula S. Edmundi*, in Herman the Archdeacon and Goscelin of Saint-Bertin, *The Miracles of St Edmund*, ed. and trans. by Tom Licence with Lynda Lockyer (Oxford: Clarendon, 2014), pp. 127–304

Goscelin, *Miracula S. Kenelmi* = *Vita et miracula S. Kenelmi*, in Rosalind C. Love, ed. and trans., *Three Eleventh-Century Saints' Lives: Vita S. Birini, Vita et Miracula S. Kenelmi, and Vita S. Rumwoldi* (Oxford: Clarendon, 1996), pp. 49–89

Goscelin, *Miracula S. Mildrethe* = *Translatio et miracula S. Mildrethe*, in David Rollason, ed., 'Goscelin of Canterbury's Account of the Translation and Miracles of St Mildrith: An Edition with Notes', *Mediaeval Studies*, 48 (1986), 139–210

Goscelin, *Miracula S. Yuonis* = *Miracula S. Yuonis*, in W. D. Macray, ed., *Chronicon Abbatiae Rameseiensis*, Rolls Series, 83 (London: Longman, 1886), pp. lix–lxxv

Goscelin, *Miraculis S. Augustini* = *Historia maior de miraculis S. Augustini*, in *Acta Sanctorum*, Maii VI, 397–411

Goscelin, *Translatione S. Ethelburge* = *De translatione uel eleuatione SS. Uirginum Ethelburge, Hildelithe ac Wlfhilde*, in Marvin L. Colker, 'Texts of Jocelyn of Canterbury Which Relate to the History of Barking Abbey', *Studia Monastica*, 7 (1965), 383–460 (pp. 435–52)

Goscelin, *Translationis S. Augustini* = *Historia translationis S. Augustini et aliorum sanctorum*, in *Acta Sanctorum*, Maii VI, 411–43

Goscelin, *Virtutibus S. Adriani* = *De Adventu, Translatione et Virtutibus S. Adriani*, in London, British Library, Cotton, Vespasian B.xx, fols 233^r–48^v and London, British Library, Harley 105, fols 205^r–18^v

Goscelin, *Vita S. Edithe* = *Vita S. Edithe*, in A. Wilmart, ed., 'La légend de Ste Édith en Prose et Vers par le Moine Goscelin', *Analecta Bollandiana*, 56 (1938), 5–101, 265–307

Goscelin, *Vita S. Ethelburge* = *Vita et uirtutes S. Ethelburge*, in Marvin L. Colker, 'Texts of Jocelyn of Canterbury Which Relate to the History of Barking Abbey', *Studia Monastica*, 7 (1965), 383–460

Goscelin, *Vita S. Mildrethe* = *Vita S. Mildrethe uirginis*, in David Rollason, *The Mildrith Legend: A Study in Early Medieval Hagiography in England* (Leicester: Leicestershire University Press, 1982), pp. 108–43

Goscelin, *Vita S. Vulfhilde* = *Vita et uirtutes S. Vulfhilde*, in Marvin L. Colker, 'Texts of Jocelyn of Canterbury Which Relate to the History of Barking Abbey', *Studia Monastica*, 7 (1965), 383–460 (pp. 418–34)

Goscelin, *Vita S. Werburge* = *Vita S. Werburge*, in Goscelin of Saint-Bertin, *The Hagiography of the Female Saints of Ely*, ed. and trans. by Rosalind C. Love (Oxford: Clarendon, 2004), pp. 25–51

Goscelin, *Vita S. Wihtburge* = *Vita S. Wihtburge*, in Goscelin of Saint-Bertin, *The Hagiography of the Female Saints of Ely*, ed. and trans. by Rosalind C. Love (Oxford: Clarendon, 2004), pp. 53–93

Goscelin, *Vita S. Wlsini* = *Vita S. Wlsini*, in C. H. Talbot, ed., 'The Life of St Wulsin of Sherborne by Goscelin', *Revue Bénédictine*, 49 (1959), 68–85

Herman, *Miracula S. Edmundi* = *Liber de miraculis S. Edmundi*, in Herman the Archdeacon and Goscelin of Saint-Bertin, *The Miracles of St Edmund*, ed.

and trans. by Tom Licence with Lynda Lockyer (Oxford: Clarendon, 2014), pp. 1–126, 337–49

Lantfred, *Miracula S. Swithuni* = *Translatio et Miracula S. Swithuni*, in Michael Lapidge, ed. and trans., *The Cult of St Swithun*, Winchester Studies, 4.II (Oxford: Clarendon, 2003), pp. 251–333

Osbern, *Miracula S. Dunstani* = *Vita et Miracula S. Dunstani*, in William Stubbs, ed., *The Memorials of St Dunstan*, Rolls Series, 63 (London: Longman, 1874), 69–161

Robert, *Translatio S. Wenefrede* = *Vita et translatio S. Wenefrede*, in *Acta Sanctorum*, Novembris, I, 708–31

William Ketell, *Miracula S. Johannis* = *Miracula S. Johannis*, in James Raine, ed., *The Historians of the Church of York and its Archbishops*, Rolls Series, 71, 3 vols (London: Longman, 1879–1894), I, 261–91

Wulfstan, *Narratio de S. Swithuno* = *Narratio metrica de S. Swithuno*, in Michael Lapidge, ed. and trans., *The Cult of St Swithun*, Winchester Studies, 4.II (Oxford: Clarendon, 2003), pp. 371–551

Wulfstan, *Vita S. Æthelwoldi* = *Vita S. Æthelwoldi*, in Wulfstan of Winchester, *The Life of St Æthelwold*, ed. and trans. by Michael Lapidge and Michael Winterbottom (Oxford: Clarendon, 1991)

Introduction

Tom Lynch

Dominic of Evesham records a miracle story from the mid eleventh century, approximately one hundred years before he composed his *Miracula S. Ecgwini*. A man from Kent who was born mute had gone on a pilgrimage to Rome in hope of a cure. He stayed there for three years, praying and waiting for the saints to aid him. One night, as he was beginning to despair, a figure dressed in white approached the man and told him to return to his country, specifically to the monastery of St Ecgwine at Evesham. The figure said that if the man went to visit Ecgwine with an offering and then prayed to the saint, he would be cured. He then left for Evesham, and with the help of God, he reached his destination. When the man arrived, the scene was one of solemn observance. It is worth quoting Dominic in full for the remainder of the story:

> Therefore, all the brethren were standing in the choir, when the man arrived carrying a candle in his hand as vespers was being sung: advancing before the altar he prayed for a long time and then offered his candle. Having made this offering he again stood in prayer. Then, a wonderful and amazing thing happened! As the dumb man was standing before them all, suddenly he fell, and began to cough up a stream of blood, and, through extreme distress, thrash around in all directions on the floor. Evening prayer being over, Æfic, prior of the place at that time, came over with certain older monks to where the man was lying and coughing; they asked what was the matter, and why he was lying there in this way coughing blood. Rising in the midst of the brethren, and raising his eyes and his hands to God, his tongue was finally loosed, and he began to make his first utterance: 'May almighty God help me as may my lord St Ecgwine, by whose merit Christ has wrought such a miracle in one so wretched as I, that I might tell you the truth.' Starting with his prayer, he revealed the whole story in detail, as has been recounted above. When his story was ended, the brethren were overjoyed, the people were also summoned, their mouths were opened in loud praises of God, beginning with the 'Te Deum Laudamus'; they rang the bells for a long time, extolling as sweetly as they could the miracles of God, who is God blessed above all things.[1]

I have chosen to begin the book with this vignette as it is representative of the subject in question, making miracles in medieval England. A person with a problem came to know of a saint, brought his problem to the saint and was cured. The story of the mute man is full of incidental details which help to show us how miracles were reported and investigated, promulgated amongst the people and celebrated on a grand scale. The narrative shows the use of material offerings, the credence given to visions and the ability of one saint to help where others had not. In addition, we have an example of the religious of a monastery performing their daily work and interacting with a particularly gruesome cure. The whole process involved the saint, the supplicant, the custodians of the shrine and the people of Evesham. In short, the whole community of the saint took part. We are presented with this unified community all contributing to the fostering of this miracle and, more generally, the cult. But there remains the potential for disruption presented by this man walking in on the monks performing vespers and then falling into a bloody seizure. Whilst the basic structure of a shrine cure was simple, a miracle story can also demonstrate the complexities and tensions underlying the cult of the saints.

The post-mortem miracles performed by the saints were central to the workings of their cults. Miracles were the main driver of pilgrimage, they provided a community with aid, they demonstrated the saint's place amongst the elect of Heaven, they showed the saint's will manifest on Earth and they provided an opportunity for storytelling, preaching and writing. In a sense miracles, made the cult of the saints,[2] but the question remains: how were these miracles made? This book is in part an attempt to answer this question. Miracles were not just down to the saints. Miracles required a subject, a person who was directly impacted by the intercession of the saint and who usually played an active role in bringing the miracle about. In order to be recorded and disseminated, a miracle needed to be recognised as such. This responsibility fell to the custodians of a saint's shrine or their proxies and was key to framing miracles. The custodians moderated not only the shrine but also the written record. The records of the cults which survive are selective, and composers of miracle accounts omitted much information. However, the sources include a great deal of useful material, intended and unintended by the authors.

Examining the petitioning of miracles allows us to explore the cult of the saints in medieval England not just as a means by which to enter reciprocal relationships but also as a field of contest. Cults could be essential to the survival of a religious house, but they could be disruptive to the religious life. Not everyone engaged with saints in a way which met with approval. Saints, supplicants and custodians had expectations which were not always met. In miracle stories, we get a view of these expectations in action, and these stories show us how miracles were made in the middle ages. I contend that the actions of the community of a saint were at the heart of the miracle-making process, and the most important of these actions was the petition. Petitions followed a basic structure and gave an active role to supplicants, allowing them a means to overcome life crises. In addition, a successful petition allowed a supplicant to demonstrate their close relationship to a saint and their ability to behave appropriately. Meaningful action was not limited to petitions, however. In the miracles of vengeance, it was often the misbehaviour of people which initiated the intervention of a saint. Here the perpetrators filled the role of the supplicants in a manner which fits with the structure of a miracle petition. No matter what the miracle, it seems the deliberate actions of human beings were the most common cause. Before proceeding to a summary of the chapters which make up this book, it will be useful to examine a few key concepts more closely, beginning with miracles.

Scholarly definitions of the miraculous in medieval Christianity were indebted to the work of Augustine of Hippo and his emphasis on the wonder of miracles.[3] Scholastic developments in the eleventh and twelfth centuries sought to build on Augustine's corpus and looked to define miracles as causally different from the everyday wonder of creation.[4] This notion is expressed by Peter Lombard, who stated that normally things acted according to nature, based on how God had created them. Miracles were special because they acted in a manner which was beyond nature (*praeter naturam*) and their causes were known to God alone.[5] Miracles can be found in Christian texts from the Bible onwards. The miracles of Jesus and the apostles were the model for saintly miracles, although the biblical miracles were usually performed by a living person with no reference to relics in the medieval sense.[6] By the time of Swithun's first miracles in the late tenth century, the idea that post-mortem miracles could be performed by saints in England was well established. The earliest evidence of post-mortem miracles in medieval England comes from the wave of hagiography which was composed in the first half of the eighth century. This includes the lives of Cuthbert, Guthlac and Wilfrid.[7] Miracles were present in other kinds of texts from this period as well. Bede includes some fifty-one miracles in the *Ecclesiastical History of the English People*, whilst hinting at the existence of more stories which could have been included but were not.[8]

What miracles meant to those who collected them is harder to uncover. There is a tendency, continuing in the tradition of Augustine, to marvel at the power of God in his saints. This is well phrased by Eadmer, who proclaimed in his miracles of Oswald, 'How wonderful is the love of God and how wondrous his awesome power!'[9] Eadmer is not alone in his amazement at the miraculous; such reactions are found throughout our period.[10] Geoffrey of Burton noted that Modwenna announced her presence in Heaven through her miracles.[11] Lantfred posited that the abundance of miracles solicited by Swithun was a means for God to lead those behaving inappropriately to 'hasten towards heavenly joys with their good works'.[12] For supplicants it is harder still to uncover what miracles meant. Miracles showed that the saint in question was powerful, and by extension the saint's custodians were powerful. Miracles would have been a cause for joy or despair, depending on the nature of the intercession. Miracles may also have indicated personal moral worth, with only the just receiving intercession.[13] What is clearer is what miracles did. Simply put, they solved problems which had been brought to a saint's attention. Whilst the majority of these miracles were beneficent a significant proportion punished negative actions. Either way, the saint could do almost anything: including controlling the weather, healing the sick, protecting their supplicants from disasters, freeing prisoners, exorcising the possessed and killing perpetrators. They could also withhold miracles, send supplicants to other saints and reverse miraculous cures. All of this was within the structure of the cult of the saints. It would be helpful to explore the history and understanding of the cult of the saints before moving on.

The cult of the saints was found throughout medieval Europe, but early medieval saints were not subject to rigorous definition. Instead, these holy people existed in a vague system and were subject to vague terminology.[14] The process of canonisation did not begin to be centrally controlled by the papacy until the twelfth century, so all the saints venerated in England during our period were saints primarily because of devotion accorded them rather than proclamation from Rome.[15] Jones has written a list including the 'expected components' of the medieval cult of the saints. These expected components are 'physical presence and perceived effect', 'celebration of the saint and the saint's doings', 'engagement and enacted supplication' and 'further commemoration in the church, the wider world and society at large'.[16] The most tangible result of these components was the attention paid to the bodies, tombs and shrines of the saints.[17]

Cults had developed by the second century at the tombs of the martyrs.[18] These early tomb cults consisted mainly of the celebration of Mass on the anniversary of the martyr's death and were necessarily small scale and clandestine prior to the Edict of Milan in 313.[19] The focus on the tomb of the saint was established in Western Europe by the sixth century, based on the idea that Heaven and Earth met at the grave of a holy individual.[20] This was tied to the concept of a saint as a human being, present both in their tomb and in Heaven, who could intercede with God on their devotees' behalf and who was best reached through proximity to their earthly remains or relics associated with them.[21] The conviction that saints listened to prayers, were in a special position to intercede with God and were particularly accessible at their relics 'was one of the dominant themes' of medieval Christianity.[22]

The cult of the saints was established in England following the mission of Augustine in 597. Bede portrayed the influence of the saints and the promise of miracles as integral to the conversion of King Æthelberht of Kent (c. 585–616), and relics were sent along with other religious supplies by Pope Gregory the Great (590–604) to Augustine.[23] Cults to local saints began to develop in the late seventh century.[24] Whilst there is hagiography and other evidence in Latin and Old English from the eighth century onwards, this study will focus on the central middle ages running from around 970 until 1170. This start date allows us to take in the results of the tenth-century monastic reforms and coincides with the first Anglo-Latin miracle collection, Lantfred's late-tenth-century *Translatio et Miracula S. Swithuni*. Finishing in 1170 allows us to consider the upheavals of the Conquest and the Anarchy as well as one of the most productive periods of miracle recording before the unrivalled 'hagiographical aftermath' of the death, miracles and canonisation of Thomas Becket.[25] Becket's death was shortly followed by a letter from Pope Alexander III (1159–1181), which included the proclamation that saints were to be canonised only by papal authority.[26] Despite the fact that saints continued to be venerated regardless of their canonisation status, 1170 stands as a watershed in the centralisation of saint making. Therefore, 1170 is a suitable end point for this study, on the eve of Becket's murder and the changes which coincided with his death. The England in the title of this book should be self-explanatory, but it is worth noting that I have designated saints as 'English' if their main shrine was in England, no matter where the saint was born or spent their career. In practice this designation applies mainly to early British and Irish figures, members of the Augustinian mission and a few Continental imports.

In his foundational work on the cult of the saints in medieval England, Ronald Finucane noted that whilst people must have visited the saints for many reasons, the sources suggest that miracles were the most common motivation. Miracles begat more pilgrims and more miracles, and miracle collections are our major source on the workings of the cult of the saints.[27] Miracle collections are one type of hagiography, a genre of text concerned with the life, death and miracles of the saints.[28] All hagiography is based on the 'historical claim' that an individual existed,[29] but it is not a work of history or biography in the modern sense. Hagiographic texts are works that are consciously, and sometimes explicitly, imitative. Earlier examples of sanctity provide ideals of behaviour that situate the subject of hagiography within the ranks of the sacred. These exemplars could include biblical figures, the Church fathers, earlier saints and Christ himself.[30]

Much early scholarship on hagiography focused on 'weakly individualized' saints in a setting where time and place were unimportant, a thin veil on which to imprint the universalising messages of the Church.[31] Hagiography has been regarded as a 'notoriously problematic' source, which can spur attempts to separate the historical 'fact' from the derivative 'fiction'. Such a separation is neither practical nor desirable, however.[32] Hagiography provides us with some of the best evidence for the lives of medieval people and their relationships with the saints.[33] But what can be gleaned from hagiography is driven by the concerns of the authors and their understanding of the genre, and this does not always line up with the concerns of the historian.[34] Hagiographers did not pick up every miracle performed or even cover every cult which was popular at the time. Miracle collecting in medieval England was not rare, but it was still a specialist interest that 'waxed and waned in tune to its own rhythms and the enthusiasms of individuals'.[35] Despite the wealth of detail contained in the evidence, hagiography is not 'a transparent window into the everyday life' of supplicants and communities.[36] This is partly because our authors had their own preoccupations and were participants in the cult of the saints, who sought the glorification of their saint, of the saint's home and of their community.[37] It is also partly because what is recorded is not the quotidian but the occasional in terms of major events, great ceremonial set pieces, life crises of supplicants and the miraculous responses of the saints.

All of this is not to say that hagiography should be avoided as a historical source, just that the genre conventions and editorial power employed by the authors should be considered.[38] Hagiography 'if handled with care may yield a great deal of information'.[39] We have presentations by monks and clerics of how a system should work,[40] what might be termed the 'ideal types' of the cult of the saints,[41] which are useful in themselves. At the same time, there is a degree of information which comes through 'behind the direct indications of the texts'.[42] The hagiographers were not impartial observers but participants embroiled in the same cultural system as the laity and the rest of the community.[43] Hagiographers chose their content, selected texts to imitate and stories to pick up or to leave unwritten, but they had to conform to social reality as well as genre expectations in order to be understood and accepted by their audience.[44] Even where hagiography is explicitly imitative, it does not necessarily mean that the incidents described did not happen in some form.[45] Thus, in spite of the 'idealizing features of the genre, we can glimpse a recognizable social reality behind these miraculous cures'.[46] We can examine the communities around specific cults, the practices of the participants and 'the circumstances of a particular miracle'.[47]

The cult of the saints has been subject to a great deal of academic attention. Since the 1960s, there has been an increased focus on the communities of the saints rather than the saints as individuals. This is reflected in the utilisation of other forms of hagiography over *vitae* and a recognition of the importance of the collective records surrounding individual cults.[48] One of the most influential authors in this new wave was Peter Brown.[49] Brown's work can be seen as a reaction to the sceptical view of the cult of the saints as expressed by Gibbon, who saw the rise of the cult as a feature of the decline of the Roman Empire.[50] Brown brought in insights from the social sciences and made the use of hagiographical sources 'respectable to a generation of historians'.[51] Brown presented the cult of the saints as integral to late-antique and medieval Christianity, a part of the 'religious common sense of the age'.[52] Part of this 'common sense' was the experience of 'new forms of the exercise of power, new bonds of human dependence, new, intimate, hopes for protection and justice in a changing world'.[53] Brown looked to emphasise the function of the cult of the saints as a means of flattening out the divisions of society in a patron-client system based around 'ties of interdependence and reciprocity'.[54]

Following Brown, many scholars have focused on the social and cultural history of the cult of the saints. Ronald Finucane and Pierre-André Sigal both produced wide-ranging statistical analyses of the cult of the saints in England and France, respectively.[55] Both of these studies look to reveal trends from the cult of the saints by extracting data from a large amount of evidence. This leads to a focus on numbers rather than individual cults, hagiographers or miracle accounts. The work of Ridyard, Rollason and Yarrow maintains a broad scope whilst focusing more on the specifics of individual cults in England. Ridyard's study of the royal cults of pre-Conquest England explores the development and continuity of those cults. Ridyard concludes that these cults, whilst perhaps popular, were only possible through the efforts of their custodians, particularly through the advertisement of hagiography. According to Ridyard, these cults were driven by the political and parochial concerns of the saints' custodians and were ultimately able to survive the Conquest due to the saints' role as monastic patrons.[56] Rollason similarly privileges the role of the religious and lay elite in his study of English relic cults. He divides the cult of the saints into two stages, before and after 850, with the earlier stage dominated by the clergy and the later more open to the laity following the monastic reforms. Like Ridyard, Rollason points out the continuity of cults after the Conquest and emphasises the useful role saints could play as moral authorities and 'undying landlords'.[57] Yarrow's work uses six cults as examples of the cult of the saints in the twelfth century. His focus is on the communal nature of the cult of the saints, the forms of behaviour and the 'ritual significance' of a cure.[58] More recently there has been a turn in studies to focus on the development, recitation and recording of miracle stories, as presented by Koopmans.[59] Here the stories told by supplicants are presented as the central feature of the cult of the saints, a great foundation of 'personal stories' from which hagiographers took a selection to record.[60] Whilst this focus maintains the important position of the custodians of a saint, it also allows for any supplicant to contribute to the cult of a saint and its interpretation.

Like Brown and many other historians of the cult of the saints, I have taken influence from the social sciences. My understanding of reciprocity and social relations is based upon the work of Mauss as well as that of his critics, particularly Graeber.[61] The work of Mauss is behind my conception of education and change in a social system, too, and so is the work of Bourdieu.[62] In terms of the shrine as a liminal space which is presented as harmonious, I heavily reference Turner.[63] In addition, I have incorporated a selection of ethnographic studies which critique Turner's view for a more nuanced approach to the supposed social cohesion of shrines. My comprehension of structure, contingency and agency is indebted to the writing of Sahlins on the interaction between European explorers and the peoples of the Pacific Islands.[64] Sahlins' conception of the 'structure of the conjuncture', the interaction between social structures and events,[65] has been helpful in shaping my ideas about the flexibility of the cult of the saints and the agency of its participants. These ethnographic and theoretical studies help to show the possibilities for how the cult of the saints could function in practice, how a cult might be understood by its participants and how social structures and the actions of people are informed by one another.

This book takes inspiration from all of the previously mentioned authors and many others on the subject of the cult of the saints. Three main points differentiate this book from previous work in the field. Firstly, my time frame and selection of texts: no major study I have read takes into account the primary sources that I do here, including all the English-miracle collections produced from 970 to 1170.[66] I believe that examining multiple cults across two centuries allows us to look for more examples of how the cult of the saints worked. This involves the examination of a great deal of primary source material, but my goal is to be representative rather than exhaustive.[67] All aspects of miracle stories can be potentially useful, and I do not attempt only to extract data for statistical analysis or to separate 'fact' from 'fiction'.

Secondly, I have chosen to examine three elements in the miracle-making process: beneficent miracles, miracles of vengeance and thanksgiving. Most studies revolve around the beneficent miracles, using punitive material selectively if at all. Thanksgiving is sometimes mentioned, but again this is usually in the context of beneficent miracles. I have also considered miracles performed away from the main shrine of the saint. These miracles raise questions about the tension between specificity and universality in the cult of the saints but are often passed over in favour of shrine cures. Likewise I have included miracles which concern all manner of crises, not just illness, injury and possession. In order to more fully represent the special role of the custodians of the saints, I have attached an appendix on the English saints in the liturgy.[68] This allows me to touch upon the liturgy throughout without moving away from the focus on making miracles.

Thirdly, I centre this study on the agency and actions of the people involved in the cult of the saints. This communal aspect of the cult of the saints includes the supplicants, the custodians and the saints. The saint was the wellspring of miracles and a person who had to be kept happy in order for the cult to succeed. Saints were thought to be aware of the actions taken by and against the members of their community and could react accordingly. Custodians kept the holy places of a saint, they observed the liturgical components of the cult and they commissioned or composed the hagiography and other relevant texts. These guardians sought to represent, defend and maintain an idealised form of the cult of the saints. Supplicants exerted a great deal of energy in prayers, praise and thanksgiving to the saints. Indeed, it is my contention that the petitionary process, the ways in which supplicants solicited miracles from the saints, was at the heart of the cult of the saints. All sections of the community of a saint and even external threats to that community had agency. No one was forced to engage a saint, although they could sometimes be persuaded. The cult of the saints in medieval England was about this choice over how to engage such powerful people in human relationships. How you acted mattered a great deal.

The first chapter concerns miracle collections – their authors, audience and the recording of them. The miracle collections and other hagiography shed light on the cult of the saints, the lives of its participants and Christianity in England more generally. As a part of this chapter, we will consider the authors of the hagiography, their backgrounds, their methods and their motivations for miracle collecting. The hagiographers were involved in the cults they represented; they took part in miracle stories, argued over their saints and wrote down their patrons' deeds against oblivion. Their narratives were the preferred version of events addressing the interests of the saints and their custodians.

The second chapter is on the saints' shrines: their development and location and how they were founded, moved and contested. A majority of miracles were effected at the shrines of the saints, and this detail seems to have focused the attentions of hagiographers and pilgrims. People visited the shrines for a great many reasons, which could lead to problems of overcrowding and access, and all manner of supplicants came in search of the miraculous. These same people flocked to witness and take part in the movement of relics, whether permanently in translations or temporarily in processions. Just as supplicants competed for access to shrines, so, too, did different communities compete over the relics of the saints when they were translated. In the end, the tacit approval of the saint would be known by their acceptance of their resting place. At these resting places, people could meet with the saints and personally interact with them.

Chapter three concerns the petitioning of the saints for miraculous aid. Whilst there is a bias towards shrine petitions, we will also examine petitions at alternative locations, petitions using relics and petitions at a distance. All petitions follow a basic structure in spite of how or where they were carried out. Various forms of elaboration could be included in a petition, such as vigils, prostration and physical interaction with the shrine. However, in its most simple form, a petition consisted of a person who knew of a saint asking that saint for help with a problem. These problems were often illness or injury but could include all manner of other issues. The petition allowed a supplicant to perform their misfortune, to show the saint and the community both that they were in crisis and that they knew how to deal appropriately with that crisis. No matter how grave the problem, there was a practical step that a devotee of a saint could take to help themself.

Following the discussion of beneficent miracles is a chapter on punitive miracles. This fourth chapter focuses on inappropriate behaviour and its consequences. Throughout the period, saints reacted to slights against their communities and cults with miracles of vengeance. Such miracles include psychological and physical assaults by the saints, which could then be the catalyst for the redemption of the perpetrators. Saints took part in legal disputes, punished thieves, made sure their people were secure and protected themselves from mockery and mistreatment. Miracles of vengeance could be petitioned like any other miracle, but they could be produced reactively by a saint as well. Either way, these intercessions were triggered by human actions taken with a foreknowledge of the saint in question, thus following the structure outlined in chapter three. The misbehaviour of these people shows not only what a saint could not tolerate and what a hagiographer found instructive; it also highlights the elements of the cult of the saints which people resisted. The cult of the saints was a ubiquitous feature of life based on an understanding that the saints were known to be powerful thaumaturges. Despite this, people were willing to defy, attack and ignore the local saint, perhaps enacting a critique of the cult and its workings.

Chapter five concerns the act of thanksgiving that regularly came after a miracle. Whilst it was never required to give thanks to a saint after an intercession, thanksgiving was common and expected. A saint who was not properly thanked could reverse a miracle or stop interceding for future supplicants. Thanksgiving stood as a conclusion to the petitionary process, an act which showed that the preceding ordeal was over. These acts could be as simple as an individual cry of thanks, but if a miracle was picked up by the custodians of a shrine, thanksgiving could become prolonged and elaborate. Some people included material offerings as part of their thanksgiving, from a memento of a miracle to a rebuilding programme for the local church. Whatever a person did and gave in thanks, a supplicant's thanksgiving could never truly live up to the miraculous favour the saint had performed for them. There was a development of a reciprocal relationship between saint and beneficiary, but it was profoundly uneven, and each individual had to come to terms with this debt. As long as they made an effort, however, a

10 *Introduction*

supplicant could leave happy that they had been deemed worthy of intercession and that they had behaved graciously following their miracle.

Finally I conclude that miracles were made in medieval England through a collaborative endeavour which revolved around a basic structure. A person had a problem, and acting upon their knowledge, they brought that problem to a saint in the hope and expectation of intercession. This was a communal event involving supplicants, custodians and the saint. The cult of the saints was flexible, but it maintained this basic structure despite the range of events and experiences brought to bear. Unacceptable behaviour was punished, but people could be redeemed. Tensions were present within communities and between the communities and external threats. By petitioning a saint, a person could take an action to improve their lot whilst demonstrating their piety publicly. A successful petition marked the end of a crisis and showed that an individual had a relationship with the saint. Ultimately the cult of the saints was driven by these communal actions. The saints, custodians, hagiographers and supplicants were all focused on making miracles.

Notes

1 'Igitur cunctis fratribus in choro astantibus, uenit predictus uir candelam manu gestans cum uespertina sinaxis decantaretur, pergensque ante altare diutius orauit, sicque candelam optulit. Qua oblata, rursus ad orationem stetit. Res mira et uehementer stupenda! Cum coram cunctis astaret mutus, subito cadens riuum sanguinis ex ore cepit excreare, nimiaque pre angustia in pauimento circumquaque uolutare. Finita ergo uespertina prece, accessit ad illum qua excreans iacebat domnus Aeuicius, ea tempestate prior loci, cum quibusdam senioribus, interrogans quid haberet, aut cur sanguinem excreans sic iaceret. Surgens itaque homo in medio fratrum, oculosque cum manibus ad Deum intendens, demum lingua resoluta, hanc primam ita cepit uocem formare: 'Sic me adiuuet omnipotens Deus, meusque dominus sanctus Ecgwinus, per cuius meritum in me misero tale miraculum operatus est Christus, sicut uobis uera dixerim.' Sumensque principium orationis omnia seriatim pandit, ut supra habetur comprehensum. Qua narratione finita, fratres exhilarantur, conuocatur etiam populus, ora relaxantur in summis Dei laudibus; incipientesque 'Te Deum laudamus', classicum sonant diutius, extollentes Dei miracula quam poterant dulcius, qui est super omnia benedictus Deus.' Dominic, *Miracula S. Ecgwini*, pp. 88–91.
2 William Christian, *Local Religion in Sixteenth-Century Spain* (Princeton, NJ: Princeton University Press, 1981), p. 63.
3 For example Augustine of Hippo, *De utilitate credendi*, in *Patrologia Latina*, 42, col. 90.
4 Robert Bartlett, *The Natural and the Supernatural in the Middle Ages: The Wiles Lecture Given at the Queen's University of Belfast, 2006* (Cambridge: Cambridge University Press, 2008), pp. 4–9.
5 Peter Lombard, *Sententiarum Libri Quatuor*, in *Patrologia Latina*, 192, col. 688–89.
6 Ronald C. Finucane, *Miracles and Pilgrims: Popular Beliefs in Medieval England* (London: Dent, 1977), pp. 49–50. As Finucane notes, the closest we come to a post-mortem miracle is the resurrection of a man when he was thrown into Elisha's tomb and touched the prophet's bones, Kings 13. 21.
7 See for example Bede's *Vita Cuthberti*, Bertram Colgrave, ed. and trans., *Two Lives of St Cuthbert: A Life by an Anonymous Monk of Lindisfarne and Bede's Prose Life* (Cambridge: Cambridge University Press, 1985), pp. 290–307; Felix's *Vita Guthlaci*,

Bertram Colgrave, ed. and trans., *Felix's Life of Saint Guthlac* (Cambridge: Cambridge University Press, 1956), pp. 160–7; Stephen's *Vita Wilfridi*, Bertram Colgrave, ed. and trans., *The Life of Bishop Wilfrid By Eddius Stephanus* (Cambridge: Cambridge University Press, 1985), pp. 142–7.
8   Joel T. Rosenthal, 'Bede's Use of Miracles in "The Ecclesiastical History"', *Traditio*, 31 (1975), 328–35 (p. 329).
9   'Mira Dei pietas, mira et tremenda potestas!' Eadmer, *Miracula S. Oswaldi*, pp. 318–19.
10 For example, the wonder expressed by Wulfstan at the healing of a child after Swithun's translation, Wulfstan, *Narratio de S. Swithuno*, pp. 462–3, is matched by that expressed by Aelred in the persistence of the miracles performed by the saints of Hexham, Aelred, *De sanctis Hagustaldensis*, pp. 173–6.
11 Geoffrey, *Miracula S. Modwenne*, pp. 202–5.
12 'festinent ad celestia bonis operibus gaudia', Lantfred, *Miracula S. Swithuni*, pp. 294–5.
13 Ethnographic studies show that many supplicants conceive of miracles as evidence of a divine presence with the potential for that presence to bestow gifts upon them, often based on their behaviour. See for example Alexandra Kent, 'Divinity, Miracles and Charity in the Sathya Sai Baba Movement of Malaysia', *Ethnos*, 69 (2004), 43–62 (p. 48); Anthony Shenoda, 'The Politics of Faith: On Faith, Skepticism, and Miracles among Coptic Christians in Egypt', *Ethnos*, 77 (2004), 477–95 (p. 478). See also Victor Turner and Edith Turner, *Image and Pilgrimage in Christian Culture: Anthropological Perspectives* (Oxford: Blackwell, 1978), p. 71 on Christian miracles as evidence of God, particularly through the person of Jesus, working in the world. On the anthropologist as participant observer to a miracle, see Bruce Grindal, 'Into the Heart of Sisala Experience: Witnessing Death Divination', *Journal of Anthropological Research*, 39 (1983), 60–80.
14 David Rollason, *Saints and Relics in Anglo-Saxon England* (Oxford: Blackwell, 1989), p. 3.
15 Antonia Gransden, *Historical Writing in England c. 550 to c. 1307* (London: Keegan & Paul, 1974), p. 67. The first English saint afforded papal canonisation was Edward the Confessor in 1161. See Robert Bartlett, *England Under the Norman and Angevin Kings, 1075–1225* (Oxford: Clarendon, 2000), p. 461.
16 Graham Jones, 'Introduction: Diverse Expressions, Shared Meanings: Surveying Saints across Cultural Boundaries' in Graham Jones, ed., *Saints of Europe: Studies towards a Survey of Cults and Culture*, ed. by Graham Jones (Donington: Tyas, 2003), pp. 1–28 (p. 11).
17 Rollason, *Saints and Relics*, p. 4.
18 Robert Bartlett, *Why Can the Dead Do Such Great Things?: Saints and Worshippers from the Martyrs to the Reformation* (Princeton, NJ: Princeton University Press, 2013), p. 3.
19 G. J. C. Snoek, *Medieval Piety from Relics to the Eucharist: A Process of Mutual Interaction*, Studies in the History of Christian Thought, 63 (Leiden: Brill, 1995), p. 9.
20 Peter Brown, *The Cult of the Saints: Its Rise and Function in Latin Christianity* (London: SCM, 1981), pp. 1–3.
21 Martin Biddle, 'Archaeology, Architecture, and the Cult of the Saints in Anglo-Saxon England', in *The Anglo-Saxon Church: Papers on History, Architecture, and Archaeology in Honour of Dr H. M. Taylor*, ed. by L. A. S. Butler and R. K. Morris, CBA Research Report, 60 (London: Council for British Archaeology, 1986), pp. 1–31 (pp. 1–3).
22 Finucane, p. 39.
23 Bede, *HE*, I.23–30, pp. 70–107.
24 Alan Thacker, '*Loca Sanctorum*: The Significance of Place in the Study of the Saints', in *Local Saints and Local Churches in the Early Medieval West*, ed. by Alan Thacker and Richard Sharpe (Oxford: Oxford University Press, 2002), pp. 1–43 (pp. 38–9).
25 Robert Bartlett, 'The Hagiography of Angevin England', *Thirteenth-Century England*, 5 (1995), 37–52 (p. 40).

12 *Introduction*

26 E. W. Kemp, *Canonization and Authority in the Western Church* (Oxford: Oxford University Press, 1948), p. 99.
27 Finucane, p. 83.
28 Thomas D. Hill, '*Imago Dei*: Genre, Symbolism and Anglo-Saxon Hagiography', in *Holy Men and Holy Women: Old English Prose Saints' Lives and Their Contexts*, ed. by Paul E. Szarmach (Albany: State University of New York Press, 1996), pp. 35–50 (p. 35).
29 Ibid., p. 47.
30 Thomas J. Heffernan, *Sacred Biography: Saints and Their Biographers in the Middle Ages* (Oxford: Oxford University Press, 1988), pp. 5–16.
31 Régis Boyer, 'An Attempt to Define the Typology of Medieval Hagiography', in *Hagiography and Medieval Literature: A Symposium*, ed. by Hans Bekker-Nielsen and others (Odense: Odense University Press, 1981), pp. 27–37 (pp. 28–9).
32 Hilary Powell, '"Once Upon a Time There Was a Saint . . .": Re-evaluating Folklore in Anglo-Latin Hagiography', *Folklore*, 121 (2010), 171–89 (p. 171).
33 Peregrine Horden, 'What's Wrong with Early Medieval Medicine?', *Social History of Medicine*, 24 (2009), 5–25 (p. 18).
34 Anne E. Bailey, 'Wives, Mothers and Widows on Pilgrimage: Categories of "Woman" Recorded at English Healing Shrines in the High Middle Ages', *Journal of Medieval History*, 39 (2013), 197–219 (pp. 217–19).
35 Rachel Koopmans, *Wonderful to Relate: Miracle Stories and Miracle Collecting in High Medieval England* (Philadelphia: University of Pennsylvania Press, 2011), p. 45.
36 Patrick J. Geary, *Living with the Dead in the Middle Ages* (Ithaca, NY: Cornell University Press, 1994), p. 12.
37 Koopmans, pp. 61–2; Geary, *Living with the Dead*, pp. 22–3.
38 Aron Gurevich, *Medieval Popular Culture: Problems of Belief and Perception*, trans. by János M. Bak and Paul A. Hollingsworth, Cambridge Studies in Oral and Literate Culture, 14 (Cambridge: Cambridge University Press, 1988), p. 20.
39 James Howard-Johnston, 'Introduction', in *The Cult of Saints in Late Antiquity and the Middle Ages: Essays on the Contribution of Peter Brown*, ed. by James Howard-Johnston and Paul Antony Hayward (Oxford: Oxford University Press, 1999), pp. 1–24 (p. 19).
40 Paul Antony Hayward, 'De-mystifying the Role of Sanctity in Western Christendom', in *The Cult of Saints in Late Antiquity and the Middle Ages*, ed. by Howard-Johnston and Hayward, pp. 115–42 (p. 130).
41 Geary, *Living with the Dead*, p. 11.
42 Gurevich, p. xix.
43 John Arnold, *Belief and Unbelief in Medieval Europe* (London: Hodder Arnold, 2005), pp. 5–12.
44 Simon Yarrow, *Saints and Their Communities: Miracle Stories in Twelfth Century England* (Oxford: Clarendon, 2006), p. 16. For more on the audience of hagiography, see chapter I.
45 Lawrence P. Morris, 'Did Columba's Tunic Bring Rain? Early Medieval Typological Action and Modern Historical Method', *Quaestio*, 1 (2000), 45–65 (p. 64).
46 Barbara Newman, 'Possessed by the Spirit: Devout Women, Demoniacs, and the Apostolic Life in the Thirteenth Century', *Speculum*, 73 (1998), 733–70 (p. 737).
47 Michael Goodich, '*Mirabilis Deus in Sanctis Suis*: Social History and Medieval Miracles', in *Signs, Wonders, Miracles: Representations of Divine Power in the Life of the Church*, ed. by Kate Cooper and Jeremy Gregory, Studies in Church History, 41 (Woodbridge: Boydell, 2005), pp. 135–56 (pp. 144–5).
48 Geary, *Living with the Dead*, pp. 9–17.
49 Brown's first published work on the cult of the saints is Peter Brown, 'The Rise and Function of the Holy Man in Late Antiquity', *Journal of Roman Studies*, 61 (1971), 80–101.

50 Hayward, 'De- mystifying', pp. 115–17.
51 Geary, *Living with the Dead*, p. 13.
52 Peter Brown, *The Rise of Western Christendom*, 2nd edn (Oxford: Blackwell, 2003), p. 19.
53 Brown, *The Cult of the Saints*, p. 22.
54 Anne E. Bailey, 'Peter Brown and Victor Turner Revisited: Anthropological Approaches to Latin Miracle Narratives in the Medieval West', in C*ontextualizing Miracles in the Christian West, 1100–1500: New Historical Approaches*, ed. by Matthew M. Mesley and Louise E. Wilson, Medium Aevum Monographs, 32 (Oxford: The Society for the Study of Medieval Languages and Literature, 2014), pp. 17–39 (pp. 20–1).
55 Finucane's *Miracles and Pilgrims* concerns the years 1066 to 1300 and Pierre-André Sigal, *L'homme et le Miracle dans la France Médiévale, XIe-XIIe Siècle* (Paris: Cerf, 1985) concerns the eleventh and twelfth centuries.
56 Susan J. Ridyard, *The Royal Saints of Anglo-Saxon England: A Study of West Saxon and East Anglian Cults*, Cambridge Studies in Medieval Life and Thought: Fourth Series, 9 (Cambridge: Cambridge University Press, 1988), pp. 234–52.
57 Rollason, *Saints and Relics*, pp. 182–205.
58 Yarrow, pp. 14–21.
59 Koopmans, pp. 9–27. See also Aviad M. Kleinberg, *Flesh Made Word: Saints' Stories and the Western Imagination*, trans. by Jane Marie Todd (Cambridge, MA: Harvard University Press, 2008), pp. 279–85; Bailey, 'Peter Brown', pp. 36–9.
60 Koopmans, pp. 25–7.
61 Marcel Mauss, *The Gift: The Form and Reason for Exchange in Archaic Societies*, trans. by W. D. Halls (London: Routledge, 1990); David Graeber, *Toward an Anthropological Theory of Value: The False Coin of Our Own Dreams* (Basingstoke: Palgrave, 2001).
62 Marcel Mauss, *Sociology and Psychology: Essays*, trans. by Ben Brewster (London: Routledge, 1979); Pierre Bourdieu, *Outline of a Theory of Practice*, trans. by Richard Nice (Cambridge: Cambridge University Press, 1977).
63 Victor Turner, *The Ritual Process: Structure and Anti-Structure* (New York, NY: Aldine de Gruyter, 1969); Victor Turner, 'Betwixt and Between: The Liminal Period in the *Rites de Passage*', in *Reader in Comparative Religion: An Anthropological Approach*, ed. by William A. Lessa and Evon Z. Vogt, 4th edn (New York, NY: Harper, 1979), pp. 234–43.
64 Marshall Sahlins, *Historical Metaphors and Mythic Realities: Structure in the Early History of the Sandwich Islands Kingdom* (Ann Arbor: University of Michigan Press, 1981); Marshall Sahlins, *Islands of History* (Chicago, IL: University of Chicago Press, 1985).
65 Sahlins, *Islands of History*, pp. xiii–xv.
66 The closest to my date range is Koopmans, who actually extends her perspective to the end of the twelfth century to include the Becket material and other later miracle collections. However, Koopmans primarily considers the work of Lantfred, Goscelin, Osbern and Eadmer before going on to look at the hagiographers of Becket. See Koopmans, pp. 112–15. Other studies tend to fall either side of the Norman Conquest.
67 Although I have surveyed all of the hagiography produced in this period, there are certain texts I return to more than others, as indicated by the list of abbreviations. This date range was chosen to include the most source material whilst having a clear cut-off point. In practice this has led to my not including borderline texts like Reginald of Coldingham's *Miracula S. Cuthberti*, composed 1165–1174, and Thomas of Monmouth's *Vita S. Gulielmi Nordowicensis*, composed 1150–1173. See Michael Lapidge and Rosalind C. Love, 'England and Wales (600–1550)', in *Hagiographies: histoire internationale de la littérature hagiographique latine et vernaculaire, en Occident, des origines à 1500*, ed. by G. Philippart and M. Goullet, 7 vols (Turnhout: Brepols,

1994–2018), III, 203–325 (pp. 262, 276). Reginald's *Miracula S. Cuthberti* is edited by James Raine, ed., *Reginaldi Monachi Dunelmensis Libellus de Admirandis Beati Cuthberti Virtutibus quae Novellis Patratae sunt Temporibus*, Publications of the Surtees Society, 1 (London: Nichols, 1835). Thomas's *Vita S. Gulielmi Nordowicensis* can be found in Thomas of Monmouth, *The Life and Miracles of William of Norwich*, ed. and trans. by M. R. James and Augustus Jessopp (Cambridge: Cambridge University Press, 1896).

68 This is mainly concerned with material found in liturgical books intended for use on the feast days of the saints. I have also added some comment on the marking of feast days in the calendar as well as the place of English saints in the litany. See Appendix I.

1 Writing Miracles

Tom Lynch

The writing down of miracle stories was both a means of recording and a means of reproducing the wonders performed by the saints. Each collection, no matter how it was consumed, demonstrated to its audience the prior glories and the future possibilities of a saint's cult. Eadmer described some of the impetus and process behind miracle collecting in the introduction to his *Miraculi S. Dunstani*:

> A number of things concerning the life of blessed Dunstan and his departure from life, which I learnt either from written records or from those who have handed down accounts through successive generations from his time right up to our day, I have recounted succinctly to the extent that God has deigned to permit me because of Dunstan's intercession and merit. And so it now pleases me no less to relate concisely what deeds I have learnt either from writings, from the accounts of truthful men, or by my own sight, were brought about in proximity to his most sacred body or through the blessed memory of his holy name.[1]

Together with the liturgy, miracle petitions and thanksgiving, miracle stories contributed to a 'sacred history' of a cult centre which could then serve as the basis for further miracle making.[2] In order to consider the conditions of the composition of our sources, it is useful to look at the lives and careers of the relevant hagiographers of our period, where they can be identified.[3] For this we will follow a rough chronology beginning with the first miracle collections and translation accounts from Winchester.

Our earliest source is Lantfred's *Translatio et Miracula S. Swithuni*, which records the miracles of Swithun and his translation at Winchester on 15 July 971. The text was composed sometime between the translation and 975.[4] Lantfred was a Frankish monk and priest, associated with Fleury and resident at Winchester at the end of the tenth century.[5] He was a part of a greater hagiographical scene at Winchester, under Bishop Æthelwold (963–984), who was one of the architects of the Benedictine reforms in England. Two anonymous authors composed verse hagiography about Eustace and Judoc around the same time, most probably in Winchester.[6] Whilst Lantfred was working in a climate of monastic reform and was probably brought to England to help with Æthelwold's project,[7] there is little evidence of the influence of the reform movement in his work. Instead Lantfred brings his Frankish sensibilities, including an understanding of miracle collecting and its importance, to a country with many saints but few hagiographers. In a sense, this coincidence of author and place helped to reinvigorate English hagiography after the hiatus of the Viking age.[8] That such an approach was endorsed by the English can be seen from the writing of Wulfstan, a monk, priest and eventually precentor of the Old Minster,[9] who wrote two texts which concern us. The earliest of these compositions is the *Narratio metrica de S. Swithuno* written in the 990s, which closely follows Lantfred but includes additional details and an account of a second translation.[10] Wulfstan appears to have been an eyewitness to many of the events he described and took part in both translations.[11] Wulfstan's other composition of note here is his *Vita S. Æthelwoldi*, written to accompany the Bishop's translation in 996.[12] This was undoubtedly coloured by the personal relationship between Æthelwold and his student Wulfstan, and Wulfstan seems to have been the major proponent of the Bishop's post-mortem cult.[13]

Ramsey was another centre of hagiographical production around this time, though on a smaller scale than Winchester. Whilst visiting Ramsey Abbey and acting as the schoolmaster between 985 and 987, Abbo of Fleury composed his *Passio S. Eadmundi* at the request of his hosts.[14] Drawing on local traditions regarding the killing of Edmund of East Anglia by the Danes in 869, the text focuses on positioning Edmund as a Christian king and martyr.[15] Despite this focus, Abbo does describe some of the post-mortem miracles of the saint and stated that Edmund's relics were to be found at Bury.[16] The other major author active at Ramsey at this time was Byrhtferth, a student of Abbo in the monastic school.[17] Relatively little is known for certain about Byrhtferth. He was probably born in the 960s, and in terms of hagiography, he composed a *Passio SS. Æthelredi et Æthelberhti* c. 991, a *Vita S. Oswaldi* around the turn of the eleventh century and a *Vita S. Ecgwini* between 1016 and 1020. We do not know whether Byrhtferth spent time at Evesham when he composed his life of Ecgwine, nor are the details of the author's death known to us.[18]

Looming large over our evidence is Goscelin of Saint-Bertin, a prolific author who came to England before the Conquest and worked in the country for several decades, dying after 1107.[19] Goscelin has had more than thirty texts assigned to him, the majority of which contain post-mortem miracles performed by the saints in question.[20] Whilst some of these texts were quite short, Goscelin's miracles of Ivo stretch to more than thirty chapters, and his miracles and translation of Augustine and the other saints of St Augustine's Abbey includes more than fifty chapters.[21] Goscelin's reputation was recognised in medieval England, and William of Malmesbury described him as second only to Bede in his hagiographical endeavours.[22] Goscelin's texts show a great interest in circumstantial detail and are full of 'little vignettes' which help bring to life the cults he describes.[23] Goscelin is thought to have been Flemish, and he came to England from the Benedictine community of Saint-Bertin at Saint-Omer, in the Pas de Calais. Goscelin came to England to become a part of the household of Bishop Herman, who combined his sees of Ramsbury (1045–1075) and Sherborne (1058–1075) and transferred them to Salisbury in 1075.[24] Goscelin's hagiographical career contained several stages. His earliest work was composed in the area of Wessex around Salisbury. Amongst the items that Goscelin composed at this time, the 1070s and 1080s, were his *Vita S. Wlsini*, *Vita S. Edithe* and *Vita et miracula S. Kenelmi*. Goscelin then seems to have moved on to Barking, where he composed the *Vita et uirtutes S. Vulfhilde* and *De translatione uel eleuatione SS. Uirginum Ethelburge, Hildelithe ac Wlfhilde*, along with other texts about the saints of Barking around the time of their translation in 1086. During this period, Goscelin also penned a *Vita et Miracula S. Yuonis* for Abbot Herbert of Ramsey (1087–1091). Goscelin produced hagiography on the saints of Ely around this time as well, including the *Vita S. Werburge* and *Vita S. Wihtburge*, although the latter was completed after the 1106 translation. During the 1090s, Goscelin was probably resident at Canterbury, where he produced several texts including his *De Adventu, Translatione et Virtutibus S. Adriani*, *Translatio et miracula S. Mildrethe*, *Historia maior de miraculis S. Augustini* and *Historia translationis S. Augustini et aliorum sanctorum*. Following this Goscelin went to East Anglia and rewrote the *Miracula S. Edmundi*, which had been written previously by Herman, archdeacon of Bury and erstwhile associate of Bishop Herfast of Elmham and Thetford (1070–1084/5).[25]

Roughly contemporary with Goscelin were the two hagiographers of Christ Church, Canterbury, Osbern and Eadmer. Both of them were brought up and educated in the Benedictine community at Christ Church with Osbern, the senior of the two, dying around 1095 and Eadmer dying after 1128.[26] Osbern spent some time at Bec as a young man[27] and went on to become precentor and subprior at Christ Church. His surviving hagiographical works are the *Vita et translatio S. Aelphegi* and the *Vita et miracula S. Dunstani*. Osbern composed his text on Archbishop Ælfheah (1006–1012) shortly after the doubts raised over the saint's sanctity in 1079. Ælfheah had been killed by the Danes in 1012 and his translation from London to Canterbury occurred in 1023.[28] Osbern wrote about Dunstan, his place in the history of Canterbury and his post-mortem miracles in the 1080s, using the work of Adelard and the author known as 'B' as well as the traditions of Christ Church.[29] Eadmer was an associate of Archbishop Anselm (1093–1109) and was elected Bishop of St Andrews in 1120, although he was never consecrated. Eadmer's reworking of Osbern's collection of Dunstan's miracles demoted Archbishop Lanfranc (1070–1089) from a quasi-saint to an admirable archbishop and removed Osbern himself from the narrative.[30] Eadmer composed his *Vita et miracula S. Dunstani* between 1105 and 1109, and his other major hagiography appropriate for our purposes, the *Vita et miracula S. Oswaldi archiepiscopi* and the *Vita S. Anselmi*, were written before 1100.[31]

During the first half of the twelfth century, there were numerous named authors about whom we know relatively little. Arcoid, who wrote a miracle collection on Erkenwald in the early 1140s, was a canon of St Paul's and nephew of Bishop Gilbert of London (1128–1134).[32] Slightly earlier than this, William Ketell, a cleric of Beverley Minster, wrote his *Miracula S. Johannis*.[33] Abbot Geoffrey of Burton (1114–1151) wrote of the life and miracles of Modwenna whilst he was in office.[34] Another Abbot, Robert of Shrewsbury (c. 1140–1168), composed his *Vita et translatio S. Wenefrede* based on an earlier Welsh model combined with an account of the 1138 translation of the saint from Gwytherin to Shrewsbury.[35] Dominic of Evesham was Prior of Evesham and completed his *Miracula S. Ecgwini* after the death of Abbot Walter of Evesham (1077–1104).[36]

Three later figures can be examined in a little more detail – Osbert of Clare, William of Malmesbury and Aelred of Rievaulx. Osbert of Clare was a monk and Prior of Westminster who wrote a *Vita S. Edwardi confessoris*, which he finished in 1138. At the time of composition, Edward the Confessor's (1042–1066) cult was not well established, but on the back of Osbert's work, a first petition for canonisation was made to Rome.[37] Osbert also rewrote some of the miracles of Edmund and wrote lives of Æthelberht and Eadburh,[38] but his contribution to the canonisation of Edward the Confessor and the textual tradition about the saint is most pertinent here. William of Malmesbury was a monk at Malmesbury Abbey from his youth and an author of great industry, whose most prolific period was between 1124 and 1137. Amongst his compositions during this time were lives of Patrick, Dunstan, Indract and Benignus and a compilation of the miracles of the Virgin Mary.[39] Other texts concerning the cult of the saints include his *Gesta Pontificum Anglorum* and the lives of Bishop Aldhelm of Sherborne (706–709/10) and Bishop Wulfstan of Worcester (1062–1095).[40] Finally, Aelred of Rievaulx was a Cistercian who was likely raised at Hexham, went on to spend his youth in the Scottish court and entered the new foundation at Rievaulx, Yorkshire, around 1134. He became the first Abbot of Revesby, a daughter house of Rievaulx, in 1143 and returned to Rievaulx to become abbot there in 1147. He took a part in the politics of his day and died in 1167. Aelred was asked by the canons of Hexham to produce a work on their saints after the translation of 1155, which resulted in the *De sanctis ecclesiae Hagustaldensis*. He was also asked by Abbot Lawrence of Westminster (1158–1173), a relative of Aelred, to compose another life of Edward the Confessor which would update and improve Osbert's attempt.[41]

Not all texts from our period have a named author, whether they were noted in the manuscripts or assigned at a later date. The context for their composition appears to be similar, however. Our primary sources were written by male religious who were either members of the community in possession of the saint's relics, were commissioned to work for the community or were otherwise inspired to write down the saints miracles.[42] All of our named authors were Benedictines, with the exception of Arcoid, who was a secular canon, and Aelred, who was a Cistercian monk. Likewise, the majority of communities which housed the saints and commissioned this hagiography were Benedictine, mainly male monastic communities and cathedral priories but including nunneries like Wilton and Barking.[43] The only notable exceptions were the Augustinian canons of Hexham, the secular canons of St Paul's and Beverley and the Cluniacs of Much Wenlock.

In the accounts of post-mortem miracles, it is not uncommon for the author to appear in the narrative. In our earliest source, Lantfred is a central player in one of the miracles of Swithun. Having travelled to France, Lantfred was asked to help the sick wife of a friend, and he suggested that Swithun, who had been performing many miracles among the English, could help. Lantfred suggested ordering a candle to be made and burning it in a local church whilst the woman's husband prayed to Swithun. Lantfred had inscribed a prayer to Swithun on the candle, asking for the saint's help in this case. The woman was cured, and she gave thanks to God.[44] Wulfstan enters his narrative of the translations of Swithun as a young witness to the events, and he claimed to have personally seen more than two hundred miracles in the year following the first translation in 971.[45] In his *Vita S. Æthelwoldi*, Wulfstan also presents himself as a part of the cult of the saint when he led a blind man to Æthelwold's shrine.[46] Goscelin, or perhaps an earlier author that Goscelin used as a source, was cured of gout by Ivo at Ramsey.[47] In the *Liber Eliensis*, it is claimed that Goscelin was present at Ely when Æthelthryth performed a miracle.[48] Additionally, Goscelin mentions the major source for his Edmund material, Herman. Whilst Herman was preaching at Pentecost, he had the bloody underclothes of Edmund shown to the crowd. This was done in a disorderly and disrespectful fashion, and Herman was killed by the saint for his part in it.[49] Osbern claimed to have witnessed the cure of a blind girl by Dunstan, as well as claiming to have led another girl and her mother to Dunstan's shrine so they could petition the saint.[50] Eadmer features in his own writing on Anselm as the custodian of the saint's belt. Eadmer lent this relic out to those who needed it and even cut off a portion to help ease the suffering of a knight named Humphrey.[51] Eadmer claimed to have witnessed the translation of Dunstan at Canterbury too.[52] Arcoid appears in his own work as host to a doctor cured by Erkenwald, who stayed at the author's house in London.[53] These examples demonstrate that the authors of our primary sources did not portray themselves as impartial observers but as a part of the cult of the saints in practice. Most often this was as witnesses or facilitators of miracles, but they took part in grand occasions and could be the subject of a saint's intercession.

Thus, authors drew on their own experience of the cult of the saints in their miracle collections. They also drew on earlier traditions circulating at the home of the saint. This is most obvious where a miracle collection has been added to an earlier text or in the reworking of a previous collection. Wulfstan versified and added to Lantfred's material on Swithun. Ælfric then wrote an epitome of Lantfred's *Translatio et Miracula S. Swithuni*, and the anonymous author of the c. 1100 *Vita et Miracula S. Swithuni* depended on Lantfred, Wulfstan and Ælfric.[54] Goscelin used earlier sources in the composition of his hagiography as well. He relied on Bede and perhaps a *libellus* of Hildelith's miracles for his work at Barking, a lost life of Ivo by Abbot Withman of Ramsey (1016–1020) and again on Bede for much of his St Augustine's material.[55] Goscelin made use of an earlier collection of Juthwara's miracles in his *Vita S. Wlsini*, an Old English account of a miracle of Edith and various writings in Latin and Old English, including a letter from Heaven, for his *Vita et miracula S. Kenelmi*.[56] Goscelin's other major rewriting project was the miracle collection of Edmund, working from and expanding Herman's earlier composition.[57]

Whilst Osbern claimed there was no previous text on Ælfheah's life, he tried to incorporate some written material into his *Vita et translatio* of the saint.[58] The Dunstan material can be traced from the work of the author known as 'B' through

Adelard, Osbern and finally Eadmer. Eadmer used Byrhtferth as the main source for his life and miracles of Oswald, as did Dominic for his miracles of Ecgwine.[59] Arcoid added his miracles of Erkenwald to an existing *vita*, as did William Ketell with his miracles of John of Beverley.[60] Geoffrey of Burton reworked an earlier Irish life of Modwenna, attributed to Conchubranus, and William depended on the Welsh *Vita prima S. Wenefrede* for his version.[61] As well as his rewritten Edmund material, Osbert of Clare was a part of a tradition of writing about Edward the Confessor, which began with the anonymous *vita*, went through Osbert's version and ended with Aelred's text, which was the most widely circulated.[62] William of Malmesbury relied on earlier texts for his hagiography too, specifically Faricius' work on Aldhelm and a lost Old English life of Wulfstan of Worcester.[63] Our authors were, therefore, not only a part of the cult of the saints but also part of a self-referential literary tradition of English hagiography. Their use of texts was not only as source material, however, and when houses competed over the patronage of a saint and the possession of their relics, they could take to writing.

The body of Alban was claimed both by the foundation at the site of his martyrdom, St Albans Abbey, and by the abbey at Ely, where the *Liber Eliensis* records that Alban was translated under the instruction of Archbishop Stigand (1052–1070) during his persecution by King William I (1066–1087).[64] The counterclaim of St Albans was focused around a translation on 2 August 1129, the account of which includes an explanation of how Ely came to think they possessed Alban's relics. Concerned with Danish incursions, Abbot Ælfric (c. 968–990) had walled up Alban's relics and sent a dummy set to Ely. When the troubles were over, Ælfric requested the relics back, and the monks of Ely, wishing to keep their prize sent a second dummy corpse back to St Albans. Ælfric realised the deception but remained quiet, retrieved the genuine relics from their hiding place and replaced Alban's shrine in the centre of the church. The *Gesta Abbatum Monasterii Sancti Albani* then claims that Abbot Frederick (c. 1072) fled to Ely because of the persecutions of William I but that he did not take Alban with him. The translation of 1129 was prefigured by a thorough inspection of Alban's bones, which were all present bar a shoulder blade which had been given away by King Cnut (1016–1035). The translation narrative highlights concern over claims from both Ely and Denmark, but the St Albans version is brought to a close when, at the behest of Abbot Robert (1151–1166), three bishops with the authority of Pope Adrian IV (1154–1159) had the Ely monks confess to their duplicity.[65] The first book of the *Gesta Abbatum Monasterii Sancti Albani* was composed by Matthew Paris approximately seventy years after the 1129 translation and around thirty-five years after the supposed enquiry, although he may have been dependent on earlier material written when these issues came to a head in the mid twelfth century.[66] What remains to us is a fairly one-sided counterclaim against Ely from the perspective of St Albans.

In the eleventh century, there were also two contradictory traditions regarding Mildrith's body, both centring on Canterbury. The regular canons of St Gregory's and the monks of St Augustine's both claimed to have the body of the eighth-century Abbess. The tradition at St Gregory's was that Mildrith was translated to Lyminge from Thanet. Then, in 1085 Mildrith was translated to St Gregory's along with the remains of Eadburg, Mildrith's successor, who was thought to be responsible for the first translation of the saint. The tradition at St Augustine's was that Mildrith remained at Thanet following a translation there until her remains were translated to St Augustine's in 1030. The argument over Mildrith is recorded by Goscelin in his *Libellus Contra Inanes Sanctae Virginis Mildrethae Usurpatores*, from the perspective of St Augustine's but quoting the St Gregory's evidence.[67] Goscelin wrote a *vita* and *miracula* of Mildrith as well and included her in his account of the translations at St Augustine's in 1091, both of which confirm St Augustine's as Mildrith's ultimate resting place. The evidence of the tradition at St Gregory's is limited to what can be gleaned from Goscelin's narrative and the evidence from the cartulary of St Gregory's, which simply claims that the relics were translated as a part of Lanfranc's foundation of St Gregory's.[68]

The body of Dunstan was claimed both by Christ Church, Canterbury and Glastonbury Abbey. Both sides agreed that Dunstan was originally buried at Canterbury, but his subsequent movements were disputed. The Glastonbury tradition claims that Dunstan's body was originally translated to Glastonbury in 1012 under the orders of Edmund Ironside and during the upheaval related to the Danish incursions. The narrative explains that the remains were hidden for one hundred and seventy-two years following this translation for fear that the relics would be demanded back by the Archbishop of Canterbury once order had been re-established. The body of Dunstan is said to have remained hidden until the relics were rediscovered following the fire of 1184.[69] Although the details of this tradition originate from a later interpolation in William of Malmesbury's *De Antiquitate Glastonie Ecclesie*, there must have been a claim from earlier in the twelfth century which Eadmer of Canterbury felt he had to refute in a letter to the monks of Glastonbury. Eadmer claimed to have witnessed the translation of Dunstan at Canterbury himself along with a multitude of people and claimed it was a falsehood that Dunstan's body was substituted for that of another by some thieving monks from Glastonbury. Eadmer also cited the lack of opportunity and the fact that a hundred years had passed since the supposed theft, yet no one had mentioned it until near the time of his composition, c. 1120. Eadmer finally asked for some written evidence of the translation to Glastonbury and prayed that the monks of Glastonbury would give up their libellous claim.[70]

There are other contradictory claims over translated relics, though we do not have any material containing the invective which may have been used to attack or defend them. Symeon of Durham records the translation of the remains of Oswine of Deira from Tynemouth to Jarrow, whilst the Tynemouth tradition maintains that Oswine remained there following the invention of his relics in 1065.[71] Similarly the remains of King Edward the Martyr (975–978) were translated to Shaftesbury and translated there again in 1001 according to his *passio*, but there was a slightly later claim from Abingdon that the relics of Edward were taken there in the time of King Cnut.[72] Several of the great number of relics claimed by Glastonbury were claimed elsewhere. When it came to main shrines, the account in *De Antiquitate Glastonie Ecclesie* records the translation of relics of Aidan and the bodies of Ceolfrith, Benedict Biscop, Eosterwine, Hwaetberht, Selfrith, Bede, Æbbe,

Begu, Boisil and Hilda from Northumbria in the eighth century.[73] This exodus of saints was apparently facilitated by Abbot Tyccea (754–760) under the pressure of Danish raids. Of these saints, Benedict Biscop was claimed by Thorney, Æbbe was claimed by Coldingham and the bones of Aidan, Boisil and Bede were claimed by Durham.[74] A similar claim for northern saints can be found in Symeon of Durham's *libellus* on the church of Durham. In Symeon's example, the collector is named as Elfred. This collector went out to the neglected churches and monasteries of Northumbria at the behest of a vision to elevate and translate relics.[75] Elfred is said to have uncovered the relics of Balthere, Billfrith, Acca, Alchmund, Oswine, Æbbe and Æthelgitha and brought back to Durham 'a certain part of all these relics'.[76] He was also supposedly responsible for the translation of the whole of Boisil and Bede's remains to Durham from Melrose and Jarrow, respectively.[77] It is difficult to know exactly what was meant by 'a certain part' of the relics, but in Aelred of Rievaulx's account of the miracles of the Hexham saints, he reveals that Elfred attempted to take away a finger bone of Alchmund but was foiled by the intercession of the saint himself. Aelred notes that Eata appeared in a vision to stop his translation from Hexham to York as well.[78]

These conflicting stories show the importance attributed to specificity in the cult of the saints. Whilst it would be possible for God or a saint to grant a miracle when a person was mistaken, it seems that the best approach was to know who you were asking for help and where their body was interred.[79] People had relationships with their saints, identified with them and did not want to find out they had been mistaken or misled. These literary debates also show that the resting places of saints were not considered folk tales or legends. Authors thought they could prove, through evidence and argument, where a saint reposed and how they came to be there. Perhaps more importantly, they thought they could convince others of this fact and therefore convince them of the location of the earthly centre of the saint's cult. Knowing that a thaumaturgic saint rested in your community would have been of great spiritual, and potentially material, comfort. Convincing everyone else of the presence of a holy body would have been a source of personal pride. Saints were worth arguing over, and in the end, the victor could infer the saint's consent by their continued presence in their community.

The evidence of earlier hagiography was not the only kind of source open to hagiographers. More basic shrine records could be used as well or indeed replace hagiography at a shrine which could not recruit an appropriate author. For instance the shrine to Leofwynn in Sussex, most likely in the minster at Bishopstone, contained notes detailing the miracles of the saint in English which visiting Flemish monks could not understand.[80] Aside from shrine records and previous hagiography, the compilers' main source must have been the complexes of stories surrounding the shrine. For example, after the cure of three blind women and a mute man by Swithun, the man, now able to speak, informed the sacristan about the miracle.[81] So, too, the Saxon man Leodegar cried so loudly at the wonder of his cure at St Augustine's that he attracted the sacristans and raised others from their beds. He then explained the saints' intercession to them.[82] Miracles performed away from the shrine could be collected in this manner, as was the case of Wulmar the villein, who lay sick for four days and was cured with a vision of Edmund. Upon his cure, Wulmar got out of bed, went to Edmund's shrine, gave the saint four pieces of crystal rock and thanked God and the saint. Wulmar then told the story to the sacristan, and later he was brought in to address the monks with the story. Believing him, Abbot Baldwin (1065–1097) had a sermon preached, rang the bells and led the monks in the *Te Deum*.[83] These stories help to emphasise the role of the sacristan not only as guardian of the relics but also as an announcer, investigator and repository of miracle stories.[84]

The stories told and retold at shrines could be old tales that had circulated for years or reports of more recent events. Koopmans has written extensively on the interplay between spoken and written miracle stories in medieval England. She points out that most miracle collectors relied on the 'personal stories' of supplicants, which had found favour with the community.[85] Koopmans states that we should believe authors when they say that they had heard about many more miracles than they recorded.[86] She goes on to claim that the 'animating essence' of the cult of the saints was this circulation of personal stories.[87] Whilst I disagree slightly with this assessment, I do believe that a great deal of oral stories lie behind the hagiography and that many accounts which could have been written down have been lost to us. Major occasions like feast days would have provided many opportunities for sharing old stories about the saints and composing new ones.

The celebration of a saint's feast could be relatively simple, relying on a calendar and common of the saints to modify a few elements of the day's liturgy.[88] At a cult centre, the observances would have been much more involved.[89] Whilst supplicants would have been a common fixture at a major shrine, judging by the miracle accounts, there would be a spike in attendance on a saint's feast. This attendance would begin on the eve of the feast and could last until the following week when the octave was celebrated. There is a rather detailed description found in the *Vita Beate Sexburge Regine*:

> The solemn festival day of the blessed Seaxburh dawned, on which the religious common folk are joined in equal devotion with the religious of the community who attend to the rites of the church. They are all suffused with immense joy, and extol the wonderful works of the Creator in songs of praise. To the eternal glory of the noble queen, they pass in procession arrayed in festive garb. Praising God, they are dressed in tunics with gold ornament and purple border. The weakness and idleness of the human mind is far removed from their observance. Holy devotion grows, and all sides of the church resound with ringing music. The holy assemblies rejoice, and are charmed by hymns to God on all sides. They carry out the festal day with rejoicing, triumphing in the good favour of blessed Seaxburh. When at length the holy rites were completed and solemn sacrifices had been offered up to God, a solemn banquet was fitting for the brothers in their solemnity.[90]

Although it might be expected that the feast of a local saint would be remembered, proclamations were made to remind the people.[91] Feast days provided a 'change in the pattern of life' for both the religious community and the surrounding laity,[92] an event which would reverberate beyond the shrine and throughout the local area.[93] Common additions included a procession of the saint's relics, the wearing of ceremonial dress and the reading of lessons on the saint's life and virtues. Such readings came both in the form of specially composed lections and excerpts from longer hagiographical works. These texts were used as part of liturgical celebrations and in the refectory to accompany the meals of the religious.[94] For example, the acts of Augustine as written by Bede were read during the Mass on the saint's feast day.[95] It seems that not only were the deeds of the saints read aloud, but they were also incorporated into sermons and homilies. By the eleventh century, such liturgical elements could be performed in English,[96] and the vernacular sermon could be a feature of a saint's feast.[97]

Sermons and preaching about the saints are recorded in the hagiography as well. Æthelwold instructed the laity on Swithun and his miracles before the saint's first translation in 971.[98] Such sermons could be more ad hoc affairs, as is indicated by Herman's inclusion of contemporary miracles being worked into feast day preaching at Bury. A boy, also called Edmund, was cured of warts between the eyes and sight problems. He had previously kept vigil in a church at Binham, to no avail, but he was cured in vigil at Edmund's shrine on the eve of his feast. At daybreak the details of the miracle spread, and a sermon was incorporated into the Mass, detailing the cure. So, too, a blind girl named Lyeveva was healed on the saint's feast by spending the night in vigil. Herman himself and Abbot Baldwin saw the girl prostrate at vespers. Lyeveva was the subject of a sermon during Mass the next day, and God was praised for the miracle. Herman also includes the story of the crippled woman Brihtgyfa. After Brihtgyfa had been cured and after the prior had been reassured by witnesses, a sermon was preached about the miracle.[99] The role of the clergy could be supplanted, and the recipients of miracles could recount their experience themselves, as the little girl Amelia did at Mildburh's shrine, presumably in English rather than Latin.[100] Such personal stories helped to enliven the cult of the saints with contemporary evidence and facilitated a dialogue that was not reliant on anything beyond hearing of a miracle and talking about it.[101] Thus, a feast day or other major occasion would be an opportunity to share stories of the saint, both oral and written.

Often a degree of investigation was inserted between the personal story and the hagiography. There are elements of witness testimony in Lantfred and Wulfstan with the crowds present for the wonders of Swithun and the reaction of the monastic community to the saint's deeds.[102] The sense of witness interrogation is more obvious in the late-eleventh-century anonymous collection of miracles of Swithun, particularly the final two miracles of the text. In the first of these, a pilgrim from the Isle of Wight who was blind in one eye came to Swithun on his feast day. He visited the church on the eve of the feast, and following divine guidance, he went to the statue of Swithun found before his tomb. The man kissed the statue's feet, prayed and found himself unexpectedly healed. The day after the feast, the miracle was extensively investigated, involving the testimony of witnesses under oath. In the second story, a lame youth from an estate close to Winchester was taken to Swithun on his feast day. He was placed before Swithun's tomb and was healed, and this, too, was confirmed by witnesses.[103] Likewise, in Geoffrey of Burton's miracles of Modwenna, five of the six detailed contemporary miracles included some investigation. In fact, the one miracle that was not investigated further – the release of a penitent from his iron bonds – occurred before witnesses present at the shrine.[104] Like the arguments over the resting places of the saints, the investigation of a miracle shows a concern over accuracy. It was important, where it was possible, both to ascertain that a miracle had occurred and to correctly attribute the miracle.

When Swithun first performed miracles there was some confusion over which saint had interceded for the supplicants. There were several saints with relics in the Old Minster, Judoc in the New Minster and a tower dedicated to Martin of Tours, upon whose feast one of the miracles occurred.[105] Such confusion could also potentially arise when a person was aided at multiple sites or at a place with many saints like Hexham, Ely or Canterbury.[106] In general it was easy to attribute a miracle accurately, however, as the saint prayed to either provided aid or indicated where aid could be sought. But custodians seem to have thought it important to confirm that anything miraculous had occurred at all and to understand the circumstances surrounding a miracle. This allowed the community to record the incident accurately and react appropriately, and it gives us an opportunity to see how a supplicant could be embroiled in the composition of a miracle story.

Our authors were dependent on the traditions of the communities they were concerned with, including the testimony of custodians and supplicants. The process of sourcing miracle collections is discussed by Eadmer in the quote at the beginning of this chapter, particularly the desire 'to relate concisely what deeds I have learnt either from writings, from the accounts of truthful men, or by my own sight'.[107] Such an approach was endorsed by Byrhtferth, who claimed that he used both old charters and reliable witnesses for his life of Ecgwine, and Osbern, who relied on unnamed witnesses and trusted sources for his work on Ælfheah.[108] We have a picture of the method of the miracle collector, but before moving on, we should consider their motivations.

Abbo and Lantfred both wrote about their saints for the edification of future generations.[109] This sense of obligation is found in Osbern's presentation of Dunstan's miracles as things which ought to be written down.[110] Eadmer, too, felt 'compelled to write down a few of the many' miracles of Anselm.[111] Dominic of Evesham sought to remedy the neglect of earlier authors in recording Ecgwine's miracles.[112] Likewise, William Ketell, Geoffrey of Burton, Herman and Arcoid wrote their collections with a sense of preservation against previous neglect.[113] Generally our authors seem to have been concerned with creating a permanent record of events and to have been 'distressed by the loss of stories about their saints' miracles'.[114]

Other motivating factors for the creation of these miracle collections were the requests of custodians and other influential people, a desire to please these people and attempts to secure patronage. Abbo dedicated his *Passio S. Eadmundi* to Dunstan and wrote it in thanks to the monks of Ramsey for their hospitality, fulfilling their requests for such a text.[115] Lantfred dedicated his miracles of Swithun to the monks of the Old Minster, and he was apparently encouraged by them.[116] Wulfstan recreated Lantfred's letter to the monks of the Old Minster but added a dedicatory preface to Ælfheah, then Bishop of Winchester (984–1006), which also includes praise for the late Bishop Æthelwold.[117] Goscelin regularly named his patrons and dedicated his texts to specific individuals. His work on Edith was composed at the urging of Herman of Salisbury and dedicated to Archbishop Lanfranc.[118] Goscelin dedicated his *Vita S. Wlsini* to Osmund of Salisbury (1078–1099) and stated that his collection of Edmund's miracles was the result of a request from an anonymous prelate.[119] Herman states that he was asked to compose his *Liber de miraculis S. Edmundi* by Abbot Baldwin of Bury.[120] Eadmer wrote that anonymous friends encouraged him to write the lives of Anselm and Oswald.[121] Aelred was commissioned to write his *De sanctis ecclesiae Hagustaldensis* by the canons of Hexham and the text was intended to be read on the feast of the translation of their saints.[122] Aelred's version of the life of Edward the Confessor was more plainly commissioned by and dedicated to Abbot Lawrence of Westminster.[123]

In cases of rewriting, the reviser sometimes indicates why they were undertaking this specific type of collecting. Goscelin seems to have been inspired to rewrite Herman's miracle collection mainly on stylistic grounds.[124] Eadmer, too, disapproved of Osbern's style as well as his historical accuracy. He also took the time to remove Osbern from the narrative as a witness and a participant.[125] In reworking the life and miracles of Aldhelm for his *Gesta Pontificum*, William of Malmesbury commented that whilst Faricius' style was fine, there were stories he omitted and knowledge he lacked. William put this down to Faricius' position as a foreigner who could not speak English.[126] Aelred does not directly criticise his predecessors in his work on Edward the Confessor, but he updated Osbert's style and sought to improve the historical narrative through the use of other sources.[127]

Our authors' more explicit motives, then, were concerns for the preservation of miracle stories, the fulfilment of the wishes of the community, the encouragement of friends and notables, the patronage of superiors and a desire to record events with greater accuracy or in a clearer manner. We may consider the nature of their audience more generally: who was hagiography intended for and how was it intended to be used? The audience question is still debated among scholars.[128] Van Egmond has identified three major ways hagiography could have been consumed in the medieval period. The first is through private reading, the second is through reading aloud to an audience and the third was through a recounting of the text by someone already familiar with it. These activities could take place anywhere and did not necessarily have to be limited to a church. Van Egmond uses the example of Alcuin's *Vita S. Willibrordi*, which included a prose version intended for reading aloud in church, the metrical version for private study and the homily which was to be preached.[129] Taking these three categories of consumption individually, private study of a text is the most difficult method to find evidence for. The text itself could only be accessed by a few people, and composition in Latin was obviously a bar to access for most of the laity and some religious. Even if a person had a grasp of Latin, an appreciation of the style and technique of an author would have been beyond all but the most educated.[130] This would lead to an immediate audience focused on the custodians of the saint.[131] Monastic and clerical readers did not limit themselves to private readings of the hagiography, however. Our second mode of consumption, reading aloud, was also used by the religious.

In monasteries and cathedral priories, a primary use of these texts would have been in the observance of the liturgy.[132] The main need would have been for lections to read as part of the office of a saint. These lections could be composed specially or extracted directly from a text. For example, Lantfred's *Translatio et Miracula S. Swithuni* is marked up for lections in the manuscript London, British Library, Royal 15.C.VII, whereas the lections found in Lincoln, Cathedral Library, 7 were composed separately by an author working from Lantfred's text.[133] Goscelin himself is described in the *Liber Eliensis* as composing liturgical material for Æthelthryth,[134] and he was the author of lections for Seaxburh, Eormenhild and Hildelith and a sermon for the feast of Augustine.[135] Such material could have been read aloud in the refectory or used in a monastic school as well as in the liturgy.[136] There was also room for the third mode of consumption, recounting a text within a religious context. This could see the custodians of a shrine recounting the deeds of their saint, as recorded, to pilgrims and other visitors.[137] As has been previously mentioned, Bede's material on Augustine was recounted to visitors to the saint's shrine.[138] It is likely, too, that miracle stories were recounted at court and other noble settings.[139] Our closest instance in the hagiography comes from Geoffrey's miracles of Modwenna, when the Abbot describes the healing of a man who had swallowed a brooch. The man was later brought before Queen Matilda (1100–1118), Henry I's first wife, by Geoffrey, who then told the Queen of other miracles of Modwenna.[140] Such retelling can be linked to the recounting of miracles by their recipients mentioned previously.

If we include these three modes of consumption, the audience of hagiography was a multifaceted community made up of slightly overlapping groups. Each individual could take more or less from the hagiography based on their training and inclinations. As Geary has pointed out, all hagiography was 'occasional literature' composed in response to a 'specific need'.[141] It could subsequently be mobilised in all manner of endeavours: in the liturgy, as an object of study, as a source of stories or even in a petition itself.[142] It is possible that saints were meant to be exemplars and that miracle stories were meant to be didactic. Certainly the punitive miracles demonstrated the potential consequences of the saints' power much more clearly than the beneficent ones.[143] But who was the hagiographer trying to teach a lesson to, if anyone, when they wrote down miracle stories? The people who would have got the full force of the stories, the rhetoric and the references would have been those who could examine the text directly – that is, the religious custodians of a saint and members of houses with a copy of the text in question. This is not to say that the second-hand audience was blind to the lessons of a text, but hagiography was not necessary for a supplicant to engage in a petition. A layperson would likely focus on the role of the saint as 'a healer and fixer' over the details of holy lives or the moralising of a text.[144]

The community of a saint did not need to be told of the saint's greatness and power – they had first-hand experience of it – but stories could help to reinforce the reputation of a saint, particularly with newcomers. Hagiography allowed the community of a saint to tell the stories it wanted to about itself,[145] leaving a written record which could help to authenticate the local cult. Hagiography could tell other communities more about your saint, but first they had to have heard of your saint or otherwise have had the text forced upon them.[146] Hagiography could also be used to try and influence the dealings of the aristocracy and royalty with your foundation. But at its most foundational level, hagiography was about collecting the deeds of the saints for posterity and the glory of God.[147] Its first audience was the community of the saint, both the custodians directly and the other members through recitation, who were a 'collection of experts' on the saint and their miracles. This audience of experts would have been considered at all stages of composition and acted as 'resource, censor, critic and arbiter' for the hagiographer.[148]

With these and doubtless other motivations in mind, the miracle collectors took experiences, memories and interpretations and produced a record of the shrine's 'official discourse'.[149] We rely on this official discourse as evidence, but it was also a part of how custodians tried to control the cult of their saint and the interpretations of them.[150] These attempts at control were sometimes contested, as in the debates over saints' resting places, and unintended information is included in much of the hagiography.[151] We have texts about local interests and events, with universalising characteristics and populated with characters, named and unnamed, who had encounters with the saints which resulted in miracles. The behaviour of these miracle seekers is our primary concern, but before we examine their petitions, we have to consider the shrines of the saints. For the majority of miracle making, the shrine played a crucial role as the domain of the saint and their custodians and as a site of pilgrimage.

Notes

1 'Nonnulla quae de uita beati Dunstani uitaeque decessu aut scripto, aut ab iis qui ab eius tempore usque ad nos per successus aetatum fluxere accepimus, in quantum Deus, illius interuenientibus meritis, concedere dignatus est, succincte digessimus. Nichilo igitur minus succincte digerere placuit quae uel ad sacratissimum corpus eius, uel ad beatam memoriam beati nominis eius partim scripto, partim ueracium uiuorum relatu, partim proprio uisu gesta didicimus.' Eadmer, *Miracula S. Dunstani*, pp. 160–1.
2 Christian, *Local Religion*, p. 3.
3 This will not be an exhaustive examination of hagiographical production in our period, nor will it contain complete career information and lists of works for each individual. For a more comprehensive overview, see Lapidge and Love, pp. 216–68; J. E. Cross, 'English Vernacular Saints' Lives before 1000 A.D.', in *Hagiographies*, ed. by G. Philippart and M. Goullet (Turnhout: Brepols, 1994–2018), II, 413–28; E. Gordon Whatley, 'Late Old English Hagiography, ca. 950–1150', in *Hagiographies*, ed. by G. Philippart and M. Goullet (Turnhout: Brepols, 1994–2018), II, 429–500; M. Thiry-Stassin, 'L'hagiographie en Anglo-Normand', in *Hagiographies*, ed. by G. Philippart and M. Goullet (Turnhout: Brepols, 1994–2018), I, 407–28.

4   Lantfred, *Miracula S. Swithuni*, pp. 235–7.
5   Koopmans, p. 49.
6   Lapidge and Love, pp. 217–18.
7   Michael Lapidge and others, *The Cult of St Swithun*, Winchester Studies, 4.II (Oxford: Clarendon, 2003), pp. 223–4.
8   Koopmans, p. 50.
9   Lapidge and Love, p. 219.
10 Lapidge, *Swithun*, p. 335.
11 Wulfstan, *Narratio de S. Swithuno*, pp. 452–61, 492–7.
12 Lapidge and Love, p. 219.
13 Wulfstan, *Vita S. Æthelwoldi*, p. 99.
14 Carl Phelpstead, 'King, Martyr and Virgin: *Imitatio Christi* in Ælfric's *Life of St Edmund*', in *St Edmund, King and Martyr: Changing Images of a Medieval Saint*, ed. by Anthony Bale (Woodbridge: York Medieval Press, 2009), pp. 27–44 (pp. 30–1).
15 Lapidge and Love, pp. 220–1.
16 Abbo, *Passio S. Eadmundi*, pp. 82–3.
17 Lapidge and Love, pp. 220–2.
18 Byrhtferth of Ramsey, *The Lives of St Oswald and St Ecgwine*, ed. and trans. by Michael Lapidge (Oxford: Clarendon, 2009), pp. xxviii–xxx.
19 Koopmans, pp. 60–3.
20 Lapidge and Love, pp. 225–33; Koopmans, pp. 60–1.
21 Koopmans, p. 61.
22 William of Malmesbury, *Gesta Regum Anglorum*, ed. and trans. by R. Mynors, and others, 2 vols (Oxford: Clarendon, 1998–1999), I, 592–93 (IV.342).
23 Rosalind C. Love, trans., 'The Life of St Wulfsige of Sherborne by Goscelin of Saint-Bertin', in *St Wulfsige and Sherborne: Essays to Celebrate the Millennium of the Benedictine Abbey, 998–1998*, ed. K. Barker, and others (Oxford: Oxbow, 2005), pp. 98–123 (p. 101).
24 Koopmans, pp. 60–3.
25 Lapidge and Love, pp. 225–33; Koopmans, pp. 60–4; Herman the Archdeacon and Goscelin of Saint-Bertin, *The Miracles of St Edmund*, ed. and trans. by Tom Licence with Lynda Lockyer (Oxford: Clarendon, 2014), pp. xxxvi–liv and cxiv–cxvi.
26 Lapidge and Love, p. 237.
27 Koopmans, pp. 81–2.
28 See chapter II.
29 Lapidge and Love, pp. 238–9.
30 Koopmans, pp. 92–4.
31 Lapidge and Love, pp. 240–1.
32 Ibid., p. 247.
33 Susan E. Wilson, *The Life and Afterlife of John of Beverley: The Evolution of the Cult of an Anglo-Saxon Saint* (Aldershot: Ashgate, 2006), pp. 9–10.
34 Lapidge and Love, p. 252.
35 Ibid., p. 260.
36 Ibid., pp. 242–3.
37 Koopmans, pp. 98–9.
38 Lapidge and Love, pp. 257–8.
39 Rodney M. Thomson, *William of Malmesbury*, rev. edn (Woodbridge: Boydell, 2003), pp. 3–7.
40 Lapidge and Love, pp. 258–60.
41 Ibid., pp. 260–1.
42 Whilst none of our named authors were female, it is possible that the author of the *Passio S. Edwardi regis et martyris* was a nun of Shaftesbury Abbey. See Koopmans, p. 80; Paul Antony Hayward, 'Translation-Narratives in Post-Conquest Hagiography

and English Resistance to the Norman Conquest', *Anglo-Norman Studies*, 21 (1999), 67–93 (pp. 85–6). See also Paul Antony Hayward, ed., 'The *Miracula Inventionis Beate Mylburge Virginis* Attributed to the Lord Ato, Cardinal Bishop of Ostia', *English Historical Review*, 114 (1999), 543–73, pp. 548–50 on the potential Cluniac identity of the author of the miracles of Mildburh.

43 Barking began life as a double house but was refounded as a women's community following the Viking incursions. See Donna Alfano Bussell and Jennifer N. Brown, 'Introduction: Barking's Lives, the Abbey and its Abbesses', in *Barking Abbey and Medieval Literary Culture: Authorship and Authority in a Female Community*, ed. by Jennifer N. Brown and Donna Alfano Bussell (Woodbridge: Boydell, 2012), pp. 1–30 (p. 3).
44 Lantfred, *Miracula S. Swithuni*, pp. 320–3.
45 Wulfstan, *Narratio de S. Swithuno*, pp. 455–6, 495–6, 568–9.
46 Wulfstan, *Vita S. Æthelwoldi*, pp. 64–7.
47 Goscelin, *Miracula S. Yuonis*, p. lxiii.
48 *Liber Eliensis*, pp. 213–16.
49 Goscelin, *Miracula S. Edmundi*, pp. 278–99.
50 Osbern, *Miracula S. Dunstani*, pp. 136–9.
51 Eadmer, *Vita S. Anselmi*, pp. 159–65.
52 William Stubbs, ed., *The Memorials of St Dunstan*, Rolls Series, 63 (London: Longman, 1874), pp. 412–22.
53 Arcoid, *Miracula S. Erkenwaldi*, pp. 144–7.
54 Lapidge and Love, pp. 217–20, 234–5.
55 Ibid., pp. 229–32.
56 Koopmans, pp. 66–7.
57 Licence, *Edmund*, pp. cxiv–cxvi.
58 Osbern, *Vita et translatio S. Aelphegi*, in *Patrologia Latina*, 149, col. 375–76.
59 Lapidge and Love, pp. 222–3, 237–42.
60 Ibid., pp. 247–8.
61 Richard Sharpe, *Medieval Irish Saints' Lives: An Introduction to Vitae Sanctorum Hiberniae* (Oxford: Clarendon, 1991), pp. 25–6; Lapidge and Love, p. 260.
62 Lapidge and Love, pp. 257–61.
63 Ibid., p. 259.
64 *Liber Eliensis*, pp. 176–7.
65 *Gesta Abbatum Monasterii Sancti Albani a Thoma Walsingham, Regnante Ricardo Secundo*, ed. by Henry Thomas Riley, Rolls Series, 28, 3 vols (London: Longman, 1867–1869), I, 33–8, 51, 85–8, 175–7.
66 Mark Hagger, 'The *Gesta Abbatum Monasterii Sancti Albani*: Litigation and History at St Alban's', *Historical Review*, 81 (2008), 373–98 (pp. 382–4).
67 Marvin L. Colker, ed., 'A Hagiographic Polemic', *Mediaeval Studies*, 39 (1977), 60–108.
68 Audrey M. Woodcock, ed., *The Cartulary of the Priory of St Gregory, Canterbury*, Camden Third Series, 88 (London: Royal Historical Society, 1956), p. 1.
69 *The Early History of Glastonbury: An Edition, Translation and Study of William of Malmesbury's De Antiquitate Glastonie Ecclesie*, ed. and trans. by John Scott (Woodbridge: Boydell, 1981), pp. 72–9.
70 Stubbs, *St Dunstan*, pp. 412–22.
71 Symeon of Durham, *Libellus De Exordio Atque Procursu Istius, Hoc Est Dunhelmensis, Ecclesie*, ed. and trans. by David Rollason (Oxford: Clarendon, 2000), pp. 234–5. The invention of Oswine at Tynemouth is described in his anonymous vita, as is a later 1110 translation at Tynemouth itself. See *Miracula S. Oswini*, pp. 11–17, 24–5.
72 *Passio S. Edwardi*, pp. 10, 12–13. There is a manuscript of Edward's *passio* from Abingdon, but it does not mention any of the translations. See Christine E. Fell, ed., *Edward, King and Martyr* (Leeds: University of Leeds, 1971), p. vi. The Abingdon

claim is in John Hudson, ed. and trans., *Historia Ecclesie Abbendonensis*, 2 vols (Oxford: Clarendon, 2002–2007), I, 182–3, 358–9.
73 *De Antiquitate*, pp. 68–9.
74 On Benedict, see William of Malmesbury, *Gesta Pontificum Anglorum*, ed. and trans. by M. Winterbottom, 2 vols (Oxford: Clarendon, 2007), I, 496–7 (iv.186); Walter de Gray Birch, ed., *Liber Vitae: Register and Martyrology of New Minster and Hyde Abbey* (London: Simpkin, 1892), p. 289. On Æbbe, see Robert Bartlett, ed. and trans., *The Miracles of St Æbbe of Coldingham and St Margaret of Scotland* (Oxford: Clarendon, 2003), pp. 20–7. On Boisil and Bede, see Symeon, *Libellus*, pp. 164–7. On Aidan, see Symeon of Durham, *Historia Regum*, in *Symeonis Monachi Opera Omnia*, ed. by Thomas Arnold, Rolls Series, 75, 2 vols (London: Longman, 1882–1885), I, 252–3.
75 Symeon, *Libellus*, pp. 162–3.
76 'De quorum omnium reliquiis aliquam secum partem', Symeon, *Libellus*, pp. 164–5.
77 Symeon, *Libellus*, pp. 164–7.
78 Aelred, *De sanctis Hagustaldensis*, pp. 195–9, 202–3.
79 This point is also borne out by the relic and resting place lists. See for example David Rollason, 'List of Saints Resting-Places in Anglo-Saxon England', *Anglo-Saxon England*, 7 (1978), 61–93. Hugh Candidus contains a later relic and resting place list in his twelfth-century chronicle, *The Chronicle of Hugh Candidus, a Monk of Peterborough with La Geste De Burch*, ed. by W. T. Mellows and Alexander Bell (London: Oxford University Press, 1949), pp. 52–64.
80 John Blair, 'A Saint for Every Minster? Local Cults in Anglo-Saxon England', in *Local Saints and Local Churches*, ed. by Alan Thacker and Richard Sharpe (Oxford: Oxford University Press, 2002), pp. 455–94 (p. 479). See also John Blair, 'A Handlist of Anglo-Saxon Saints', in *Local Saints and Local Churches*, ed. by Alan Thacker and Richard Sharpe (Oxford: Oxford University Press, 2002), pp. 495–565 (p. 543).
81 Lantfred, *Miracula S. Swithuni*, pp. 288–9.
82 Goscelin, *Miraculis S. Augustini*, p. 398.
83 Herman, *Miracula S. Edmundi*, pp. 104–9.
84 On the sacristan as a guardian of relics, see Herman, *Miracula S. Edmundi*, pp. 28–39, 346–9; William of Malmesbury, *Gesta Pontificum*, I, pp. 642–3 (V.270); Goscelin, *Vita S. Ethelburge*, p. 415. On the sacristan as a source of knowledge of their saint, see Herman, *Miracula S. Edmundi*, pp. 58–9; Lantfred, *Miracula S. Swithuni*, pp. 330–1. For more on the role of the sacristan, see chapter V.
85 Koopmans, p. 18.
86 Ibid., p. 14. For examples of authors claiming they could have included more miracles in their collection, see Osbern, *Miracula S. Dunstani*, p. 160; Eadmer, *Miracula S. Dunstani*, pp. 208–11; Geoffrey, *Miracula S. Modwenne*, pp. 214–25.
87 Koopmans, p. 25.
88 See Appendix I for the ubiquity of the common of the saints and on the liturgical celebration of a feast day more generally.
89 For example, at Winchcombe Abbey, by the 1170s there was a full Mass-set for Kenelm, with an extra prayer for vespers as well as a mention of the saint in the Mass in honour of the abbey's relics. The office material for Kenelm included a full twelve lessons, which were drawn from the eleventh-century *Vita* of the saint, as well as the collects, chapters, psalms and other chants required to celebrate the office on the saint's feast day. See Anselme Davril, ed., *The Winchcombe Sacramentary*, Henry Bradshaw Society, 109 (London: Boydell, 1995), p. 170; Richard W. Pfaff, *The Liturgy in Medieval England: A History* (Cambridge: Cambridge University Press, 2009), p. 175; Victor Leroquais, *Les Bréviaires Manuscrits des Bibliothèques Publiques de France*, 6 vols (Paris: Leroquais, 1934), IV, 283–5; Rosalind C. Love, ed. and trans., *Three Eleventh-Century Saints' Lives: Vita S. Birini, Vita et Miracula S. Kenelmi, and Vita S. Rumwoldi* (Oxford: Clarendon, 1996), pp. 130–4.

32 Writing Miracles

90 'Solennis beate Sexburge dies natalis illuxit quo ecclesiasticis intendentes officiis religiosos conuentus plebs religiosa pari deuotione comitatur. Immensa uniuersi perfunduntur letitia, et canoris laudibus mirabilia conditoris attollunt. Pro eterna gloria regine insignis festiuo ornatu gradiuntur amicti. Toga deaurata et pretexta purpurea Deum laudantes induuntur. Languor et desidia mentis humane ab eorum officio penitus remouetur. Crescit pia deuotio, et tinnula modulatione latera sonant ecclesie. Gaudent sancta collegia, et ymnis hinc inde mulcentur diuinis. Festiuum cum tripudio diem deducunt, in beate Sexburge fauore triumphantes. Expletis demum sacris et solennibus Deo sacrificiis immolatis, solennes fratres solenne decebat conuiuium.' *Vita Sexburge*, pp. 184–5.
91 Arcoid, *Miracula S. Erkenwaldi*, pp. 108–9. See also the anger of the locals when a priest refused to proclaim the upcoming feasts of Wihtburh and Seaxburh at Ely, *Liber Eliensis*, pp. 370–1.
92 David d'Avray, 'Popular and Elite Religion: Feastdays and Preaching', in *Elite and Popular Religion*, ed. by Kate Cooper and Jeremy Gregory, Studies in Church History, 42 (Woodbridge: Boydell, 2006), pp. 162–79 (p. 179).
93 Ben Nilson, *Cathedral Shrines of Medieval England* (Woodbridge: Boydell, 1998), pp. 92–3.
94 Thomas Head, *Hagiography and the Cult of the Saints: the Diocese of Orléans, 800–1200*, Cambridge Studies in Medieval Life and Thought: Fourth Series, 14 (Cambridge: Cambridge University Press, 1990), pp. 121–5.
95 Goscelin, *Translationis S. Augustini*, pp. 423–4.
96 M. T. Clanchy, *From Memory to Written Record: England 1066–1307*, 2nd edn (Oxford: Blackwell, 1993), p. 237.
97 Head, p. 132.
98 Wulfstan, *Narratio de S. Swithuno*, pp. 452–3.
99 Herman, *Miracula S. Edmundi*, pp. 98–109, 122–5, 340–2.
100 *Miracula S. Mylburge*, pp. 568–70.
101 Koopmans, p. 25.
102 Lantfred, *Miracula S. Swithuni*, pp. 292–307; Wulfstan, *Narratio de S. Swithuno*, pp. 462–3.
103 *Miracula S. Swithuni*, pp. 692–7.
104 Geoffrey, *Miracula S. Modwenne*, pp. 164–219.
105 Lantfred, *Miracula S. Swithuni*, pp. 266–87.
106 For example Byrhtferth, *Vita S. Ecgwini*, pp. 280–7; Goscelin, *Miracula S. Yuonis*, pp. lxvii–lxix; Goscelin, *Vita S. Wlsini*, pp. 84–5. On praying to the many saints of Hexham, Ely and Canterbury and their intercession, see Aelred, *De sanctis Hagustaldensis*, pp. 177–81; *Liber Eliensis*, pp. 212–13; Goscelin, *Miraculis S. Augustini*, pp. 397–8; Goscelin, *Translationis S. Augustini*, pp. 435–42.
107 'partim scripto, partim ueracium uirorum relatu, partim proprio uisu gesta didcimus.' Eadmer, *Miracula S. Dunstani*, pp. 160–1.
108 Byrhtferth, *Vita S. Ecgwini*, pp. 208–9; Osbern, *Vita et translatio S. Aelphegi*, in *Patrologia Latina*, 149, col. 375–76.
109 Abbo, *Passio S. Eadmundi*, pp. 67–9; Lantfred, *Miracula S. Swithuni*, pp. 252–3.
110 Osbern, *Miracula S. Dunstani*, pp. 129–30.
111 Eadmer, *Vita S. Anselmi*, p. 152. See also Eadmer's motivation to write about Dunstan due to his miracle working and worthiness, Eadmer, *Miracula S. Dunstani*, pp. 160–1.
112 Dominic, *Miracula S. Ecgwini*, pp. 76–7.
113 William Ketell, *Miracula S. Johannis*, pp. 261–2; Geoffrey, *Miracula S. Modwenne*, pp. 180–1; Herman, *Miracula S. Edmundi*, pp. 2–3; Arcoid, *Miracula S. Erkenwaldi*, pp. 102–3.
114 Koopmans, p. 98.
115 Abbo, *Passio S. Eadmundi*, pp. 67–9.

Writing Miracles 33

116 Lantfred, *Miracula S. Swithuni*, pp. 252–5.
117 Wulfstan, *Narratio de S. Swithuno*, pp. 372–401.
118 Goscelin, *Vita S. Edithe*, pp. 5–6.
119 Goscelin, *Vita S. Wlsini*, pp. 68–9; Goscelin, *Miracula S. Edmundi*, pp. 130–1. The anonymous prelate was probably Herbert of East Anglia (1094–1119). See Licence, *Edmund*, pp. cxv–cxvi.
120 Herman, *Miracula S. Edmundi*, pp. 2–3.
121 Eadmer, *Vita S. Anselmi*, p. 1; Eadmer, *Miracula S. Oswaldi*, pp. 216–17.
122 Aelred, *De sanctis Hagustaldensis*, pp. 173–6.
123 Aelred of Rievaulx, *Vita Sancti Edwardi confessoris*, in *Patrologia Latina*, 196, col. 737–40.
124 Licence, *Edmund*, p. cx.
125 Eadmer, *Miracula S. Dunstani*, pp. 44–5; Eadmer of Canterbury, *Lives and Miracles of Saints Oda, Dunstan, and Oswald*, ed. and trans. by Andrew J. Turner and Bernard J. Muir (Oxford: Clarendon, 2006), p. lxxvii.
126 William of Malmesbury, *Gesta Pontificum*, I, pp. 498–501 (V.prol).
127 Lapidge and Love, p. 261; Frank Barlow, *Edward the Confessor* (London: Eyre & Spottiswoode, 1970), p. 281.
128 On this debate see Anne E. Bailey, 'The Rich and the Poor, the Lesser and the Great', *Cultural and Social History*, 11 (2014), 9–29 (p. 11).
129 Wolfert S. van Egmond, 'The Audience of Early Medieval Hagiographical Texts', in *New Approaches to Medieval Communication*, ed. by Marco Mostert, Utrecht Studies in Medieval Literacy, 1 (Turnhout: Brepols, 1999), pp. 41–67 (pp. 42–3).
130 Hayward, 'Demystifying', p. 128.
131 Koopmans, pp. 133–4.
132 John Reuben Davies, 'Cathedrals and the Cult of Saints in Eleventh and Twelfth Century Wales', in *Cathedrals, Communities and Conflict in the Anglo-Norman World*, ed. by Paul Dalton, and others, Studies in the History of Medieval Religion, 38 (Woodbridge: Boydell, 2011), pp. 99–115 (p. 114).
133 Lapidge, *Swithun*, pp. 104–5. For more on the use of lections see Appendix I.
134 This text is now lost. See *Liber Eliensis*, p. 215.
135 Lapidge and Love, pp. 228–9, 232. On Goscelin as liturgist see Richard Sharpe, 'Words and Music by Goscelin of Canterbury', *Early Music*, 19 (1991), 94–7; Shannon Ambrose, 'The Social Context and Political Complexities of Goscelin's Sermon for the Feast of Saint Augustine of Canterbury, the "Apostle of the English"', *Studies in Philology*, 109 (2012), 364–80.
136 Egmond, p. 50.
137 Bailey, 'Rich and Poor', p. 11.
138 Goscelin, *Translationis S. Augustini*, pp. 423–4.
139 Yarrow, p. 21; Hayward, 'Demystifying', p. 128.
140 Geoffrey, *Miracula S. Modwenne*, pp. 202–5.
141 Geary, *Living with the Dead*, pp. 20–3.
142 See the miraculous application of a book of Oswine's passion in a miracle petition, *Miracula S. Oswini*, pp. 46–7.
143 Gábor Klaniczay, 'Healing with Certain Conditions: The Pedagogy of Medieval Miracles', *Cahiers de Recherches Médiévales et Humanistes*, 19 (2010), 237–48 (pp. 241–2).
144 Kleinberg, pp. 191–3.
145 Davies, p. 114.
146 Goscelin composed abbreviations of his work on the saints of Barking and St Augustine's. The St Augustine's works, at least, were composed for visitors to the abbey and for use beyond St Augustine's. See Lapidge and Love, pp. 229–32. Ælfric also provided epitomes of the Winchester texts Lantfred's *Translatio et Miracula S. Swithuni*

and Wulfstan's *Vita S. Æthelwoldi*, Lapidge and Love, p. 220. Conversely, Goscelin appears to have considered some of his compositions as intended for use by a saint's custodians specifically. In the preface to his *Vita S. Mildrethe*, Goscelin refers to the *domestici* whom he has prepared the text for, Goscelin, *Vita S. Mildrethe*, p. 109.
147 Geary, *Living with the Dead*, p. 22; Koopmans, pp. 97–9, 109–11.
148 Heffernan, p. 20.
149 John Eade, 'Order and Power at Lourdes: Lay Helpers and the Organisation of a Pilgrimage Shrine', in *Contesting the Sacred: The Anthropology of Christian Pilgrimage*, ed. by John Eade and Michael J. Sallnow (London: Routledge, 1991), pp. 51–76 (pp. 73–5).
150 Anne E. Bailey, 'Modern and Medieval Approaches to Pilgrimage, Gender and Sacred Space', *History and Anthropology*, 24 (2013), 493–512, pp. 497–9.
151 Gurevich, p. xix. For contests between and within communities of the saints, see chapter II.

2 Making Shrines

Tom Lynch

So far we have explored the process of recording miracles, the position of the hagiographer and their motivations for writing. When it came to miracles, a major source of information for the hagiographer was the shrine of the saint. The shrines of the saints were the primary location for their cults.[1] That saints, who were believed to be present in Heaven and on Earth, were particularly responsive to supplication in proximity to their relics was central to people's engagement with them.[2] Shrines, then, acted as a 'symbolic physical point' where people met their saint.[3] The saints themselves were an active presence in these places, as described by Eadmer in his *Miracula S. Dunstani*:

> Then the abbot, who had raised his eyes to the heavens, saw a great light shine down from there upon that church and penetrate it from above. When he saw this and pointed it out to his companions, who merited to see it with him, sighing with devout feeling he said: 'Truly our loving father Dunstan comes now to his own festival, wishing to be present at the show of reverence which his sons are about to perform for God and him on this night.' The brothers, who deserved to be present on this festive occasion, were witnesses that this occurred just as he had said. For they sensed his sacred presence amongst them from the sweet and holy feeling there, which made them delight in God and in his servant.[4]

Most shrines were within churches and sacred both through the holiness of the saint and the consecration of the church.[5] God and the saints were participants in the actions performed at a shrine, and they helped to construct this sacred space with the communities of the saints.[6] The vast majority of supplicants 'were neither theologians nor hagiographers',[7] and it is impossible to know how the average religious understood the ideas behind miracles, let alone the laity. What is evident is the popularity of saints' cults and the expectation that such saints could perform miracles, especially at their shrines.[8]

Such sentiments are borne out by the hagiographical evidence. In Lantfred's miracles of Swithun there are two hundred and forty-nine individual beneficent miracles successfully petitioned. Of these some two hundred and sixteen miracle stories were no more than lists of cures with little detail, leaving thirty-three longer form descriptions of miracle petitions. All of the short-form miracles and twenty-one of the thirty-three long-form miracles occurred at Swithun's resting place, at first his tomb outside the Old Minster and then his shrine inside the church. Goscelin's *Historia maior de miraculis S. Augustini* and his *Historia translationis S. Augustini et aliorum sanctorum* contain fifty-eight detailed accounts of successful miracle petitions, of which twenty-eight occurred at one of the saints' shrines at St Augustine's. From the end of our period, there is no collection to rival Lantfred's or Goscelin's in terms of size, but there are many shorter ones. Arcoid's miracles of Erkenwald include fifteen successful miracle petitions, of which twelve were at Erkenwald's shrine. William Ketell's miracles of John of Beverley contain nine successful miracle petitions, of which six occurred at his shrine. Finally the anonymous miracles of Oswine include fifteen successful miracle petitions, of which eight occurred at the shrine. Taken together from this sample, excluding Lantfred's short-form entries, 57.7% of successful petitions occurred at shrines. Shrines were not only a centre for miracles but also a centre for miracle stories. People who had experienced miracles elsewhere came to shrines to give thanks and tell the custodians and other supplicants what had happened to them.[9]

Shrines were important from the beginning of the cult of the saints. The early martyrs were first venerated wherever they had been buried, with an altar built without disturbing the grave. By the fourth century, this association between a saint and an altar had led to the inclusion of relics in new altars and the demand for relics as a part of the consecration of churches.[10] The altars at tombs began to be elaborated into substantial monuments usually built over an undisturbed grave, what Crook calls a 'tomb-shrine'.[11] The prime example of a tomb-shrine in pre-Conquest England is that of Swithun in the Old Minster at Winchester. Lantfred describes the tomb as the site of the first post-mortem miracles prior to the 971 translation of the saint.[12] This tomb-shrine appears to have developed into a chapel, which was combined into the western end of the Old Minster, perhaps as a part of the westwork itself.[13] Certainly Swithun's original tomb attracted attention long after the saint was translated. Burials were made around the tomb from the thirteenth century onwards, and a modest chapel was built at the site, which lasted until the Reformation.[14] An empty tomb could provide a secondary focus for pilgrims attending Winchester in hope of intercession from Swithun. Whilst we lack archaeological evidence of other alternative sites, they can be found described in the textual sources.

Lantfred also describes how Swithun performed a miracle at St Swithun's church on the Isle of Wight.[15] Some of Wulfhild's miracles were effected in her old oratory at Horton, where she spent some time as abbess.[16] In Constantinople a church was built to Augustine and Nicholas. There a miraculous icon of Augustine was kept, candles were lit and the saint was memorialised by English exiles.[17] Miracles occurred at Augustine's church in Exeter and an unspecified ruined church which had an altar dedicated to Augustine in it too.[18] A statue of Swithun, donated by the monks of Winchester and erected in Sherborne Cathedral, was a site of pilgrimage and miracles as well.[19] Erkenwald granted cures beyond St Paul's too, and he healed a crippled nun at Barking Abbey, which was founded by the Bishop for his sister, Æthelburh.[20] Other saints' previous resting places were likewise thought to be sites of healing. Like Swithun, Erkenwald's old tomb was the source of miracles at the time of his translation.[21] The church at Thanet where Mildrith was buried remained a place of miracles even after the translation of the saint's remains to Canterbury.[22] So, too, the old tombs of the Archbishops at St Augustine's, Canterbury, remained sites of intercession,[23] and a blind man was cured by spending a night with his guide in the chapel where Edmund was originally buried.[24]

Alternative sites of intercession did not have to be within a religious house, however, and the saintly presence could change the landscape itself. In England, Kenelm's death site near Clent remained associated with the saint because of the holy spring which erupted from the old grave. The *Vita Brevior*, a short passion in the form of eight lections roughly contemporary with Goscelin's life and miracles, adds that a chapel was built at the site of the spring where miracles occurred. Love points out that a twelfth-century chapel survives at a spot north-west of Romsley which once housed the holy spring.[25] A healing spring was also associated with Wihtburh's original burial place at Dereham.[26] The surviving Wihtburh's well is found to the west of St Nicholas' in East Dereham. The church contains some Norman sections and the well architecture itself is dated to the fourteenth century.[27] Ivo's remains, and those of his companions, were discovered at Slepe and translated to Ramsey. A daughter house was constructed at Slepe on the site of the old burial, where a miraculous spring flowed. Several of the miracles recorded by Goscelin involve this spring at Slepe, and it must have drawn as many people to the church there as to Ivo's remains at Ramsey. As a sign of the importance of Slepe, even without Ivo's remains, two of his companions were translated back there from Ramsey.[28]

The building of churches and chapels at these sites announced the Church's authority over the sacred landscape and the incorporation of that particular saint into the official local observance.[29] Here we can consider Gregory the Great's decree to Christianise the pagan holy sites of England with altars, relics and holy water.[30] The Church sought a monopoly over the cult of the saints, and architecture was one way this could be expressed. I do not suggest that this was the case for every site associated with the saints, merely that it was the case for the major miracle centres of medieval England. The saintly presence appears to have had a sacralising effect, which could be seen as a part of the dangerous potential of saints to circumvent the liturgical and pastoral work of the Church.[31] This danger was contained by a physical incorporation of those most special sites of the cult of the saints, the sites where miracles were petitioned and performed. The relics of a saint could be moved into a church, but the landscape required that architecture be brought to it. Whilst these alternative sites are found throughout the evidence, the shrine of the saint was the most commonly recorded location for pilgrimage and miracles.

In general shrines were above-ground structures upon which a reliquary was placed. Depending on the state of the saint's remains, these reliquaries could range from full coffins to small chests which could fit onto an altar.[32] The shrine itself varied but was usually some form of table or an arrangement of pillars. These shrines were built in the vicinity of the high altar, sometimes to the south but most often behind, to the east.[33] From the early eleventh century onwards, these shrines developed in height, and some allowed access below them for pilgrims, with an altar incorporated into the structure or found nearby and dedicated to the saint. During the twelfth century, these shrines became more elaborate, but it is difficult to chart an evolution of the form.[34] A feature which may have been quite common is a beam over the shrine from which votives and reliquaries could hang. Crook has identified such beams at Bury and Worcester,[35] and they could have provided a means to display the votives recorded in the miracle collections.[36] Shrines also seem to have been lavishly decorated with silver, gold and gems. Unfortunately we have no complete English shrines surviving from this time, but there are descriptions in the hagiography.[37] The cult of the saints impacted church architecture beyond the shrine itself. The key elements were apses, which were sometimes used to house shrines and/or altars, and ambulatories, which increased access to the shrine without having to pass through the choir. In England these elements were employed in a 'haphazard' manner. For example, important cult sites like Christ Church, Canterbury, St Albans Abbey and Durham Cathedral lacked ambulatories after their initial Anglo-Norman remodelling, whilst Bury and Winchester Cathedral included them.[38]

The only surviving elaboration of a shrine from our period is the 'holy hole' at Winchester Cathedral. The shrine of Swithun was raised in the 1150s as part of rebuilding work, which made the shrine inaccessible to lay pilgrims. The holy hole was a solution to these access problems, allowing a supplicant to crawl under the large elevated shrine and get as close as possible to the relics. Today the holy hole is visible as a small passage through the thirteenth-century retrochoir.[39] It is possible that *foramina* shrines, with their series of small openings in the supporting structure, came into use in England in the late twelfth century. *Foramina* shrines were first attested in the report of Abbot Daniel's visit to the Church of the Holy Sepulchre in Jerusalem, between 1106 and 1112. Perhaps such a shrine was used for Edward the Confessor following his translation of 1163, as depicted in the thirteenth-century manuscript of the life of Edward.[40] The idea of a *foramina* shrine also brings to mind Bede's description of Chad's tomb at Lichfield, which had holes from which people collected dust used for miraculous cures.[41] With or without elaboration, the most common place for a saint's shrine was in the vicinity of the high altar, usually to the east, and it at least consisted of a structure to support a saint's coffin or reliquary. Such a position kept the holy remains in a reverent and secure location close to the working heart of the church.[42] Before continuing, it is useful to consider the implications of such a location for the most important site of an apparently popular cult.

In larger churches, a saint's shrine could be made more accessible through the use of apses and ambulatories, but as we have seen, the use of these elements was inconsistent in our period. Without these features, a supplicant had to walk through or very close to the choir in order to access a shrine. Regular traffic through the choir would have been disruptive to the observance of the liturgy. In theory, the choir of a church, particularly in Benedictine foundations, was closed to the laity, but this practice would have been in tension with the desire of supplicants to get closer than the nave in order to interact with a saint.[43] The very crowds emphasised by the hagiographers could also be problematic. Arcoid states that the doors of St Paul's were torn off their hinges by the great crowd who assembled for Erkenwald's translation.[44] When the crowd that gathered for the translation of the saints of Barking was deemed too large by the Archdeacon of London, he limited access by stating that only those who had confessed could approach.[45] During the procession performed on the feast of the Purification at Sherborne, people were pushed around by the crowd, including five disabled people who were cured when they came into accidental contact with Wulfsige's feretory.[46] If we follow Lantfred's calculations, as many as twenty-five people could be cured in one day by Swithun in the Old Minster, with other high points including fifteen in a day, thirty-six in three days and one hundred and twenty-four in two weeks.[47] Wulfstan confirms these observations, stating that he witnessed over two hundred cures in ten days at Swithun's shrine and that countless cures occurred in the year 971–972.[48] Bearing in mind the probability that not every pilgrim sought a miracle, not every petition was successful, that supplicants did not always come alone and many spent more than a day at a shrine, we are presented with serious potential disruption to the liturgical workings of a church with a popular shrine.[49] At least in the case of the Old Minster – and probably more generally – each recognised miracle would come with the additional burden of corporate thanksgiving, which itself interrupted the daily lives of the custodians.[50] It is unsurprising, therefore, that there is also hagiographical evidence of individuals being barred from shrines.

Goscelin includes the story of a lame girl who was often brought by her family to Æthelburh at Barking in the hopes of help. This girl asked if she could spend the eve of Æthelburh's feast in vigil, but the sacristan Judith would not allow it and told the girl to pray outside. The girl did so, and during her vigil at the monastery doors, she was cured despite her separation from the saint. Presumably Judith had her reasons for this denial, and she stated that Æthelburh would heal the girl from outside if the saint willed it.[51] Perhaps the girl would have gotten in the way of the preparations for the saint's feast, perhaps the shrine area was already full or perhaps Judith just felt that a lay presence on this special night would have been inappropriate.[52] The next entry in Goscelin's account is the healing of a blind man at Æthelburh's shrine whilst the nuns were singing psalms, and the miracle before records the healing of three blind women, one at each of the shrines of Æthelburh, Hildelith and Wulfhild.[53] In Osbern's life and miracles of Dunstan, a girl asked for permission to keep vigil on the eve of the feasts of Ouen and Bartholomew (both at this time celebrated on 24 August). This was granted, and Osbern himself witnessed the miracle.[54] Evidently access to the saints' shrines was possible at Barking, and requests to engage in vigils were granted elsewhere. Goscelin frames this event in terms of the power of Æthelburh whilst maintaining the authority of Barking and the custodians. The miracle is changed in character if one interprets Judith's statement not as reconciliatory but as a quick termination to an annoying and persistent distraction. In that case, by healing the girl, Æthelburh may have subverted the authority of her sacristan slightly. The custodians could be seen as having washed their hands of the problem and to have continued the preparations for the feast day regardless. The onus would then have been on the girl to effectively petition the saint even though she was left exposed to the elements on an October night. The cure of the girl demonstrates the power of Æthelburh, but it undermines the primacy of the shrine. It shows, too, that the shrine was not open all the time to everyone.[55] Custodians were not alone in exerting control over who could visit a saint. The saints themselves could also intercede.

Cuthbert took a more active part in moderating who had access to his shrine. In Bede's *Life*, Cuthbert asked to be buried in his oratory rather than the monastery on Lindisfarne, in hopes that he would spare his community the bother of dealing with sanctuary seekers and the authorities pursuing them. In the end, Cuthbert consented to being buried at the monastery with the stipulation that he be interred in the church so that the monks could control access to his tomb.[56] Symeon of Durham also reports that access was denied to women wishing to visit Cuthbert's shrine or any of the churches where he previously lay.[57] This practice was traced by Symeon to Cuthbert himself, who declared, after he was made Bishop of Lindisfarne, that his followers should not mix with women and that women would not be admitted to the church on Lindisfarne. Symeon then brings in the fire which destroyed the double foundation at Coldingham on account of the inappropriate behaviour of the monks and nuns.[58]

In later times, Cuthbert even took miraculous vengeance against certain women who ignored his ban. Judith, wife of Earl Tostig of Northumbria (1055–1065), was devoted to Cuthbert but unable to pray at his shrine. She sent a maid to test the extent of the ban, and when the maid entered the graveyard of the church in Durham, she was pushed back by an unseen force and died of her injuries. Judith then sought to propitiate Cuthbert with gifts, including a decorated crucifix.[59] Another woman, Sungeoua, was killed for cutting through the same cemetery, and an unnamed woman killed herself after being driven insane for trying to enter the church.[60] It seems that the goal of the saint was to keep his monks chaste, and his misogyny was focused on those who would violate his shrine.[61] Here the will of the saint is interpreted by Symeon in a manner consistent with the will of the custodians. Deadly repercussions were to be expected for defying such a long-term interdiction. Yet women still tried to gain access to the nexus of the cult of Cuthbert. They contested not only the custodians but also their interpretation of the will of the saint. This leaves two obvious options for their behaviour – either they were ignorant of the interdiction, or they doubted it was truly the will of the saint in their particular case. Whilst ignorance is a possible cause in the case of Sungeoua and the unnamed woman, Judith sent her maid to probe the ban and showed remorse towards the saint when it proved deadly to her maid. For Judith another arrangement seemed possible, although it did not prove to be the case.

Even those who gained access to a shrine did not necessarily behave correctly. A woman named Mazelina struck her child in St Augustine's for interrupting her at prayer. For this inappropriate action, she was partially paralysed by Augustine. Upon realising what she had done, she cried out in anguish, plucked at her hair and appeared insane to the monks. The brothers took pity on her, and by common consent, they went to the church and tearfully sung the seven penitential psalms before Augustine's shrine on behalf of Mazelina. She shortly stood up cured and rejoiced.[62] Goscelin shows that unbecoming behaviour at a shrine would be punished by the saints but also that such punishment need not be the end. People could learn from their mistakes and be corrected into a more acceptable relationship with the saints. But even devout people did not behave correctly all the time.

Mazelina's case is also a rare example of a person praying at a shrine without a life crisis going on around them, until she brought one upon herself through her behaviour. Maybe she was praying for the remission of previous sins, as the family of Abbot Guthlac of Glastonbury did at Indract's shrine. Like Mazelina's case, this was only recorded within the context of a miracle. Whilst the family slept at the tomb, Guthlac had a vision of Indract in which the Abbot, then a child, was miraculously taught to read.[63] It is probable that many visitors to the saints were likewise simply praying or following up on the promise of an indulgence or performing a penitential pilgrimage with no miraculous content. People sought alms from those gathered at Swithun's statue at Sherborne, and a beggar at Winchester was diverted to the saint's shrine, where he was cured.[64] And then there would be sanctuary seekers not mentioned in the miracle collections as their cases were handled less dramatically.

The idea that criminals could claim sanctuary in a church was established in pre-Conquest England. The laws of Ine are the first to endorse sanctuary, with later references to the practice in the laws of Alfred, Æthelstan, Æthelred and Cnut. The practice of sanctuary is also recorded in the Anglo-Norman law code and was maintained after the Conquest.[65] Ordinarily sanctuary could be claimed at any church and relied on the holiness of a consecrated space and the authority of the local bishop.[66] In these cases, the saint and their resting place must have been conflated into a single authority, with the miraculous ability to punish transgressors with more than a mere fine. Indeed, the 'mobile charisma' of the saints could extend sanctuary beyond the confines of the church; in the province of York in the early twelfth century, a person wearing or in possession of relics could claim sanctuary.[67] Generally sanctuary was employed not as an end to legal proceedings but as a temporary period of immunity from prosecution, during which the crime and proposed punishment could be assessed. A sanctuary seeker would be expected to confess, disarm and surrender to the clerics of the church.[68] In the hagiographical accounts, criminals dominate, but any people in real need could claim sanctuary at a shrine and reasonably expect the local saint and their community to intervene if anybody tried to violate this understanding.

All of these people, with their various concerns and reasons for attending, were set against the daily liturgical backdrop of a working church. The nuns, monks, canons and other religious custodians may not have always been focused on their saints, but if their saints had any degree of fame, they would have noticed their presence daily. The exact nature of the attendees of the saints' shrines is difficult to determine. Kings, archbishops, nobles, bishops and abbots all visited shrines in search of aid or to give thanks for aid received.[69] These were relatively uncommon events, however, and the majority of supplicants seem to have been commoners and low-ranking religious. In Finucane's analysis of saints' cults in England in the twelfth and thirteenth centuries, he found that 61% of supplicants were male and 39% were female. Of the women. some 86% were of the 'lowest class', and 56% of men were of the 'lowest class'.[70] Sigal found that some 61.7% of recipients of post-mortem miracles in French saints' cults in the eleventh and twelfth centuries were of the 'classes populaires'. The next largest group was monks and clerics at 16.8% and then the aristocracy at 12.7%. The gender split for the 'classes populaires' was 66.6% male and 33.3% female.[71] Bailey has performed a statistical study using sixteen miracle collections from the long twelfth century and finding 1027 pilgrims in total. Of these 52% were female and 48% were male. Where possible Bailey also examined the age of pilgrims using the six ages of man and four familial categories. Focusing on female pilgrims, she found that children, mothers and wives dominated the narratives, although many stories lacked basic social information about supplicants.[72] Using the same data, Bailey has found that 319 pilgrims could be identified along social-functional lines, using the classes of *bellatores* (warriors), *oratores* (preachers) and *laboratores* (workers). Amongst male pilgrims, there was a roughly even distribution between each class. For female pilgrims, the majority were to be found in the *bellatores*, with slightly fewer in the *laboratores* and nine in the *oratores*.[73] In both studies, Bailey is keen to point out the limits to such analysis for representing reality.[74]

The notion of the shrine as a place for the poor is borne out by a story found in both versions of the miracles of Dunstan. A certain Ceolwulf, provost of Folkestone, was paralysed in his whole body. The provost was persuaded to go to Dunstan although he was concerned about mixing with commoners, and he was healed at the saint's tomb. Ceolwulf praised God and Dunstan for his healing and held a feast in celebration, where he was asked if he had been cured like the poor were. The provost replied that he would have been healed even without Dunstan, and he was stricken again with paralysis and died. People feared such miraculous vengeance and venerated Dunstan, and many gathered at the saint's shrine for healing and the remission of sins.[75] Ceolwulf's concern over mixing with the poor cannot have been unique. There was a presumption that a saint's shrine was a place for the poor masses, and Ceolwulf was pleased that God, through his saints, cured the powerful as well as the meek.[76] All kinds of people with all kinds of problems visited shrines. To be cured by Dunstan was fine – Ceolwulf thanked God and the saint for it – but to be cured like the poor was too much. Ceolwulf denied not only the saint but also his commonality with all those who went to Dunstan as supplicants. Such commonality has been framed by Victor Turner as *communitas*.

Turner's conception of *communitas* was indebted to the work of van Gennep on rites of passage. Van Gennep recognised that the stages of life, usually linked to age or social groups, are marked with 'ceremonies whose essential purpose is to enable the individual to pass from one defined position to another which is equally well defined'.[77] Each rite of passage can be understood to have an integral three-part structure – preliminal or separation, liminal or transition and postliminal or incorporation.[78] Van Gennep did not claim that all ceremonies are only rites of passage or that all societies elaborate each stage to the same degree, but he saw the pattern of rites of passage underlying many different forms.[79] Van Gennep noted that liminal periods regularly become extended and elaborated.[80] This state of extended liminality can be seen as being 'betwixt and between' social groups or situations.[81] Following Turner, transitional beings are seen as dangerous and polluting and are often physically separated off or exiled to the margins of society.[82] Within these ambiguous conditions, people will bond with each other regardless of previous status or grouping, in a state that Turner refers to as *communitas*.[83]

Turner saw this anti-structural moment in contrast to the structure behind everyday life, but both phases were required in the correct balance to maintain a functioning society.[84] These liminal periods are integral to Turner's understanding of cultural reproduction. The Turners recognised the act of pilgrimage as a 'liminoid' process, an extended period which took people out of structured society and into a state of equality and united purpose.[85] Pilgrims had essentially left 'a domain where relations are complex, for one where they are simple'.[86] This notion was explicitly applied by the Turners not only to contemporary practice but also to medieval pilgrimage. The medieval experience was pseudo-liminal focusing on relics, rituals and miracles at places associated with the saints.[87] The special dead mediated on behalf of supplicants, who were in a liminal condition of coping with illness or other life crises.[88] With them being united by their devotion and suffering and marginalised by their afflictions, it seems possible that the amorphous liminal period of supplication at saints' shrines, often extended over several days, could have resulted in a bond of *communitas*. Certainly this theory influenced Brown and Mayr-Harting in their conceptions of the saint's shrine as a place of social cohesion and reincorporation.[89] Turner's vision of the *communitas* of pilgrims has been challenged, however.

Sallnow has labelled pilgrimage as a 'polymorphic phenomenon' which denies the deterministic view of Turner's *communitas*. For Sallnow, who studied Andean penitential pilgrimage in the 1970s, pilgrimage did move people out of existing power structures but did not replace them with *communitas*. Instead pilgrims created new social relationships at shrines. These holy places had their own 'rudimentary structures of authority and control for keeping order amongst the assembled pilgrims'.[90] The shrine is presented as 'a ritual space capable of accommodating diverse meanings and practices' for a 'variety of clients'.[91] Eade emphasised the place of 'official discourse' at shrines, with behaviour and interpretation dominated by shrine keepers at Lourdes.[92] Bailey has linked this 'official discourse' to the evidence we rely on for medieval shrines, with both hagiography and the built environment, controlling access to relics for medieval pilgrims and guiding our interpretations of them.[93] This official discourse is a synthesis of the 'shared cultural mentality' of the cult of the saints and the 'individual historical circumstances' of a particular shrine.[94] Through this prism, Bailey sees a two-tiered system of positive anti-structural 'paradise' for the devout and negative structural 'hell' for those who behaved inappropriately.[95] I believe the hagiographers looked to portray a kind of *communitas* at their shrines, a utopian social order coalesced around the remains of their saint and under the control of their custodians. Ceolwulf disrupted this portrayal and was shown to have been punished. The story of Ceolwulf, like the misogyny of Cuthbert and the restrictions of the sacristan Judith, also shows how different members of a community could interpret a saint's shrine differently and act upon these interpretations. There were real communities focused on the saints and their shrines, but it did not level social differences or apply equally to everyone. Saints' cults were contested, and so were their shrines.

Shrines were not fixed in the landscape, and many burials had to be moved into churches before they became shrines proper. This was achieved through a translation, a formal ceremony which drew on liturgical trappings to sanctify the exhumation, transportation and reburial of a saint. The earliest recorded example of a translation is that of St Babylas, who was translated from his grave to a new church opposite a temple to Apollo at Daphne, a suburb of Antioch.[96] Following developments in the Eastern Empire, translations began to be performed in the Western capital, Milan, which suffered from a lack of local saints. This project was begun by Bishop Ambrose's translation of the martyrs Gervase and Protase to the Ambrosian Basilica in 386. Paulinus's account of the translation included the healing of many people triggered by the placing of the holy bodies on the biers and the cure of the blind man Severus when he touched the martyrs' clothes.[97] Ambrose took part in another translation at Bologna in 393 with the local Bishop Eusebius, removing the bodies of Vitalis and Agricola from their original burial site among Jewish people.[98] This translation was occasioned by miraculous cures. Ambrose's 395 translation of Nazarius and Celsus into the Basilica of the Apostles in Milan is noteworthy for the state in which Nazarius was found. In the martyr's grave, there was blood which appeared to be fresh, and Nazarius' severed head was found to be intact and incorrupt, with his beard and hair washed.[99] The translation of Nazarius and Celsus was also marked by a sweet odour, which became linked with the opening of saints' shrines, especially when they were found incorrupt.[100]

In Rome the reluctance to disturb the physical remains of the dead appears to have held out until the seventh century. The majority of Rome's saints were entombed in the catacombs of the city, and the popes of the sixth and early seventh centuries built and renovated churches in order to incorporate the resting places without disturbing them.[101] Amongst these careful popes was Gregory the Great, who describes the process of creating *brandea* in a response to Empress Constantina's request for the head of St Paul and his handkerchief. A *brandeum* was made by putting a piece of cloth into a special box which was placed near to the body of a saint. According to Gregory, after this procedure was followed, the *brandea* were potent enough to be used in the dedication of churches and were as good as bodily relics.[102] The holiness of the *brandea* is also picked up on in the *Life of Gregory the Great* by the anonymous Whitby monk, who records that Gregory cut open a *brandeum*, which bled, in front of some doubters, saying, 'When the relics are placed on His holy altar as an offering to sanctify them, the blood of the saints to whom each relic belongs always enters into the cloth just as if it had been soaked in blood.'[103] This story is related in Gregory's letters as well, although

Gregory states that the Pope involved was not himself but his predecessor, Leo I (440–461).[104]

Translation at Rome was still rare in the seventh century and only became common in the 750s due to the incursions of the Lombards on Papal territory.[105] Translation was firmly established by Pope Paul I (757–767), who, in 756, prior to becoming pope, moved the remains of many saints from extra-mural cemeteries by procession accompanied by hymns and chants.[106] Despite the well-documented influence of Rome on the development of Christianity in early medieval England, within a hundred years of the conversion, the English were translating their native saints without any qualms. Thacker traces the development of translation as practised by the English to fifth-century Francia, with the translations of Saturninus at Toulouse and Martin at Tours.[107] Bede notes several translations of the saints, including those of Augustine, Cedd, Chad, Aidan and Æthelthryth.[108] Other saints who were translated during this period include Cuthbert and Guthlac.[109] Whilst elevation and translation never became a necessity for all saints, before papal legislation, they acted as formal recognition of status, particularly suitable to a new foundation or expansion of a church.[110] Indeed, all of the saints whose cults I have referenced in this book received a translation either before or during the two centuries between 970 and 1170. The first translation recorded in England for our period was that of Swithun in 971.

Lantfred's account of the translation itself is fairly short. Following a series of visions and miracles at Swithun's original burial site, the remains of the saint were moved into the Old Minster, under the instruction of King Edgar (959–975), by Bishop Æthelwold of Winchester, the Abbots Ælfstan of the Old Minster and Æthelgar (964–980) of the New Minster and the monks of both houses.[111] Here we have the oversight of secular and religious authority figures and due reverence, but the brevity of the description makes it doubtful that Lantfred was present at the translation itself.[112] More instructive for our purposes here is the translation as recorded by Wulfstan from the later tenth century. Wulfstan may well have been an eyewitness to Swithun's translation, and his description of the event certainly contains more detail than Lantfred's version.[113] According to Wulfstan, crowds were summoned by the ringing of bells, filling the Old Minster. Æthelwold celebrated Mass, during which he admonished those gathered to observe a three-day fast and to beg God to be worthy to translate Swithun and benefit from his holy presence. The people assembled agreed and began their fast on the following Wednesday with prayers and psalms and broke it on the Friday. At this time, a blind woman approached Swithun's tomb and, following prayers and petitions, was cured of her condition. Bells were rung, and the people again assembled to give thanks, including Æthelwold, who then ordered the translation to begin.

The shrine was removed, and tents were set up around the tomb to prevent the crowd rushing the remains, but the process was halted to mark vespers. Following this, a procession of monks – with candles, incense and scripture books and led by a cross – chanted praises to Swithun and approached the saint's tomb with Æthelwold. When they had completed their hymns and prayers at the tomb, they continued into the Old Minster as dusk fell. The crowd approached the tomb, and lights were lit. Prayerful vigil was kept through the night, which the monks interrupted to perform the office. In the morning, Æthelwold, Abbot Ælfstan and the priests were vested, and they were accompanied by Abbot Æthelgar of the New Minster and the communities of both monasteries. All went in procession with candles and incense led by the Gospel-book and cross whilst they sung the chant *Iustum deduxit Dominus*. They approached the tomb with some trepidation, and after the crowd had been removed, the procession entered the tented area, which had been erected around the tomb.

As the communities chanted the psalms in order, Æthelwold ceremonially broke ground and then left the remainder of the digging to his attendants. The coffin was uncovered and opened, and all of Winchester was filled with the odour of sanctity. The remains were carefully washed and wrapped in a new shroud and then put into a shrine which was placed on a bier. Once the psalms were finished, the two abbots bore Swithun aloft to the rejoicing of the crowd. Æthelwold led the procession in the hymn, *Te Deum Laudamus*, and the doors to the Old Minster were opened. After this it seems the gathered crowd were permitted to enter the Old Minster following the procession, and they rejoiced with bells ringing. Æthelwold placed Swithun down, presumably near the high altar as he then celebrated Mass near to the saint and gave a sermon on God's deigning to allow such ceremonies and wonders to take place through his saint.[114]

Wulfstan shows how a major translation was performed and how Æthelwold aligned such an event with the observance of the divine office. The reform programme of Æthelwold and his allies was not suspended even for such an occasion. There is a tone of awe and a great deal of spiritual preparation before the grave is even approached. The presence of a great many laypeople and their participation in the ceremony is central to Wulfstan's narrative. Not only is the translation prefaced by the healing of a woman, but the people take part in the preparatory fast, the vigil and the singing of psalms and hymns. After the translation proper but on the same day, a miracle was petitioned by another woman, whose son was cured of a deformity of his hands. Word spread quickly, and many people returned to see the marvel with bells ringing and praises being given to God and Swithun.[115] Æthelwold's place as master of ceremonies is emphasised in his leading of the Masses before and after the translation, his beginning the *Te Deum* and his ground breaking at the saint's tomb. There is an obvious processional element to the translation, and the monks of the Old Minster were joined by their neighbours from the New Minster, uniting the neighbouring foundations in honouring Swithun. This was not the end for the relics of Swithun as there was a second translation, also recorded by Wulfstan.

King Edgar had vowed to have a fitting shrine made for Swithun, although it was evidently not complete by the first translation. Wulfstan notes that it was made from three hundred pounds of gold, silver and gems and that the work was carried out at a royal estate to the west of Winchester. Either a part of Swithun's body was taken inconspicuously to this estate, or perhaps the relics were moved with some formality which Wulfstan was not party to. However the relics got there, they then became the focus of a kind of second translation. Æthelwold placed a part of Swithun's body in the new shrine and announced the completion of King Edgar's request. Edgar inspected the finished work and was so pleased that he dispatched members of his retinue to Winchester. These messengers were to instruct all the people of Winchester, from slave to noble, to proceed to meet the new shrine, walking barefoot so that Swithun could arrive in the city with appropriate acclaim. The people, including Wulfstan himself, did as they were instructed, chanting the psalms on the way. The great crowd went slowly, and the people rejoiced on reaching the saint. The monks prostrated themselves before the new shrine and then rose and sang a hymn, following the feretory in procession towards Winchester. They made their way to the west gate of the city, where a blind girl was healed by praying before the relics. The monks sang thanks and praises, and the shrine was taken to the Old Minster and deposited on the altar by Æthelwold. The whole day was spent singing, and King Edgar gave thanks that his gift was deemed acceptable.[116]

Again Wulfstan emphasises popular involvement and excitement at the occasion of the translation, apparently including all of Winchester's population. The dual procession is important, as such a treasure could not pass by unheralded and without the appropriate reverence. This time the processional element was over a much longer distance and lacked the clerical vanguard with their cross, scriptures and incense. However, there was a more active royal involvement in the second translation. The main markers of reverence here were the prostration of the monks, the barefoot condition of the people and the singing of hymns and psalms performed as part of the movement of the feretory. Wulfstan's description has the feeling of a parade or an Imperial triumph, with less formality than the first translation. If we are to believe Wulfstan, much labour must have ceased as all the people of Winchester, no matter their social position or wealth, are reported as engaging in the translation. In this respect, it would have been much like a feast day, with the people given over to the work of God. Exactly how this day was regarded is difficult to say; the first translation is the date that is marked liturgically, and the relics were not moved to a new place so much as moved to a new shrine. Once the relics had been removed, it would have been impossible to return them quietly in their new feretory of sparkling metalwork and gems. It would also have been undesirable as this was an opportunity for all those involved to gain in prestige and to honour Swithun, and the event had to be carried out and stage managed appropriately.

Our latest datable translation was that of Edward the Confessor in 1163, which is recorded rather tersely by the monks of Winchester.[117] Most of the translations from the period between these events were documented similarly with little to no detail appended. The latest full account is that of Aelred of Rievaulx describing the translation of the saints at Hexham in 1154. It was decided by the canons at Hexham that their saints, who had been enshrined together at a previous translation in a wooden casket, were due higher honour. Prior, Richard was consulted and gave his permission, and the date was set as 3 March. The canons prepared with psalms and prayers, and on the day itself, they assembled in the church at the third hour after dawn. They prostrated themselves barefoot before the altar and then prayed and chanted the seven penitential psalms and the responsory used to honour confessors by the canons at Hexham. When they had finished, they carried the relics in procession to the altar, still barefoot and dressed in albs, and reverently emptied the relics onto a cloth next to the altar. The bones of four individuals were found. Three of them were identified by the labels found with their bundles as Acca, Alchmund and Frithuberht. The fourth was deduced to be Tilberht, and the separate shrine of Eata was also opened at this time so that the saint could be translated as well. All of these saints were Bishops of Hexham, a see which disappeared with the last Bishop, Tidfrith, in the early ninth century.[118] When the tombs were opened, the odour of sanctity poured forth from both of them.

Once the relics had been properly identified, the canons gave thanks and began to redeposit them. They had had three new shrines constructed, one large one coated with silver and gold and adorned with gems of the highest quality and two smaller ones which were less expensive but of the same beauty. Into the larger one they placed the remains of Acca, Alchmund, Frithuberht and Tilberht. In one of the smaller shrines, they placed Eata, and into the other, they placed some fragments of the local saints and some relics of Babylas, the same third-century Bishop of Antioch and martyr who was subject to the first recorded translation. These relics of Babylas may have been part of the relics of the apostles and martyrs that Bede claims were collected at Hexham by Acca.[119] The three shrines were arranged on three columns near the altar, the largest in the middle with the one containing Eata to the south and the one containing the loose relics to the north. This new table or shelf was decorated with images and statues. A Mass was then sung after which the people of Hexham were sent away, and the canons resumed their daily observances.[120]

The 1154 translation of the saints of Hexham shares a lot in common with the 971 translation of Swithun at Winchester. In both cases, saints were moved with great care in a short procession with various liturgical trappings. The ceremonies were overseen and approved by the local religious hierarchy, and both translations culminated in the deposition of the saints close to the high altar. The major points of difference were the practicalities of the locations, the motivations for the translations and the degree of lay participation. Swithun was translated from his original burial place following a series of miracles which revealed the power of Swithun and his presence in the graveyard of the Old Minster. The saints of Hexham were moved due to the requests of the prior and canons rather than a miraculous revelation. Miracles are much more important to Wulfstan's narrative in general, with the two cures before and after the translation as well as in the prelude to the translation. The only miracle common to both narratives was the dispersal of the odour of sanctity once the remains were uncovered.

More generally, motivations for translation seem to have been linked to concerns over appropriate reverence. This could be a vague notion as with the translation of Birinus from Dorchester to Winchester and the translation of Guthlac at Crowland under Abbot Waltheof (1124–1138).[121] Such concerns would be more focused following rebuilding schemes, which were common in the Anglo-Norman period. For example, Erkenwald, Ithamar and the saints of Bury, St Augustine's, the New

Minster and Barking were all translated into new or renovated homes in the century following 1066.[122] Of course the saints could spur on the actions of their custodians with visions and miracles, as was the case with Æthelburh at Barking as well as with Æthelwold, Edith, Kenelm, Wulfsige, Ithamar and Wenefred.[123] Even where there were miracles leading up to a translation, the hagiographers often portray a translation as a turning point resulting in more miracles. Goscelin describes crowds coming to Wulfsige's shrine after the translation and states that the majority of them went away healed.[124] Lantfred and Wulfstan describe the large number of miracles which followed Swithun's translation.[125] Miracles also flowed after the translations of Rumwold, Modwenna, Erkenwald, Æthelwold, Birinus, Wulfsige and the companions of Ivo.[126]

In terms of lay participation, Wulfstan shows the deep involvement of the crowd in the whole process, whereas in Aelred's narrative, the crowd seems to have been witness to some of the proceedings and the concluding Mass but was then sent away. Crowds seem to have been quite common at translations. Wulfstan also describes a great gathering of monks and minor clerics at the translation of Æthelwold.[127] Goscelin claimed a great crowd assembled for the translation of the saints at Barking Abbey, Æthelburh, Hildelith and Wulfhild.[128] Eadmer notes the presence of many people, including bishops, abbots, nobles, religious and common folk, at the translation of Oswald of Worcester. In fact, Archbishop Ealdwulf of York (995–1002) seems to have sought the assent of the people of Worcester before the translation was undertaken.[129] The new silver shrine for Erkenwald's translation under Bishop Gilbert of London was paid for by a collection taken amongst the people of London. Arcoid goes on to describe a great crowd on the day of Erkenwald's translation. All of this was apparently carried out under hurried conditions with no prior announcement of the translation made.[130] Crowds also gathered for the translations of Edith, Edmund, Guthlac, Osyth and the saints of St Augustine's.[131]

As with the motivation of custodians to translate their saints, the motivation of the crowds in attendance is difficult to assess. Eadmer states that the people present for Oswald's translation were gathered to witness a great event and for the sake of their souls and bodies. The people are described as having differing expectations as well as differing levels of belief. An unnamed abbot in particular was unconvinced of Oswald's power until a man was cured of leprosy during the translation.[132] Miracles certainly played a part in many translations and acted as a means of interaction between the saint and the faithful. As a coda to Edmund's translation, his relics were carried out to end a drought, whilst Wenefred kept the attendees of her translation dry despite the heavy rain clouds.[133] Wenefred cured a crippled man on her translation route as well, whilst Edward the Martyr cured two people during his translation procession.[134] People were also healed during the translations of Æthelburh, Edmund, Mellitus, Laurence and Hadrian.[135] Thus, the draw of a miracle-inducing spectacle could account for the attendance of many people. The translation of Edmund, with Jurmin and Botulf, contains an element which is worth discussing further. Bishop Walkelin of Winchester (1070–1098) granted an indulgence for the people in attendance at the translation.[136]

We are not given the details of Bishop Walkelin's indulgence beyond the fact that it began on the translation, lasted for some time afterwards and applied to all pilgrims within a fixed time. This is the only reference to an indulgence I have found in the hagiographical material composed between 970 and 1170. This is not to say that Walkelin's indulgence was unique. Indulgences emerged in the mid eleventh century as grants pardoning a portion of penance, assigned by bishops or the Pope.[137] Indulgences developed in response to a system of penance based on days of fasting or other abstention, which could easily accumulate to exceed the remaining life of a sinner.[138] The most famous early example of this reduction in 'earthly mortification' is the 1095 declaration by Pope Urban II (1088–1099) of an indulgence for those travelling to the Holy Land for the First Crusade.[139] That the Bury translation was roughly contemporary with Pope Urban's pronouncement shows that the principle had been well established by the end of the eleventh century.

The chanceries of English bishops show that indulgences were granted across the country for a variety of reasons. For our purposes, the indulgences related to translations, relics and feast days are most relevant. Richard, Bishop of London (1108–1127), granted an indulgence of twenty days for those present at St Paul's for the translation of the arm of Osyth and of seven days for those who attended the anniversary feast.[140] Bishop Richard of Hereford (1131–1148) granted an indulgence to benefactors of Leominster Priory in relation to the establishment of a feast day in honour of the church's relics.[141] Between 1158 and 1165, Bishop Josceline of Salisbury (1142–1184) granted an indulgence of forty days to attendees of the vigil and feast of Mary Magdalene at a church dedicated to the saint in Bucklebury.[142] Under the auspices of Thomas Beckett, an indulgence of forty days was granted for pilgrims visiting Chichester on the feast or in the octave of Denis.[143] Bishop Gilbert of London (1163–1187) granted an indulgence of twenty days for visitors to St Martin-le-Grand who attended within twenty days of the anniversary of the reception of fragmentary relics of Cuthbert at the collegiate church.[144] Two high-profile saints attracted indulgences from more than one see. Reading Abbey had received the hand of St James from King Henry I (1100–1135) at the request of his daughter Matilda, who had brought the relic back with her on her return to England in 1126. The relic was removed by Henry of Blois in 1136, but it was eventually returned to Reading in 1155.[145] It is probable that the great proliferation of indulgences for visiting the hand of James at Reading in the mid twelfth century were linked to this return, including grants from the bishops of Bath, Canterbury, Durham, Lincoln, London, Norwich and Salisbury.[146] Visits to the tomb of Edward the Confessor at Westminster Abbey to commemorate his deposition and translation were also encouraged with indulgences from multiple bishops.[147]

Therefore, the laity came to see their saints translated for the sake of their souls and their bodies, as well as to witness such elaborate religious performances. They could join in with elements of the ceremony, but as we have seen, their great numbers could be disruptive. This could take the form of damaging the fabric of the church, injuring one another or just getting in the way of the procession.[148] Some people asked for and were granted preferential access to the saint and their tomb during a translation. A noble woman was allowed to approach Oswald's old tomb as it was being excavated at Worcester.[149] Likewise Alwold, an architect of Crowland Abbey, was given permission by Bishop Alexander of Lincoln (1124–1148) to have the head reliquary of Guthlac placed on him to cure a brain lesion.[150] High-ranking clerics and religious could gain close access to the saints by taking on a role within the translation. If a saint was thought to be incorrupt, an inspection might take place, which happened for Cuthbert, Wihtburh and Edmund.[151] If not, the remains would be elevated, often washed and placed in a new shrine, and then carried to their new resting place. All of these actions allowed custodians and their proxies to get close to the saints in a way that the crowd could not. These close encounters could also lead to miracles.[152] Miracles drew in people of all kinds to translations, and proximity to the body of a saint was highly prized. The custodians ran the show, screened off excavations and tried to moderate participation, but it was a contest. Occasionally this contest was between potential custodians rather than between the custodians and the crowd.

Ælfheah, Archbishop of Canterbury, was murdered at the hands of the Danes in 1012. He was buried at St Paul's and soon proved to be a miracle worker. In 1023 King Cnut gave permission for the remains of Ælfheah to be translated to Christ Church, Canterbury. This event was recorded both in the *Anglo-Saxon Chronicle* and in a translation account written by Osbern in the late eleventh century. According to Osbern, Cnut sent for Archbishop Æthelnoth (1020–38) in London and told him of his plan to fulfil a vow to translate Ælfheah's remains to Canterbury. Miraculously the stone sealing the saint's tomb was moved by two monks and they found Ælfheah incorrupt. The King, the Archbishop and the monks then took the body to a boat on the Thames. They crossed the river and could hear the distraction being laid on by Cnut's troops and see the armed men holding the nearby bridge and riverbank. The body was dispatched south with an armed escort as an attack by the citizens of London was predicted. The Archbishop joined the monks whilst the King remained in London, and as he still feared an attack, the body was sent on ahead with a small group and was eventually met by a large crowd of people from Kent. There appears to have been little ceremonial to this smuggling operation, besides the prayers of Archbishop Æthelnoth, until they reached the outskirts of Canterbury several days later. Here they were met by the monks of Christ Church, who formed a procession dressed in the vestments of priests and deacons and led by brothers carrying candles, Gospel-books and jewelled crosses accompanied by the crashing of cymbals and chanting.[153]

Such tales of relic theft were incorporated into English hagiography from the eleventh century onwards. When Felix's body was stolen away from Soham to Ramsey by boat, the pursuing competitors from nearby Ely became lost in the fog.[154] The three-way struggle over Erkenwald's body between Barking, Chertsey and London was solved when the saint parted a river allowing the canons of St Paul's to carry the saint into the City.[155] The party sent to translate Kenelm to Winchcombe were intercepted on their return journey by an armed band from Worcester. After an altercation, it was decided that whichever group awoke first should take the martyr's remains with them. The Winchcombe party awoke and carried off Kenelm, pursued by the Worcester band, and eventually made it home by leaving the road.[156] When Abbot Byrhtnoth (c. 970–996/99) translated Wihtburh from Dereham to Ely under the cover of darkness, he had time to observe some of the expected ceremonial forms. Whilst the people of Dereham feasted, Byrhtnoth prayed to the virgin, approached the tomb with incense and greeted the holy body with awe. They carefully placed her coffin onto their vehicle and sang psalms as they made their way out. They were then met by soldiers and were harried by the people of Dereham, when they discovered the ruse. A miraculous star followed their progress to Ely, and this and the fear of Wihtburh put off the crowds. This whole episode seems to have been triggered by the acquisition of the monastery at Dereham by Ely and the refoundation under Byrhtnoth.[157] Before her death, Wærburh had foreseen that she would come to rest at Hanbury despite her love for all of her communities and the fact that she died at Threekingham. Her body was kept locked up at Threekingham, but when the people of Hanbury came to claim Wærburh, the locks and bars fell to the ground, and the doors were opened. The people of Hanbury entered whilst the guards slept and they carried the saint away without open conflict.[158] Finally, as noted previously, the competition over Mildrith's body resulted in a war of words between St Gregory's and St Augustine's. In Goscelin's description of the translation to St Augustine's, the people of Thanet also put up resistance to the removal of their patron.[159]

As these examples show, the theft motif was used when relics were travelling over a relatively long distance and were being transferred between communities. Tactics generally revolved around either subterfuge or armed force, though these two methods could be combined as in Ælfheah's translation. What is paramount in all these descriptions is that the will of the saint could not be denied. Where it was not initially clear who or where a saint favoured, their will would be made manifest through miraculous aid for their chosen community. There were obvious benefits to stealing the relics of a known thaumaturge. It showed not only the saint's approval but also dominance over the community from which the saint was taken. Saints brought with them the potential for financial rewards, miracles and attention from people of every social position. Theft of relics was in a sense a 'kidnapping and a seduction', as people interpreted how and why relics had moved over large distances and had been allowed to escape from their erstwhile custodians.[160] If a saint did not wish to be moved, they would make it known. Goscelin describes several saints weighing down their coffins, including Æthelburh, Wulfhild and Ywi.[161] In Herman's account of the 1095 translation of Edmund, the saint makes his body easy for the six brothers to carry despite the fact that in the past, he would make himself very heavy when leaving the old church.[162]

When a saint 'moved home' in medieval England, they did so with a translation. Taking on liturgical trappings and being imbued with Church authority meant that in many ways, translations made 'official' cults.[163] This did not mean a translation was required for an individual to be recognised as a saint, but those saints who did receive them were physically and symbolically incorporated into a church. Taking their rightful place, generally in proximity to the high altar, saints' bodies could be afforded devotion in an environment controlled by their custodians. These consolidating rites did not bind a saint, however, and if the saint willed it, they could be moved again and again.[164] The care taken in translating the saints shows how keen custodians were to not upset them. But this same power was a large part of the attraction of the saints and their relics. To be seen at the head of a translation or handling relics or saying Mass after a successful ceremony would create deep associations between leading clerics and local saints.[165] Precedence and preference could be played out through the ordering of processions, the choosing of the bearers of the saint and granting of special access to the relics. A grand translation brought out the local populace and engaged them in the cult of the saints. This attendance appears to have been motivated largely by the likelihood of miracles on such an occasion and the attendant benefits for the locality going forward. It was probably also due to the festive atmosphere and relative rarity of such an occasion, with its powerful attendees, new shrines of precious metal and the chance of curing one's soul as well as one's body.

One did not have to move the main shrine of a saint in order to forge a connection to a new location. A direct link to a saint could be established by moving a portion of their relics. On a trip to Rome, Abbot Baldwin took relics of Edmund from Bury with him and distributed them to various churches. Amongst them was St Martin's Cathedral at Lucca, where an altar was dedicated to Edmund. A young boy was beyond the help of physicians and had been taken to numerous saints. In their travels they heard of Edmund and were directed to St Martin's. There the family held vigil before Edmund's altar, and the boy was cured by morning. The family praised God and Edmund, and news of this miracle reached Bury via travellers to Rome. Every year people went to St Martin's to thank Edmund s for the miracle.[166] As well as removing a portion of relics permanently, the remains of the saints could be taken away from their homes for a number of reasons. Even whilst they were separated from their home, the saints remained potent intercessors. Edmund's relics were taken from Bury to London by the sacristan Aelwine in order to escape the Danish incursions of 1010–1013. The saint and his guardian spent some three years based in St Paul's churchyard, and miracles were effected in proximity to Edmund's feretory.[167] The relics of Ecgwine were taken from Evesham, not for protection but on a fund-raising tour. The saint travelled through London, Rochester and Winchester amongst other places, and Ecgwine was effective as an intercessor wherever his body happened to be.[168] A more common reason for removing the body of a saint from their shrine was to take it out as a part of a procession.

Processions with relics were integral to the occasional ceremonies of translation and the dedication of a church,[169] as well as being an important part of the yearly cycle of feasts. The oldest English processional, from St Albans and dating to the third quarter of the twelfth century, does not cover the whole year, but it gives an indication as to when processions were staged.[170] The St Albans processional contains provision for processions for the feasts of Alban, John the Baptist, Peter and Paul, the translation of Benedict, Peter ad vincula, the invention of Alban, the Assumption, the decollation of John the Baptist, the nativity of Mary, the exaltation of the Cross, Matthew, Michael, Simon and Jude, All Saints and Martin of Tours.[171] Processions were also common for Candlemas, Ash Wednesday and Palm Sunday.[172] The *Regularis Concordia* states that processions should be carried out on Wednesdays and Fridays in Lent and from the Octave of Pentecost to the calends of October.[173] In his *Monastic Constitutions*, Lanfranc records that processions should be carried out on the election of an abbot, Ascension Day, Maundy Thursday, Easter Day, Palm Sunday, Holy Saturday, the Octave of Easter, Christmas, Pentecost, the Assumption of Mary, the feast of the house, Rogation Days, Ash Wednesday, Fridays and Wednesdays in Lent, when receiving a dignitary, as a part of the burial service, Candlemas and as part of the office for the sick.[174] Of these occasions, only the processions on Ascension Day, the Rogation Days and saints' feasts can firmly be linked to the cult of the saints.

In Lanfranc's *Monastic Constitutions*, there is a brief *ordo* for the procession to be carried out on Ascension Day. A procession was to be carried out in albs and could either proceed outside the cloister with banners and relics and 'all else pertaining to a festal procession' or go through the cloister without the banners.[175] That relics were paraded on Ascension Day is confirmed by William of Malmesbury, who recorded that the arm of Aldhelm was carried in procession with other relics at Salisbury on Ascension Day. In carrying the arm reliquary, Archdeacon Hubald of Sarum was healed of a recurring shoulder and neck complaint.[176] Ascension Day was also an occasion for recognition processions, when the congregation and clergy of a chapel or daughter foundation would process to their mother church. In fact, Ascension Day was only one of several occasions when these recognition processions were held, with Pentecost, Palm Sunday, Candlemas, the dedication of the mother church and local saints' days being common.[177] These recognition processions appear later in our period, after about 1100, and may have been an attempt to keep old ties between minster churches and smaller local foundations alive.[178] The season of Ascension must have been full of processions as it was customary for them to be performed on the three Rogation Days beforehand.

As early as the death of Bede in 735, there is evidence for the processions on the Rogation Days. In Abbot Cuthbert's *Letter on the Death of Bede*, he states that on the Wednesday before Ascension at nine o'clock, the monks left Bede's deathbed to take part in a 'procession with relics, as the custom of that day required'.[179] It seems that the Frankish practice of marking the three days before Ascension with processions, penance and fasting was taken up by the English church.[180] Another early reference to relic carrying on Rogation Days comes from the 747 Council of Clofesho, which exhorts that these days be kept with due reverence, including the carrying of relics amongst the people.[181] The observance of the Rogation processions appears to have been maintained throughout our period, and they are included in the St Albans processional.[182] There are six Old English homilies from the tenth-century *Vercelli Book* for the pre-Ascension Rogation Days. In the second of these, homily XII, the homilist emphasises the role of relics in the procession, that they must be carried around the land and that these relics could be remains of holy men, parts of their body, their hair or their clothes.[183]

Lanfranc records extensive instructions for the Rogation processions in his *Monastic Constitutions*, including the carrying of banners, holy water, a cross and a Gospel-book and going barefoot with staves to another church where an antiphon for the patron saint would be sung. Following this a lesson and a collect for this same saint was read. They then made ready to celebrate Mass in this church, including a prayer for the patron saint. After Mass a litany of the saints was begun, which included a double invocation of the patron saint after the choir of the prophets. Whilst chanting this litany, they returned, with the litany being shortened or lengthened based on the distance of the walk. Interestingly, no mention is made of the carrying of relics in Lanfranc's *ordo*.[184] There is also evidence from hagiographical sources of the processing with relics on Rogation Days. Byrhtferth documents the practice at Ramsey of walking barefoot to a church of the Virgin Mary on Rogation Days, with relics in tow. On this occasion, Oswald of Worcester was present and stopped a boat containing the relics from sinking on the way back to Ramsey.[185] In Goscelin's account of the translation and miracles of Liudhard, a Rogation procession was carried out, with the relics of Liudhard brought forth in a golden shrine, in order to bless the people and the produce of the land.[186]

Processions also helped to mark the feast of a saint or to otherwise honour them. As noted previously, on the feast of Seaxburh, the laity and members of the monastery at Ely went in procession in festive clothes to the sound of music and hymns.[187] The people of Dereham and the surroundings performed a recognition procession on the sixth day after Ascension, with banners, crosses, candles and offerings, dedicated to Wihtburh and ending in the church where she was buried before being translated to Ely.[188] Aldhelm's feast at Malmesbury was marked with a procession, after which the shrine was fixed above the door and the faithful passed underneath and made offerings in order to receive intercession. This was the occasion of Hubald's first cure of his shoulder and neck complaint, when he brushed the shrine when passing below it.[189] A similar practice was maintained at Beverley, where the feretory of John was held aloft on Ascension Day so that supplicants could pass under it. A crippled Irishman had come in search of a cure, and after praying to God and John and being prayed for by those who saw him, he was carried under the feretory and cured. The Irishman was taken to the altar, where he gave thanks for the miracle, which William claims became well known locally and in Ireland.[190] The shrine of Liudhard was carried out on his feast day by clerics dressed in white. On this occasion, there had been a drought, and on returning to the Church, the prior led the choir in the antiphon *Nonne vides quanta sit siccitas et tribulatio in toto mundo, et tu negligenter agis*.[191] This is usually sung on the invention of Stephen, but its content was deemed fit as a torrent of rain fell that drowned out the singing.[192] Thus, a procession of relics could be marshalled against a specific threat or problem.

The shrine of Edmund was also carried outside following his translation in order to end a drought.[193] So, too, John of Beverley's relics were carried out to alleviate a drought effecting the whole of Yorkshire on his feast day. The saint's relics were carried around the outside of the church, and the clerics were drenched by a sudden storm but their vestments were unharmed.[194] Ecgwine's relics were carried against fire on several occasions.[195] Modwenna's shrine was similarly carried out to stop a fire in its tracks and to end a great gale.[196] Oswald of Worcester's relics were taken to stop fire in Worcester twice in short succession.[197] Oswald was also mobilised against a plague in Worcester and the surrounding area:

> Wishing most fervently to remedy this evil, the brothers of the church of the Holy Mother of God and Perpetual Virgin Mary at Worcester carried the shrine of the blessed Oswald in a circuit about the city, processing and chanting litanies, and begging with loving affection for this bishop to offer his prayers to God on their behalf and for the health of the people. How wonderful is the love of God and how wondrous his awesome power! At once the plague was not only eliminated entirely in Worcester, but also in the surrounding hamlets, whose inhabitants had come to seek the help of the saint. The plague was not, however, eliminated in the same way in those hamlets whose inhabitants considered these litanies to be of little value and who refrained from taking part in them, but an equal or even more savage fate overwhelmed these people.[198]

This passage demonstrates the benefits of engaging in such a communal petition. Oswald was clearly capable of eliminating the plague from the whole area, but he only saw fit to help those who asked for help appropriately. The hint in the final sentence, that the fate of those who did not take part in the procession was perhaps worse than other victims of plague, shows that rejecting a saint could be worse than being ignorant of them.

A procession with relics could be proof against almost any harm, from the sin expiated on the Rogation Days to the suffering of a disaster. Processions allowed a saint to go beyond the confines of the church and allowed people to relate to the saint by participating in the procession. The corporate identity of the people involved could coalesce around their holy burden, and this saint could be welcomed by the surrounding community.[199] The procession of relics was also a regular opportunity to demonstrate and naturalise the powerful position of the custodians as leaders of a consensus building ceremony with an obvious end point. All participants had to go in the same direction and pass through the same places at the correct time.[200] This did not mean that consensus was necessarily achieved, however, especially as processions often went beyond the confines of the church grounds. Going out into public would have required a degree of flexibility and invited unpredictable situations.[201] This is demonstrated to a degree in the hagiography. During a Rogation procession of Liudhard's relics, a woman was struck with a fit of insanity and danced around the feretory, causing the brothers to slap her to bring her to her senses. She was healed when the relics were deposited and Mass was sung, and in thanks the woman brought a silver necklace to Liudhard.[202] As with translations, people saw processions as an opportunity to interact directly with a saint at a time of openness and vulnerability, and they were evidently not always appropriate in their behaviour.

Shrines, translations and processions were all important because they marked the location of a saint's relics. Whilst saints could work miracles anywhere, people were drawn to the saint's earthly remains to ask for help and give thanks for it. Visiting a shrine implicated you in the community of a saint in a way that distant and/or private prayer did not. The mediating relationship between the human and divine seems to have been helped by a personal visit to the saint. Although people evidently visited for indulgences, sanctuary, penance and prayer, the main draw was always the potential for miracles. Grand occasions like translations and processions focused people's attention on the saints, gave them an excuse to attend and an opportunity to take part. This taking part may not always have been what the custodians had in mind, however. People jostled for position, ran in front of processions and asked for preferential access. Crowds surged, and custodians took preventative measures to protect themselves and their saintly charges. Whole towns came out for their saints, and they also fought for possession of their saints. Ultimately the saint decided where to go, who to cure and when to intervene. But it was the hagiographers, the voices of the custodians, who interpreted and recorded the saint's will and the behaviour of the people. In their compositions, hagiographers focused on shrines as the controlled centre of a saint's cult. They made note of the miracles witnessed there and the stories which circulated there and could investigate further if they thought it necessary. There was likely a genuine focus on the shrine, but this was certainly magnified by the work of the hagiographers. The shrine was the home of the official discourse of a cult, and its main stock in trade was miracles. The following two chapters explore how the miraculous was fostered by the people who interacted with the saints.

Notes

1 Thacker, '*Loca Sanctorum*', p. 2.
2 Finucane, p. 39.
3 John Howe, 'Creating Symbolic Landscapes: Medieval Development of Sacred Space', in *Inventing Medieval Landscapes: Senses of Place in Western Europe*, ed. by John Howe and Michael Wolfe (Gainesville: University Press of Florida, 2002), pp. 208–23 (p. 214).
4 'Tunc abbas, erectis ad caelum oculis, uidit ingentem splendorem inde super aecclesiam ipsam descendere, eamque de superioribus penetrare. Quo uiso, et suis qui hoc secum uidere merebantur ostenso, pio affectu suspirans ait: 'Vere pius pater Dunstanus iam ad suam festiuitatem uadit, interesse uolens obsequio quod sui filii hac in nocte Deo et sibi exhibituri sunt.' Quod ita, sicut dixerat, actum esse, experti sunt fratres qui ipsi festo meruerunt interesse. Nam ex dulci sanctoque affectu quo in Deum et famulum eius iocundati sunt, sanctam praesentiam eius sibi adesse persenserunt.' Eadmer, *Miracula S. Dunstani*, pp. 180–1.
5 Sarah Hamilton and Andrew Spicer, 'Defining the Holy: The Delineation of Sacred Space', in *Defining the Holy: Sacred Space in Medieval and Early Modern Europe*, ed. by Sarah Hamilton and Andrew Spicer (Aldershot: Ashgate, 2005), pp. 1–23 (p. 1).
6 Adrian Ivakhiv, 'Orchestrating Sacred Space: Beyond the "Social Construction" of Nature', *Ecotheology*, 8 (2003), 11–29 (pp. 24–26).
7 Finucane, p. 55.
8 Benedicta Ward, *Miracles and the Medieval Mind: Theory, Record and Event 1000–1215* (Aldershot: Scolar, 1987), pp. 31–2.
9 See chapter V.
10 John Crook, *The Architectural Setting of the Cult of the Saints in the Early Christian West c. 300 – c. 1200* (Oxford: Clarendon, 2000), pp. 12–13.

11 Ibid., p. 5.
12 Lantfred, *Miracula S. Swithuni*, pp. 270–87.
13 Crook, *Setting*, pp. 163–4.
14 Biddle, p. 25.
15 Lantfred, *Miracula S. Swithuni*, pp. 324–7.
16 Goscelin, *Vita S. Vulfhilde*, pp. 430–1.
17 Goscelin, *Miraculis S. Augustini*, p. 410.
18 Goscelin, *Translationis S. Augustini*, pp. 427–9.
19 *Miracula S. Swithuni*, pp. 680–1.
20 Arcoid, *Miracula S. Erkenwaldi*, pp. 160–3.
21 Ibid., pp. 150–5.
22 Goscelin, *Miracula S. Mildrethe*, pp. 144–5.
23 Goscelin, *Translationis S. Augustini*, pp. 430–7.
24 Herman, *Miracula S. Edmundi*, pp. 134–7.
25 Love, *Eleventh-Century*, pp. cii–cvi, 68.
26 Goscelin, *Vita S. Wihtburge*, pp. 64–7.
27 Goscelin of Saint-Bertin, *The Hagiography of the Female Saints of Ely*, ed. and trans. by Rosalind C. Love (Oxford: Clarendon, 2004), pp. xliii, 66–7.
28 Goscelin, *Miracula S. Yuonis*, pp. lix–lx, *Miracula S. Yuonis*, p. lxxvi.
29 William R. Caraher, 'Abandonment, Authority, and Religious Continuity in Post-Classical Greece', *International Journal of Historical Archaeology*, 14 (2010), 241–54 (p. 244).
30 Bede, *HE*, I.30, p. 107.
31 Alan Thacker, 'Monks, Preaching and Pastoral Care in Early Anglo-Saxon England', in *Pastoral Care Before the Parish*, ed. by John Blair and Richard Sharpe (Leicester: Leicester University Press, 1992), pp. 137–70 (p. 167).
32 John Crook, *English Medieval Shrines* (Woodbridge: Boydell, 2011), p. 104.
33 Crook, *Setting*, pp. 76–9.
34 Ibid., pp. 243–4.
35 Ibid., pp. 192–3, 236–7.
36 See Goscelin, *Vita S. Edithe*, p. 293; Goscelin, *Translationis S. Augustini*, p. 437; Goscelin, *Virtutibus S. Adriani*, Vespasian B.xx, fols 234^v-235^r, Harley 105, fol. 206^v; Herman, *Miracula S. Edmundi*, pp. 104–5, 340–1; *Miracula S. Ithamari*, pp. 433–6; *Miracula S. Bege*, pp. 516–19; Geoffrey, *Miracula S. Modwenne*, pp. 186–9, 198–201; Dominic, *Miracula S. Ecgwini*, pp. 92–3; *Miracula S. Mylburge*, pp. 567–8; Arcoid, *Miracula S. Erkenwaldi*, pp. 128–33, 135–41.
37 Aelred, *De sanctis Hagustaldensis*, p. 194; Wulfstan, *Narratio de S. Swithuno*, pp. 494–5; *Miracula S. Guthlaci*, pp. 55–7; Arcoid, *Miracula S. Erkenwaldi*, pp. 142–5; Goscelin, *Translationis S. Augustini*, p. 443.
38 Crook, *Setting*, p. 185.
39 Ibid., pp. 218–33.
40 Crook, *Shrines*, pp. 192–5.
41 Bede, *HE*, IV.3, pp. 346–7.
42 Crook, *Setting*, p. 281.
43 Ben Nilson, 'The Medieval Experience at the Shrine', in *Pilgrimage Explored*, ed. by J. Stopford (Woodbridge: York Medieval Press, 1999), pp. 95–122 (pp. 97–8).
44 Arcoid, *Miracula S. Erkenwaldi*, pp. 152–3.
45 Goscelin, *Translatione S. Ethelburge*, pp. 435–52.
46 Goscelin, *Vita S. Wlsini*, pp. 79–80.
47 Lantfred, *Miracula S. Swithuni*, pp. 296–307.
48 Wulfstan, *Narratio de S. Swithuno*, pp. 568–9.
49 Nilson, 'Medieval Experience', p. 108.
50 Lantfred, *Miracula S. Swithuni*, pp. 292–7; Wulfstan, *Narratio de S. Swithuno*, pp. 504–7. See also the case of Abbot Scotland, whose convalescence was disturbed

by the noise of the monks of St Augustine's performing the office and of the supplicants keeping vigil, Goscelin, *Miracula S. Mildrethe*, p. 207.
51 Goscelin, *Vita S. Ethelburge*, p. 415.
52 On the liturgical celebration of a feast see Appendix I.
53 Goscelin, *Vita S. Ethelburge*, pp. 415–16.
54 Osbern, *Miracula S. Dunstani*, pp. 136–9.
55 A contrast with Judith's restriction on the shrines at Barking is the case of the painter Teodwin at St Paul's. Teodwin was renovating the area around Erkenwald's tomb. Instead of celebrating the saint's feast, Teodwin continued to paint and blocked access for the many pilgrims who wished to visit Erkenwald. As he painted, Teodwin lost strength, was gripped by pain and fell to the ground from his scaffold. He drifted into sleep and was visited by Erkenwald, who beat him with his crozier to impress Teodwin's disrespect upon him. See Arcoid, *Miracula S. Erkenwaldi*, pp. 158–61. This demonstrates the difference between the authority of the custodians and that of a lay contractor.
56 Colgrave, *Two Lives*, pp. 278–81.
57 Symeon, *Libellus*, pp. 104–5.
58 Ibid., pp. 106–7.
59 Ibid., pp. 176–7.
60 Ibid., pp. 108–11.
61 Victoria Tudor, 'The Misogyny of Saint Cuthbert', *Archaeologia Aeliana*, Fifth Series, 12 (1984), 157–67 (p. 165).
62 Goscelin, *Miraculis S. Augustini*, pp. 407–8. The penitential psalms were numbered 6, 31, 37, 50, 101, 129 and 142 in the Vulgate. They were first listed as a group by Cassiodorus in the sixth century and were used to beg for God's forgiveness and aid. See Clare Costley King'oo, *Miserere Mei: The Penitential Psalms in Late Medieval and Early Modern England* (Notre Dame, IN: University of Notre Dame Press, 2012), pp. 1–14.
63 *Passio S. Indracti*, in Michael Lapidge, *Anglo-Latin Literature, 900–1066* (London: Hambledon, 1993), pp. 442–4.
64 *Miracula S. Swithuni*, pp. 676–95; Lantfred, *Miracula S. Swithuni*, pp. 330–1.
65 J. Charles Cox, *The Sanctuaries and Sanctuary Seekers of Mediaeval England* (London: Allen, 1911), pp. 2–11.
66 John P. Sexton, 'Saint's Law: Anglo-Saxon Sanctuary Protection in the Translatio et Miracula S. Swithuni', *Florilegium*, 23.2 (2006), 61–80 (p. 62).
67 Gervase Rosser, 'Sanctuary and Social Negotiation', in *The Cloister and the World: Essays in Medieval History in Honour of Barbara Harvey*, ed. by John Blair and Brian Golding (Oxford: Clarendon, 1996), pp. 57–79 (p. 62).
68 Candace Gregory-Abbott, 'Sacred Outlaws: Outlawry and the Medieval Church', in *Outlaws in Medieval and Early Modern England: Crime, Government and Society, c.1066–c.1600*, ed. by John C. Appleby and Paul Dalton (Farnham: Ashgate, 2009), pp. 75–90 (pp. 86–7).
69 For example, see Goscelin, *Miraculis S. Augustini*, pp. 400–6; Goscelin, *Vita S. Edithe*, pp. 278–80; Goscelin, *Vita S. Wlsini*, p. 78; *Miracula S. Ithamari*, pp. 431–2; *Passio S. Edwardi*, pp. 14–15; Herman, *Miracula S. Edmundi*, pp. 58–9; *Miracula S. Yuonis*, pp. lxxvii–lxxviii; *Miracula S. Guthlaci*, pp. 57–8.
70 Finucane's evidence comes from the cults of Thomas Becket, Frideswide, Thomas Cantilupe, Wulfstan of Worcester, Simon de Montfort, William of Norwich and Godric. His designation of 'lowest class' seems to be all non-nobles and non-religious supplicants. See Finucane, pp. 143–6.
71 Sigal also includes numbers for merchants and the bourgeois, who come in at 0.86% and 0.78% respectively. The gender balance of the aristocracy was 86% male to 14% female, and the gender balance for the religious was 97.4% male to 2.6% female. See Sigal, *L'homme et le Miracle*, pp. 289–301.
72 Bailey, 'Wives', pp. 199–201, 217–19.
73 Bailey, 'Rich and Poor', pp. 12–15.

60   *Making Shrines*

74 Bailey, 'Rich and Poor', pp. 23–4; Bailey 'Wives', pp. 218–19.
75 Osbern, *Miracula S. Dunstani*, pp. 131–3; Eadmer, *Miracula S. Dunstani*, pp. 162–3.
76 Eadmer, *Miracula S. Dunstani*, pp. 162–3.
77 Arnold van Gennep, *The Rites of Passage*, trans. by Monika B. Vizedom and Gabrielle L. Caffee (Chicago, IL: University of Chicago Press, 1960), p. 3.
78 Ibid., p. 11.
79 Ibid., p. 191.
80 Ibid., p. 11.
81 Turner, 'Betwixt and Between', pp. 234–43.
82 Ibid., p. 236.
83 Turner, *Ritual Process*, p. 96.
84 Ibid., p. 129.
85 Turner and Turner, *Image and Pilgrimage*, pp. 34–5.
86 Turner, *Ritual Process*, p. 122.
87 Turner and Turner, *Image and Pilgrimage*, p. 232.
88 Turner, *Ritual Process*, p. 142.
89 Bailey, 'Modern and Medieval', pp. 495–6.
90 Michael J. Sallnow, 'Communitas Reconsidered: The Sociology of Andean Pilgrimage', *Man*, New Series, 16 (1981), 163–82 (pp. 163, 179–80).
91 John Eade and Michael J. Sallnow, 'Introduction', in *Contesting the Sacred*, ed. by John Eade and Michael J. Sallnow (London: Routledge, 1991), pp. 1–29 (p. 15).
92 Eade, pp. 73–5.
93 Bailey, 'Modern and Medieval', pp. 497–9.
94 Bailey, 'Peter Brown', p. 39.
95 Bailey, 'Modern and Medieval', p. 508.
96 *The Ecclesiastical History of Sozomen*, trans. by Edward Walford (London: Bohn, 1855), pp. 234–6.
97 *Vita Sancti Ambrosii, Mediolanensis Episcopi, a Paulino eius Notario ad Beatum Augustinum Conscripta*, ed. and trans. by Mary Simplicia Kaniecka, Catholic University of America Patristic Studies, 16 (Washington, DC: Catholic University of America, 1928), pp. 52–5.
98 Ibid., pp. 70–1, 393.
99 Ibid., p. 74.
100 Ibid., pp. 74–5.
101 Alan Thacker, 'The Making of a Local Saint', in *Local Saints and Local Churches*, ed. by Alan Thacker and Richard Sharpe (Oxford: Oxford University Press, 2002), pp. 45–73 (pp. 50–1).
102 *Gregorii I Papae Registrum Epistolorum*, ed. by Paul Ewald and Ludovic M. Hartmann, Monumenta Germaniae Historica, Epistolae 1–2, 2 vols (Berlin: Weidmann, 1891–1899), I (1891), pp. 263–6.
103 'cum supra sancta eius altaria ei in libamen ob sanctificationem illorum offerebantur reliquiarum, sanguis sanctorum quibus adsignata est semper illos intravit pannos utique tinctos'. Bertram Colgrave, ed. and trans., *The Earliest Life of Gregory the Great, by an Anonymous Monk of Whitby* (Cambridge: Cambridge University Press, 1985), pp. 108–11.
104 *Gregorii I Epistolorum*, I, pp. 263–6.
105 Ibid., p. 52.
106 Lapidge, *Swithun*, p. 10.
107 Thacker, 'Making a Saint', pp. 54–5.
108 Bede, *HE*, II.3, pp. 142–5; III.23, pp. 288–9; IV.3, pp. 344–5; III.17, pp. 264–5; III.26, pp. 308–9; IV.19, pp. 390–7.
109 Colgrave, *Two Lives*, pp. 130–3, 290–7; *Bedas Metrische Vita Sancti Cuthberti*, ed. by Werner Jaager, Palaestra, 198 (Leipzig: Mayer & Müller, 1935), pp. 120–2; Colgrave, *Guthlac*, pp. 160–3.

110 Thacker, 'Making a Saint', pp. 71–2.
111 Lantfred, *Miracula S. Swithuni*, pp. 284–5.
112 Lapidge, *Swithun*, p. 16.
113 Ibid., p. 335.
114 Wulfstan, *Narratio de S. Swithuno*, pp. 452–61.
115 Ibid., pp. 462–63.
116 Ibid., pp. 492–7.
117 Henry Richards Luard, ed., *Annales Monastici*, Rolls Series, 36, 5 vols (London: Longman, 1864–1869), II, p. 57.
118 David Rollason, *Northumbria, 500–1100: Creation and Destruction of a Kingdom* (Cambridge: Cambridge University Press, 2003), p. 247.
119 Bede, *HE*, V.20, pp. 530–1.
120 Aelred, *De sanctis Hagustaldensis*, pp. 193–200.
121 *Vita S. Birini*, pp. 46–7; *Miracula S. Guthlaci*, pp. 55–7.
122 Arcoid, *Miracula S. Erkenwaldi*, pp. 152–5; *Miracula S. Ithamari*, pp. 429–30; Herman, *Miracula S. Edmundi*, pp. 112–23; Goscelin, *Translationis S. Augustini*, pp. 413–17; Luard, II, 43; Goscelin, *Translatione S. Ethelburge*, pp. 435–52.
123 *Translatione S. Ethelburge*, pp. 435–52; Wulfstan, *Vita S. Æthelwoldi*, pp. 64–7; Goscelin, *Vita S. Edithe*, pp. 270–1; Goscelin, *Miracula S. Kenelmi*, pp. 60–9; Goscelin, *Vita S. Wlsini*, pp. 79–80; *Miracula S. Ithamari*, pp. 429–30; Robert, *Translatio S. Wenefrede*, p. 727.
124 Goscelin, *Vita S. Wlsini*, p. 80.
125 Lantfred, *Miracula S. Swithuni*, pp. 296–307; Wulfstan, *Narratio de S. Swithuno*, pp. 568–9.
126 *Vita S. Rumwoldi*, pp. 114–15; Geoffrey, *Miracula S. Modwenne*, pp. 180–1; Arcoid, *Miracula S. Erkenwaldi*, pp. 154–5; Wulfstan, *Vita S. Æthelwoldi*, pp. 64–7; *Vita S. Birini*, pp. 46–7; Goscelin, *Vita S. Wlsini*, pp. 80–1; *Miracula S. Yuonis*, p. lxxvi.
127 Wulfstan, *Vita S. Æthelwoldi*, pp. 64–7.
128 Goscelin, *Translatione S. Ethelburge*, pp. 435–52.
129 Eadmer, *Miracula S. Oswaldi*, pp. 300–5.
130 Arcoid, *Miracula S. Erkenwaldi*, pp. 132–5, 152–3.
131 Goscelin, *Vita S. Edithe*, pp. 270–1; Herman, *Miracula S. Edmundi*, pp. 112–23; *Miracula S. Guthlaci*, pp. 55–7; D. Bethell, ed., 'The Lives of St Osyth of Essex and St Osyth of Aylesbury', *Analecta Bollandiana*, 88 (1970), 75–127 (p. 116); Goscelin, *Translationis S. Augustini*, pp. 413–17.
132 Eadmer, *Miracula S. Oswaldi*, pp. 300–5.
133 Herman, *Miracula S. Edmundi*, pp. 120–1; Robert, *Translatio S. Wenefrede*, p. 731.
134 Robert, *Translatio S. Wenefrede*, p. 731; *Passio S. Edwardi*, pp. 9–10.
135 Goscelin, *Translatione S. Ethelburge*, pp. 435–52; Herman, *Miracula S. Edmundi*, pp. 118–21; Goscelin, *Translationis S. Augustini*, pp. 417, 435–6.
136 Herman, *Miracula S. Edmundi*, pp. 118–19.
137 Robert W. Shaffern, 'The Medieval Theology of Indulgences', in R. N. Swanson, ed., *Promissory Notes on the Treasury of Merits: Indulgences in Late Medieval Europe*, Brill's Companions to the Christian Tradition, 5 (Leiden: Brill, 2006), pp. 11–36 (p. 11).
138 R. N. Swanson, *Indulgences in Late Medieval England: Passports to Paradise?* (Cambridge: Cambridge University Press, 2007), p. 11.
139 Nicholas Vincent, 'Some Pardoners' Tales: The Earliest English Indulgences', *Transactions of the Royal Historical Society*, 12 (2002), 23–58 (pp. 27–8).
140 Falko Neininger, ed., *English Episcopal Acta: London 1076–1187*, English Episcopal Acta, 15 (Oxford: Oxford University Press, 1999), p. 16.
141 Julia Barrow, ed., *English Episcopal Acta: Hereford 1079–1234*, English Episcopal Acta, 7 (Oxford: Oxford University Press, 1993), pp. 30–1.
142 Brian Kemp, ed., *English Episcopal Acta: Salisbury 1078–1217*, English Episcopal Acta, 18 (Oxford: Oxford University Press, 1999), pp. 80–1.

143 C. R. Cheney and Bridgett E. A. Jones, eds, *English Episcopal Acta: Canterbury 1162–1190*, English Episcopal Acta, 2 (Oxford: Oxford University Press, 1986), p. 81.
144 *EEA London 1076–1187*, p. 93.
145 Brian Kemp, trans., 'The Miracles of the Hand of St James: Translated with an Introduction', *Berkshire Archaeological Journal*, 65 (1970), 1–19 (pp. 2–3).
146 Vincent, pp. 39, 43 and see Francis M. R. Ramsey, ed., *English Episcopal Acta: Bath and Wells 1061–1205*, English Episcopal Acta, 10 (Oxford: Oxford University Press, 1995), p. 30; *EEA Canterbury 1162–1190*, p. 21; M. G. Snape, ed., *English Episcopal Acta: Durham 1153–1195*, English Episcopal Acta, 24 (Oxford: Oxford University Press, 2002), pp. 101–2; David M. Smith, ed., *English Episcopal Acta: Lincoln 1067–1185*, English Episcopal Acta, 1 (Oxford: Oxford University Press, 1980), p. 145; *EEA London 1076–1187*, p. 109; Christopher Harper-Bill, ed., *English Episcopal Acta: Norwich 1070–1214*, English Episcopal Acta, 6 (Oxford: Oxford University Press, 1990), p. 113; *EEA Salisbury 1078–1217*, p. 80.
147 Vincent, pp. 39, 43; David M. Smith, ed., *English Episcopal Acta: Lincoln 1186–1206*, English Episcopal Acta, 4 (Oxford: Oxford University Press, 1986), p. 199; *EEA London 1076–1187*, pp. 56–7.
148 Arcoid, *Miracula S. Erkenwaldi*, pp. 152–3; Herman, *Miracula S. Edmundi*, pp. 118–21; Goscelin, *Translatione S. Ethelburge*, pp. 435–52; *Passio S. Edwardi*, pp. 9–10.
149 Eadmer, *Miracula S. Oswaldi*, pp. 300–4.
150 *Miracula S. Guthlaci*, p. 56.
151 Symeon of Durham, *Historia Regum*, in *Symeonis Opera*, I, 247–61; Goscelin, *Vita S. Wihtburge*, pp. 74–83; Herman, *Miracula S. Edmundi*, pp. 112–17; Goscelin, *Miracula S. Edmundi*, pp. 246–8, 278–86.
152 Goscelin, *Vita S. Wlsini*, pp. 84–5; *Miracula S. Mylburge*, pp. 567–8; Goscelin, *Translationis S. Augustini*, pp. 414–17, 435–6; Arcoid, *Miracula S. Erkenwaldi*, pp. 153–5; Robert, *Translatio S. Wenefrede*, pp. 730–1.
153 Osbern, 'Translatio Sancti Ælfegi Cantuariensis Archiepiscopi et Martiris', ed. and trans. by Alexander R. Rumble and Rosemary Morris, in *The Reign of Cnut: King of England, Denmark and Norway*, ed. by Alexander R. Rumble (London: Leicester University Press, 1994), pp. 283–315.
154 W. D. Macray, ed., *Chronicon Abbatiae Rameseiensis*, Rolls Series, 83 (London: Longman, 1886), pp. 127–8.
155 *Vita S. Erkenwaldi*, in E. Gordon Whatley, ed. and trans., *The Saint of London: The Life and Miracles of St Erkenwald*, Medieval & Renaissance Texts & Studies, 58 (Binghamton, NY: Medieval & Renaissance Texts & Studies, 1989), pp. 91–5.
156 Goscelin, *Miracula S. Kenelmi*, pp. 68–73.
157 Goscelin, *Vita S. Wihtburge*, pp. 68–75.
158 Ibid., pp. 44–7.
159 Goscelin, *Miracula S. Mildrethe*, pp. 170–6.
160 Patrick J. Geary, *Furta Sacra: Thefts of Relics in the Central Middle Ages*, rev. edn (Princeton, NJ: Princeton University Press, 1990), pp. 132–4.
161 Kay Slocum, 'Goscelin of Saint-Bertin and the Translation Ceremony for Saints Ethelburg, Hildelith and Wulfhild', in *Barking Abbey and Medieval Literary Culture*, ed. by Brown and Bussell, pp. 73–93 (p. 85).
162 Herman, *Miracula S. Edmundi*, pp. 118–19.
163 Thacker, 'Making a Saint', pp. 65–73.
164 As was the case with Rumwold, who predicted he would rest for a year at his place of birth and death, then move on to Brackley for two years and finally remain at Buckingham. *Vita S. Rumwoldi*, pp. 114–15.
165 Much the same could be said about clerics leading a Mass for a saint on their feast day. See Appendix I.
166 Herman, *Miracula S. Edmundi*, pp. 80–5.
167 Herman, *Miracula S. Edmundi*, pp. 28–39.

168 Dominic, *Miracula S. Ecgwini*, pp. 104–17.
169 On the consecration of a church, see Helen Gittos, *Liturgy, Architecture, and Sacred Spaces in Anglo-Saxon England* (Oxford: Oxford University Press, 2013), pp. 228–56.
170 Pfaff, *Liturgy*, p. 167.
171 K. D. Hartzell, *Catalogue of Manuscripts Written or Owned in England up to 1200 Containing Music* (Woodbridge: Boydell, 2006), p. 471.
172 Gittos, pp. 103–5.
173 Thomas Symons, ed. and trans., *Regularis Concordia Anglicae Nationis Monachorum Sanctimonialiumque* (London: Nelson, 1953), pp. 32–3.
174 David Knowles and Christopher L. Brooke, eds and trans, *The Monastic Constitutions of Lanfranc* (Oxford: Clarendon, 2002), p. 251.
175 Ibid., pp. 94–5.
176 William of Malmesbury, *Gesta Pontificum*, I, pp. 642–5 (V.270).
177 Gittos, pp. 138–9.
178 John Blair, *The Church in Anglo-Saxon Society* (Oxford: Oxford University Press, 2005), pp. 454–6.
179 'ambulauimus cum reliquiis sanctorum, ut consuetudo illius diei poscebat.' Bertram Colgrave and R. A. B. Mynors, eds and trans, *Bede's Ecclesiastical History of the English People* (Oxford: Oxford University Press, 1969), pp. 584–5.
180 Joyce Hill, 'The Litaniae Maiores and Minores in Rome, Francia and Anglo-Saxon England: Terminology, Texts and Traditions', *Early Medieval Europe*, 9 (2000), 211–46 (pp. 245–6).
181 Arthur West Haddan and William Stubbs, eds, *Councils and Ecclesiastical Documents Relating to Great Britain and Ireland*, 3 vols (Oxford: Clarendon, 1869–78), III, p. 368.
182 Hartzell, p. 470.
183 D. G. Scragg, ed., *The Vercelli Homilies and Related Texts*, Early English Text Society, 300 (Oxford: Oxford University Press, 1992), pp. 228–9.
184 Knowles and Brooke, pp. 74–9. On litanies see Appendix I.
185 Byrhtferth, *Vita S. Oswaldi*, pp. 132–5.
186 Goscelin, *Translationis S. Augustini*, p. 443.
187 *Vita Sexburge*, pp. 184–5.
188 Goscelin, *Vita S. Wihtburge*, pp. 60–5.
189 William of Malmesbury, *Gesta Pontificum*, I, pp. 642–3 (V.270).
190 William Ketell, *Miracula S. Johannis*, pp. 278–80.
191 'Surely you see the great drought and distress in the whole world, and yet you do nothing.'
192 Goscelin, *Translationis S. Augustini*, p. 443.
193 Herman, *Miracula S. Edmundi*, pp. 120–1.
194 William Ketell, *Miracula S. Johannis*, pp. 269–71.
195 Dominic, *Miracula S. Ecgwini*, pp. 120–5.
196 Geoffrey, *Miracula S. Modwenne*, pp. 210–11.
197 Eadmer, *Miracula S. Oswaldi*, pp. 315–19.
198 'Cui malo fratres aecclesiae sanctae Dei genetricis ac perpetuae uirginis Mariae Wigornensis mederi summopere desiderantes, scrinium beati Osuualdi per circumitum urbis cum laetaniis procedentes deferunt, ipsum pontificem suas preces Deo pro sua populique salute offere pio affectu postulantes. Mira Dei pietas, mira et tremenda potestas! Exemplo pestilentia tota non solum Wigornam reliquit, sed et uillas circumiacentes de quibus incolae sui aduenerant, opem sancti uiri implorantes. Villas autem, quarum cultores letanias ipsas paruipendentes eis interesse supersederunt, non ita deseruit, sed aut par aut saeuitia maior super eos efferbuit.' Eadmer, *Miracula S. Oswaldi*, pp. 318–19.
199 Sabine MacCormack, *Art and Ceremony in Late Antiquity* (Berkeley: University of California Press, 1981), pp. 18–22.

200 C. Clifford Flanigan, 'The Moving Subject: Medieval Liturgical Processions in Semiotic and Cultural Perspective', in *Moving Subjects: Processional Performance in the Middle Ages and the Renaissance*, ed. by Kathleen Ashley and Wim Hüsken, Ludus, 5 (Amsterdam: Rodopi, 2001), pp. 35–51 (pp. 39–45).
201 Kathleen Ashley, 'Introduction: The Moving Subjects of Processional Performance', in *Moving Subjects*, ed. by Ashley and Hüsken, pp. 7–34 (pp. 22–3).
202 Goscelin, *Translationis S. Augustini*, p. 443.

3 Petitioning the Saints

Tom Lynch

So far we have established the great value placed on the relics of the saints. They were argued about in texts and discussions, stolen and fought over, translated within and between locales and occasionally brought out to demonstrate their power and sanctify their surroundings. The major reason for all of this fuss and the attention of the hagiographers was the social fact of intercession. Saints could perform miracles for worthy people, and their power was awesome. This chapter focuses on the supplication which was thought to lead to a dead saint interceding on a supplicant's behalf. Whilst there is certainly evidence of miracles within a saint's lifetime, the majority of the events recorded were post-mortem miracles, as a saint's cult could last far longer than their natural life.[1] Additionally the compiler of post-mortem miracles was much more likely to have direct experience of this process of intercession, whether they had witnessed the particular miracles they wrote down or not. As demonstrated in the previous chapter, whilst saints could effect miracles anywhere, their shrines acted as a nexus for their power.[2] Therefore, we will begin with shrines as the most typical venue for post-mortem miracles and the petitions for them.

A shrine petition could be as straightforward as visiting a saint and praying for help. For example, Geoffrey of Burton records the visit of a man to Modwenna at her shrine:

> I know a man who suffered from a wart that had grown for some reason under his eye. When he felt this daily increasing in size, he showed it to the blessed virgin before her shrine, saying 'My lady, if you so wish, you can take this disfigurement from me.' The wart immediately disappeared in a wonderful way and to the astonishment of all who had seen it before, since it went away immediately and without leaving a trace.'[3]

Here the man's health was only improved by going to visit Modwenna at her shrine and asking the saint for help. Such a simple act is at the heart of all miracle petitions, a person choosing to ask for help. Yarrow has outlined how descriptions of curative miracles conform to a structure and show how 'illness [was] charged with ritual significance'.[4] We can explore this structure using the cure of the man with the wart as a guide. Firstly the wart's growth was acknowledged

DOI: 10.4324/9781003205692-4

as a problem. A 'ritual strategy' was decided upon, to go and tell his problem to Modwenna and ask for help. The saint was asked with confidence in her power, and she was engaged through prayer. The culmination of this episode is the man's cure, which was witnessed by the people present and by Geoffrey himself, who made a record of the miracle. According to Yarrow, we have a description of a patterned 'communal event', which makes up the 'social reality of a cure'.[5]

This social aspect is central to an understanding of the everyday workings of the cult of the saints. As Mayr-Harting has pointed out, the 'cure needed the crowd', and all shrine miracles were embroiled in a 'three-cornered relationship' of saint, supplicant and crowd.[6] I would reformulate this description slightly by substituting 'community' for 'crowd'. Such an understanding of a saint's community must include Mayr-Harting's 'crowd' but also includes the custodians of a saint as well as denoting the communality of all those gathered in supplication to and praise of a saint. It includes the hagiographers, too, as participants in and observers of the cult who selected the miracles which were written down. This had implications for the cult as the hagiographer's output could be incorporated into future liturgy, storytelling and hagiography.

Building on the work of Mayr-Harting and Yarrow, then, I propose a basic structure of miracle petitions which helps to demonstrate the agency of the saint, the supplicant and the community. Firstly a moment of crisis was experienced. In the case of the man with the wart, this was the daily worsening of his disfigurement. Secondly a knowledge of the saint in question was called upon. The man obviously knew of Modwenna and her power, and he also knew he could call upon her for help at her shrine. Thirdly the supplicant acted by asking for help from the saint, often in the form of a prayer like the one spoken by the man with the wart. Finally a miracle was solicited. In this case, Geoffrey and the supplicant made it clear that Modwenna was capable of such a miracle but that she had the agency to choose not to intercede. As noted in the previous chapter, access to a shrine was contested amongst different parts of the community of a saint. The successful miracle petition obfuscates a deal of negotiation and naturalises the idea of a layman simply approaching a saint and asking for help in the confines of a sacred and nominally controlled space. But ultimately a man was cured by his saintly patron after going to her and asking for help, and this idea of the shrine petition proved popular in medieval England.

Shrine and tomb cures are found throughout our period in saints' lives and miracle collections. For example, Lantfred records the healing of a hunchbacked cleric named Æthelsige. The cleric had been led by a dream to Swithun's tomb, which was located near the great door of the Old Minster among the graves of the people of Winchester. There Æthelsige prayed and fell asleep. The cleric awoke cured, and when his guide came back, he took Æthelsige inside the church, where the miracle was explained to the monks.[7] Amongst Goscelin's miracles of Augustine is the cure of a man from Thanet who had been blind for fifteen years. A great crowd of common people were in attendance of a Mass to Augustine celebrated by Abbot Wulfric (1044/47–1059/61). Among those present was the blind man who had come at the behest of a dream and who prayed for a cure from Augustine. The blind man was cured during the Gospel reading and at the end of the Mass he stood and demonstrated to those around him how he had been cured by Augustine.[8] The mid-twelfth-century anonymous collection of Oswine's miracles is one of the latest texts considered here and includes a similar cure. A pilgrim on his way to visit St Andrew in Scotland had fallen ill in Newcastle. In his illness, he had a vision of Aidan informing the pilgrim of the power of Oswine at nearby Tynemouth. Unable to make his way by foot the pilgrim explained himself to some locals, and one of them agreed to transport him by boat. They arrived during the feast of Oswine's invention, and the pilgrim prayed at the saint's tomb and was cured before the crowds present for the feast. The pilgrim got up, proclaimed the cure to those present and continued his journey north to Scotland.[9]

These examples show the persistence of the shrine petition as a means of fostering a miracle. They also show the ubiquity of the dream-vision as a means of gaining knowledge of a saint. Visions could inform people of a saint's power or direct them to their shrine specifically, but they were not a necessary step in all shrine cures. Most recorded miracle petitions skip over how the supplicant obtained their knowledge of the saint, but some narratives do include details. The paralysed and deformed man from London heard of Swithun's reputation and instructed his family to take him to Winchester, where he was cured on the day of his arrival.[10] In another story, a boy from York who had become dumb was taken to the shrine of John of Beverley by his father, who had heard of the miracles of the saint.[11] Likewise, people heard of the reputation of Oswald of Worcester, Edmund and Ivo by word of mouth.[12] At Ely a serving girl was only brought to Æthelthryth's shrine for healing when she came to the attention of some clerics who were visiting her master. The clerics refused to eat their dinner until they had carried the girl to the saint's shrine, where she was cured.[13] A vision from the saint may have been a more personal interaction, but people were cured regardless of how they came to hear of the miraculous potential of their patron.

Whilst the majority of shrine miracles involved healing, there are many instances of supplicants seeking aid with other misfortunes. Penitents and prisoners made their way to saints in hope of being freed of iron bonds, chains and fetters. Such miracles began to be documented in England in the pre-Conquest collections, with Lantfred recording three people released at Swithun's shrine and Byrhtferth including the miracle of a penitent whose final iron bond was removed by Ecgwine at Evesham.[14] Such accounts are also found in much of the later material, making them the second most frequent problem solved by the intercession of a saint at their shrine. The saints freed penitents in the work of Goscelin, Osbern, Eadmer, Dominic and Arcoid as well as in an additional miracle added to Geoffrey's Modwenna collection and in the anonymous *passio* of Edward the Martyr.[15] Penitents bound in iron were generally foreigners who had been exiled to a life of permanent pilgrimage for a serious crime.[16] Penitential pilgrimage predates the English miracle collections and was sanctioned in canon law, although binding in iron was not.[17] Penitential pilgrimage as punishment for the murder of an ordained man can be found in the *Penitential of Pseudo-Egbert*.[18] The confining of penitents with iron chains, fetters and collars, perhaps including the metal of a murder weapon, originates in Merovingian Europe, with most individual penitents originating from Scotland, France and Germany.[19] The surviving evidence largely comes from hagiography, and it is difficult to trace the practice. Whether a reflection of genuine punishment or a hagiographical invention, the freeing of penitents and prisoners indicates that saints could become involved in legal and penitential processes. It is also emblematic of the biblical inheritance of the saints as they were equipped with the power of binding and loosing.[20] Less common but still found throughout the corpus are cures of possession, malefic visions, insanity and related illnesses.[21] A variety of other misfortunes could be addressed by praying to a saint at their shrine, including lawsuits, lost property and problems with livestock.[22]

At its most basic, the engagement of a saint at their shrine took the form of petitionary prayer, but the majority of cures involved a degree of elaboration. As such, elaboration is an optional step which may be added to our structure of miracle petitions. Usually elaboration occurred as a part of asking a saint for aid or immediately before or after the request. A common elaboration was to prostrate oneself before the relics of the saints. Examples abound throughout the evidence, with people prostrating themselves at the shrines of Modwenna, Æthelburh, Guthlac, Ivo, Augustine, Mildrith, Ithamar, Edmund, Swithun, Dunstan, Anselm, Oswald, Ecgwine, Erkenwald and the saints of Hexham.[23] Another element of many supplications were tears, cries and groans. These expressions of emotion and pain would come naturally to people coping with life crises and are recorded by hagiographers throughout the period.[24] Whilst these tears could be spontaneous expressions, they could also allow the supplicant to emphasise their humble piety.

In B's version of the *Vita S. Dunstani*, Dunstan is portrayed as weeping in the performance of his pastoral duties. According to B, this signified the unseen power of the Holy Spirit in Dunstan.[25] In the medieval West, the 'gift of tears' marked a spiritual transformation of an individual, cleansing the person of sin in a similar way to baptism or penance.[26] The desirability of Christian weeping goes back to the Bible and continued throughout the medieval era.[27] Along with prostration, tears and cries also helped supplicants to demonstrate their position in relation to the saint in a conspicuous manner. Prostration and other demonstrative behaviour like weeping were practised in political contexts in early medieval England, seemingly expressive of subservience, humility or contrition.[28] As a part of the petitionary process, this behaviour demonstrated subservience of the supplicant to the saint and God and the seriousness of their condition. These supplicants showed that they were desperately in need of a miracle as well as being spiritually ready for a miracle. Sometimes tearful prayers made bowed before a saint were not deemed sufficient. On these occasions, a supplicant might conduct a vigil at the saint's shrine.

Spending a night in vigil before a saint was another of the most common forms of elaboration in shrine miracles. Lantfred records eleven vigils in his *Translatio et Miracula S. Swithuni*, one of which includes a dream-vision of the saint during the vigil.[29] Goscelin includes fourteen vigils in his corpus, of which only three feature a visitation of the saint as part of a miracle.[30] With or without a direct encounter with the saint, vigils seem to have been popular. Later examples can be found in the work of Dominic of Evesham, Arcoid, Geoffrey of Burton, Aelred and William Ketell,[31] as well as anonymous collections for saints, including Ithamar, Waltheof and Oswine.[32]

Vigils are evident from the beginning of the Christian period onwards and have been linked to the pagan practice of incubation at gods' temples in the Graeco-Roman world.[33] In the pagan and early-Christian evidence, the dream itself was the goal and the key to healing, either through a dreamed interaction or the instructions received in the dream.[34] These dreams were ideally sought out at shrines, although dreams experienced at other locations could be incorporated into a healing experience.[35] The most extensive records of Christian incubation healing are from the shrine of Cosmas and Damian at Constantinople, but they are also found quite widely elsewhere. Gregory of Tours included incubations in his writing, and some 7% of the miracles in his *Libri de virtutibus S. Martini episcopi* were dream based.[36] There appears to be a continuity between the pagan Mediterranean and the experiences of saints' supplicants in medieval western Europe. Incubation has been documented in the Mediterranean world since the classical period, but this continuity does not presuppose an unchanging ritual. Christians did not understand their practices as inherited from pagans, and they 're-crafted' the practice of cultivating healing dreams with a similar structure but a transformed meaning.[37] For our purposes, it is difficult to distinguish incubation precisely. Dream-visions of saints are common in the English hagiography, but the active seeking of saintly dreams through specific action is harder to trace. Individuals could have a vision day or night at a shrine, be instructed in a dream to visit a shrine or be otherwise admonished by a saint in a dream.[38] As sources of information, dream-visions were taken seriously, and sometimes the actions of saints in dreams had immediate physical consequences upon waking.[39] But as a systematic approach to miracle seeking, the vigil itself rather than the dream appears to have been much more reliable in medieval England.

Conducting a vigil allowed an extension of the time an individual spent in proximity to a saint. It granted a supplicant more of a chance to feel part of the community of the saint and to witness, and perhaps participate in, the liturgical life of the church in question. Vigils also showed a degree of commitment to the miracle-seeking process, a sacrifice of time and potentially income. People could be instructed to perform a vigil,[40] but it seems likely some people just extended their shrine visit until they were granted a miracle. Whilst most people found a vigil of a single night sufficient, some extended their stay with the saint. The man injured by furies was cured by Swithun on the third night of vigils, prayer and fasting, whilst a paralysed man from Rochester was cured after three nights of prayer and vigil.[41] The Saxon man Leodegar, who was crippled by deformity, had been told in a dream to go to Augustine. Once admitted into the shrine he spent three nights in prayer and vigil, and towards dawn of the third night, he had a vision of Augustine, Mellitus and Laurence, who healed him.[42] Erkenwald cured a doctor, who was unable to heal himself, after three days and nights of prayers, fasting and vigils.[43] Fasting accompanied two of these extended vigils and was also used by a crippled woman named Brihtgyfa when she sought a cure from Edmund in a single night's vigil.[44] Like a vigil, a fast was a sacrifice of sorts, an outward display of an inward commitment. Like tears and prostration, a fast was a sign of contrition and humility showing that the person was abasing themselves before the saint and relying on them in their extremity. Beyond prayers, vigils and fasting, a few individuals were able to physically interact with the trappings of a saint's shrine.

Goscelin includes four such physical interactions in his work. A cleric was cured of a swollen hand by praying prostrate at Ivo's shrine for a long time and eventually wrapping his hand in the covering of the shrine.[45] Two shrine cures from the miracles of Hadrian also include such physical interaction. A young man was cured of an eye carbuncle by wiping the protuberance on the cloth covering and bare stone of Hadrian's tomb. After a few years, the same man came back with the same complaint but worse. He remembered his old cure, rubbed his eye on the stone of the tomb again and was cured.[46] Lastly, the recluse Seitha was healed of a finger tumour by touching Edmund's bier and asking for the saint's help.[47] Osbern records that a young man who was mute and unable to walk was carried to Dunstan's tomb, and when he got there, his friends held him aloft and prayed aloud to Dunstan on his behalf. When the young man touched the saint's tomb, he was healed instantly.[48] Eadmer notes the story of a bound penitent who came to the shrine of Oswald of Worcester. This penitent pressed himself to Oswald's tomb, prayed and was set free from his bindings.[49]

Several examples of physical interaction are also found in the later material. The anonymous collection of miracles of Ithamar includes two such examples. A man was cured of fever having kissed the saint's feretory, and a monk of Rochester was relieved of extreme anxiety by kissing Ithamar's shrine and praying to the saint.[50] In the anonymous collection of Swithun's miracles, a visitor kissed the feet of a statue of the saint in the Old Minster.[51] In order to be cured of his blindness, Raven was led to the church of Hexham Abbey on Acca's feast and went to the shrine. There he prayed, kissed the altar, cried and held vigil. Raven fell asleep and saw Acca in a dream; when he awoke, he was cured.[52] There are three such physical interactions in the anonymous Oswine collection. A man blinded by a festering head wound interrupted his vigil at Oswine's shrine and felt his way to the saint's casket itself. There the man embraced and kissed the statue of Oswine that decorated the casket and, following tearful prayer, he was cured. A monk called Symeon was cured of a toothache which was not responding to medicine by kissing Oswine's casket and praying at the shrine. Finally, Prior Ruelendus was cured of a paralysed hand by praying and touching the stone support of Oswine's shrine.[53] These physical interactions were about getting as close to the saint as possible whilst they reposed in their coffins and feretories. Kissing a statue, embracing the tomb or touching your face to a shrine cloth were acceptable alternatives to kissing, embracing and touching the saint. These practices help to emphasise the desire for proximity, and their relative rarity in the corpus highlights the potential problems of every pilgrim fiddling with the shrine and its accoutrements. Five of the twelve supplicants detailed previously were religious rather than laypeople and could perhaps have expected preferential access. But people, regardless of rank or religious status, were willing to go to any length in order to engage the saint of their choice in helping them solve their crises. Such a commitment was not limited to attendance at the main shrine of a saint. Where they were available, people also visited alternative sites to petition their patrons.

As noted previously, alternative sites could be subject to pilgrimage and a place for supplication. These could include sites associated with the life, death and burial of a saint and seem to have been as miraculously potent, if not as popular, as the main shrine.[54] Other nexuses for miracle petitions included churches, altars and statues dedicated to the saint in question.[55] Behaviour at these alternative sites was much the same as at the main shrines. For example, a paralysed man on the Isle of Wight had a vision of two youths who led him to Swithun, who admonished the man to imitate Christ. On awaking the man told his wife, who suggested he go to St Swithun's church on the Isle of Wight to seek a cure. The paralysed man did this, prayed at the church for intercession and was healed.[56] Where these holy places were within the precinct of a religious foundation access must have been similarly negotiated as at a shrine. Those places which were away from clerical control would presumably have been more open to the laity. When people visited shrines and alternative sites, they often took away some token to help effect a miracle at a distance. This practice can be understood in relation to the 'holy radioactivity' of saints and their relics,[57] much like the touching of the shrine and its trappings. Places in which a saint had lived, died or been buried were infused with their power and presence. The contagious nature of the saints is perhaps not best displayed through their tombs and shrines but through the earth and water their remains came into contact with.

Taking away relics from places associated with the saints was established in Bede's work. Soil, dust and splinters could all be used in the search for miraculous cures, particularly when suspended in water.[58] Lantfred and Wulfstan are silent on these uses of relics and water, but the thread was picked up by Goscelin. Juthwara's bones were washed in the same water as Wulfsige's when they were both placed in a new shrine under Bishop Osmund (1078–1099), and Goscelin frames further miracles at Sherborne as joint efforts between the two saints. A monk of Sherborne was cured of fever by drinking some of this water on the feast of Juthwara. This miracle led to the water being used to cure several sick people at Sherborne. A mother of one of the monks was cured of a serious illness by this water, and she began to feel better as soon as the water entered her home. The mother's ailment was judged to have been beyond the skill of doctors, and all who heard of this miracle praised the two saints. Similarly a priest named Wulfric was cured on his death bed by drinking some water into which some relics of Juthwara had been dipped, which Wulfric had sent for by messenger.[59]

Here we see a differentiation between water used for ablution and relic water created for the purpose of healing. Washing is found in the acts of baptism, burial, translation and the consecration of churches.[60] As part of this Christian tradition of ablution, it made sense to wash bodily relics whenever they were removed from their shrines, as well as the shrines themselves. Water in which relics had been dipped, however, is not a by-product of washing but a substance created with the sole purpose of more easily transmitting the power of a saint. These are the two major facets of water in the Christian context, as purifier and 'transmitter of spiritual power'.[61] Relic water could be substituted by abundant miraculous water which came forth from saint's springs and wells. The water from Ivo's spring at Slepe was used to cure various ailments, including leprosy, blindness, gout, toothache and injuries sustained by falling off a horse. It also helped a girl with a pin stuck in her throat and a rich woman who had swallowed a snake.[62] A novice of Ramsey was exorcised by drinking a tonic of water and scrapings from Ivo's shrine. The exorcism of the novice was found to be too difficult for the monks of Ramsey, and this is why they resorted to their patron.[63] Perhaps such a difficult task required scrapings from the saint's tomb as a more potent or specific remedy than the water from Ivo's spring.

People used relic water from several other saints. A woman from Perkley who vomited up a worm was cured by drinking some water which the relics of Mildburh had been washed in.[64] The relics of St Augustine's were also effective in a healing tonic. Following the translations of the saints, a dying girl was cured by drinking water in which one of the handlers of the relics had washed his hands, and her family gave thanks. Elements from around the old tomb were retained as secondary relics, including tiles and bricks which were placed in water and the draught drunk as a curative. A Frenchman came from Essex to gain some of this water for his wife. A priest was cured of a long illness in the same manner, and so, too, a sick merchant staying in Canterbury who had gone to St Augustine's in search of medicine. The merchant gave thanks for his cure and presented the saint with a large candle. A girl was cured of a persistent stomach complaint after praying before Hadrian's relics just after his translation and drinking water which had washed the hands of the brothers who had touched the saint.[65] The sacristan at St Augustine's was also cured of fever by drinking the water used to wash Hadrian's tomb. This water was then used to cure others.[66] Again at St Augustine's there seems to have been a combination of using relic water created as a by-product and using tailor-made relic water.

The use of water as a transmitter of sanctity is found in the later material as well. Eadmer concludes his collection of Dunstan's miracles by referring to the saint's staff, which was adorned with a tooth of St Andrew. Countless people were healed by drinking water that the staff had been dipped into, and a vessel of this water was kept on hand at Christ Church as there was an almost daily need for it.[67] A woman whose child had died in her womb drank water which had washed the arm of Ecgwine, and her belly burst, the child's remains were extracted and she recovered.[68] Following the translation of Erkenwald, a student was healed after he had been sickening for half a year. His teacher, Canon Theoldus of St Martin-le-Grand, took some dust from Erkenwald's old tomb, gave it to the boy in some water and burnt some incense which had been found at the tomb. This drove the sickness from the boy, and he was completely healed.[69] A woman was cured of fever by drinking the water used to wash the feet of a statue of Ithamar which decorated his feretory. This same liquid was then used to cure sufferers in an outbreak of fever.[70] During Wenefred's translation from Gwytherin to Shrewsbury, a man was cured by being given some dust from Wenefred's head in a tonic made with holy water.[71] A blind woman was healed after regular visits to the saints at Hexham when Canon Edric took pity on her. Edric took a bone from Acca's reliquary and prayed, then dipped it in some water. He asked the woman to trust in Acca, she bowed her head and bent her knee, then Edric anointed her eyes with the water, signed her with the cross and asked Acca to help. Immediately she was cured, and both of them rejoiced. A craftsman of Hexham was also healed with relic water given to him by Edric. He suffered with a serious throat problem and was cured by drinking the water.[72]

The use of saints' water was common in England during our period, whether from springs, as a by-product of ablution or as a specifically created tonic. Again we come back to the contagious power of the saints. Frazer first posited the 'law of contact or contagion' in his analysis of magic and religion. He pointed out that 'things which have been in contact with each other continue to act on each other at a distance'.[73] In the Christian context, the idea that holy power could be transmitted through inanimate objects goes back to the Bible. When Jesus healed the woman of the issue of the blood, the woman touched Jesus' clothes rather than his person. Paul is also said to have been able to transmit his healing power through cloth which had previously touched him.[74] This 'chain of contact' led to early relics including the dust from tombs of the martyrs and the *brandea* mentioned by Gregory the Great.[75] If power could radiate from a saint's body through a tomb and into dust or cloth, it is not a great leap to include water. Water, as a necessity of life and a solvent, is commonly understood as a 'repository or medium of a kind of spiritual power'.[76] These natural and cultural characteristics of water lend it to democratising the direct consumption of saintly power, especially where the source of saintly power was freely available. Relic water as by-product would have been in limited supply, but dust and relic dipping could have filled the gap. People and animals could be healed of all manner of ailments even if they could not engage in prolonged petitions at the saint's shrine. It is worth considering that water from these sources in other contexts would be understood as polluted and perhaps dangerous. At best we are presented with a spring rising from a grave. The deliberate muddying of water with dust, dirt and other detritus would also be preferable to the second-hand water used for washing corpses, bones and the hands of those who had handled them. If the bodies behind such water were not saints, this used water might be considered polluted or 'dead'. Instead the special position held by the saints resulted in a 'living' water, a medium of 'transformation and regeneration'.[77] Water used in this way might more properly have been disposed in a relic grave or drained near the altar, elements which had developed into the purpose-built *piscina* by the thirteenth century.[78] But such were the benefits of saints' water that it was created, retained and distributed widely.[79]

Interactions with primary and secondary relics by supplicants themselves were less common. Once a year, on Maundy Thursday, a woman named Oswen would open the tomb of Edmund and trim his hair and nails, the clippings of which were kept in a separate reliquary which was placed on the altar of the church at Bury.[80] Presumably these relics were kept separate from Edmund himself for ease of access, requiring only the opening of a small reliquary rather than the elevation of the saint and all the ceremony that would entail. More commonly retained outside of a saint's tomb were relics like burial shrouds, clothing and other possessions. Wulfthryth's ring of office healed those with eye complaints if they looked on it with faith.[81] Erkenwald's litter was said to cure those who touched or kissed it, and splinters were taken away for use elsewhere.[82] Edmund's secondary relics also had miraculous properties. A layman named Norman was charged with bringing a phylactery containing some of Edmund's relics across the sea to Normandy, where Abbot Baldwin was attending King William I. Whilst crossing the Channel, Norman's ship was beset by a storm and was in dire straits for three days. In a vision, Norman was told to touch the phylactery around his neck and pray. He awoke and called out to the steersman, and they both prayed to God and Edmund, the sea calmed and they arrived that day. On landing in Normandy, Norman lost his travelling bag. He went into a church and prayed to God and Edmund for help and was directed to his bag by an old lady he encountered on leaving the church. Finally, Norman crossed a previously unforded section of river under the protection of Edmund.[83]

Dunstan's possessions were used as curative relics as well. First, as described by Osbern, Dunstan's processional cross was used as a part of an exorcism of Æthelweard, a young monk of Christ Church. At the climax of a long petition a monk placed Dunstan's staff on to Æthelweard and then tearfully prayed to the saint. This worked and Æthelweard thanked Dunstan and the monks of Christ Church for saving him from so strong a demon.[84] Eadmer notes the healing of a woman in London. This woman was deathly ill and had a vision of Dunstan in which the saint told her to send for and decorate his chasuble, which was kept at St Peter's Abbey, Westminster. In the morning, she sent for the chasuble. The woman kissed it and decorated it with gold, and she was healed straight away.[85]

Eadmer also records Anselm's cure of a well known knight called Humphrey, who was suffering from dropsy. Throughout his illness, Humphrey constantly prayed to Anselm. As he ailed, the knight called for his friend Haimo, a monk of Christ Church, to visit him. Haimo brought with him a belt of Anselm's which he had been left in charge of by Eadmer himself. On seeing his friend, Haimo gave the belt to Humphrey, who prayed, took the belt, kissed it and put it around himself. Humphrey's swelling began to subside, and as he felt the curative power, he moved the belt over his swollen limbs. After recovering, Humphrey went to Anselm's tomb and told his story to the brethren, asking that they would give thanks on his behalf to God and Anselm. When Eadmer went to collect the belt, he cut off a section for Humphrey to keep. Later Humphrey suffered from dropsy again and was able to cure himself through the use of his strip of Anselm's belt. Whilst Eadmer was Bishop of St Andrews (1120–1121), an English woman named Eastrilda was unwell. Eadmer had Anselm's belt with him and put it around her. Eastrilda recovered after a few days, and all who saw this miracle gave thanks to God. Back at Canterbury, Anselm's belt was used to cure a Christ Church monk of fever by placing it around his neck. He recovered quickly, and those present gave thanks to God for Anselm's help. The belt of Anselm was later called for by women having difficulty giving birth, and all who asked for the belt with proper intention and faith were helped.[86]

In his miracles of Oswald, Eadmer relates the story of Eadwacer, a monk of Worcester who suffered from a tumour in his jaw and lived in self-imposed exile. Eadwacer came to the monastery on Oswald's feast and, in a secluded spot, marked the Mass for the day and prayed. The other monks noticed Eadwacer and also prayed for him. The monks asked him to rest with them, and he agreed. The monks sat down to dine and afterwards drank from a cup which Oswald had used in his lifetime. A prayer was said, and the brothers took turns to drink from the cup. When it came to Eadwacer, he prayed, as did the other monks, and then drank his draught and placed the cup against his jaw. When he took the cup away, he was healed, and all who witnessed it or learnt of it praised God.[87] Finally, William of Malmesbury records that Wulfstan of Worcester's inner tunic was worn by a recluse who had been harassed by the Devil in his solitude. The tunic proved effective in easing the troubled monk's solitary life.[88]

The application of relics in any form allowed direct access to a saint and often resulted in a truncated petition. Whilst some of these relics could be finite and consumed on use the source of their power, the saint themself was effectively infinite. The touching of a relic, the consumption of saint's water or even just looking upon Wulfthryth's ring was enough to facilitate a cure. This is not to say that these simple actions were not proper petitions. The manipulation of a relic required a person experiencing a crisis to have knowledge of a relevant saint. They then engaged with the relic in order to gain the aid of the saint and in the belief that the saint could help. The saints seem not to have differentiated between supplicants praying at their shrines and those who interacted with them through their relics. Acceptable petitionary actions all resulted in the same ends, a miracle. In fact, the use of relics was not necessarily divorced from other means of supplication. Several miracle petitions used a combination of various methods. A woman who swallowed a snake enacted a convoluted strategy, including first visiting Edmund at Bury, then being redirected to Ivo at Ramsey, where she conducted vigils, prayers and fasting, combined with the drinking of Ivo's water, which led to her cure.[89] Æthelweard's exorcism came at the end of a long process, with the placing of Dunstan's cross on the young monk as the decisive act.[90] When Norman was in trouble at sea, he was instructed in a vision and, on waking, touched his reliquary and called on the steersman to pray with him to Edmund.[91] Many of these miracles were performed at a distance from the shrine or other locations associated with the saints, with the relics helping to forge a connection between saint and supplicant. Of course, not all distance miracles required the application of relics.

Post-mortem miracles which took place at a distance from a saint's shrine first appear in Lantfred's miracles of Swithun. A slave girl who had been shackled and was to receive a beating in the morning escaped her punishment through spending the night beseeching Swithun, who granted her intercession. Her shackles fell off, and she fled to Swithun's shrine, where her master found her but, on account of the saint, did not proceed with any other punishments.[92] This entry is followed by another distance miracle. A paralysed man from Hampshire was cured in his sickbed after having stated his intention to visit Swithun and having had the preparations begun. He jumped up from his bed and outpaced his friends on horseback on their way to Winchester, perhaps to give thanks having already been cured.[93] These two miracles are quite different in content, with one based on an invocation of the saint and the other an early reward for a promised shrine visit. Lantfred only records two other instances of an early reward. In one instance, a blind man was cured by Swithun on his way to Winchester. When he arrived at the Old Minster, he told the monks what had occurred, and they gathered in the church and praised God and chanted hymns. In the other instance, a boy of noble birth was injured falling from a horse, and it was thought that he might die. Upon seeing this, the ealdorman who led the horseback procession prayed to Swithun and promised to carry the boy to his tomb. After the ealdorman's prayer was finished, the boy sprang up and the ealdorman gave thanks to God. Related to these examples is the case of the rich woman who was healed after promising to visit Swithun with gifts, only to be struck down again with the same illness when she did not fulfil her vow.[94] The majority of distance miracles documented by Lantfred – and in the corpus more generally – were like the invocation of Swithun by the imprisoned girl.

Lantfred records the miraculous liberation of prisoners and slaves on three other occasions. In each case the supplicant prayed to Swithun for help and secured their release. One slave girl praying for release looked on the Old Minster as she prayed, whilst a criminal in France could only pray to God and the famous Swithun to be saved from execution the following day.[95] The most extensive escape miracle saw a man abscond from prison equipped only with a small knife, given to him for trimming his fingernails, and prayers to Swithun. The man faced execution for stealing four wheat sheaves, and once he had escaped, he made his way to the Old Minster to give thanks and tell his tale.[96] Related to these miracles was the intercession of Swithun in a judicial ordeal. A slave belonging to the merchant Flodoald was apprehended for a crime and was to go through an ordeal of carrying a bar of red-hot metal to determine his guilt. The slave's hand burnt and swelled up as would be expected, a sign that he was guilty. But Flodoald and his companions prayed to Swithun, stating that they would hand the slave over to Swithun's service if he would help him. When the hand was examined to determine guilt, Flodoald and his supporters saw the burn and blisters, but the others saw only an unharmed hand, and so the slave was let go. Flodoald and his companions gave thanks to God, and the slave was given over to the service of Swithun at the Old Minster.[97] The only other distance miracle found in Lantfred's collection involved the author himself, helping a friend's wife in France, as noted previously.[98]

The supplicants in these distance miracles all had a compelling reason that they could not visit the saint's shrine. In Lantfred's work, these reasons include imprisonment, severe illness and great distance. These supplicants knew of Swithun's power and asked the saint for help as best as they could away from his shrine. The deliverance of prisoners is a common form of distance miracle performed by Æthelwold, Augustine, Mildrith, Ithamar, Bege, Modwenna, Wilfrid, Oswine and John of Beverley as well.[99] The late-eleventh-century collection of Swithun's miracles also includes the account of a slave girl escaping incarceration and going to Swithun's shrine, where her chains fell off.[100] Another major example of a supplicant unable to visit the shrine were those detained at sea due to storm, becalming or other problems. Augustine was incredibly potent as an intercessor at sea. The saint was invoked to save King Cnut, Abbot Æthelwine of Athelney (c. 1020–1025), a man raised at St Augustine's named Elfnoth, a boat carrying stone for St Augustine's from Normandy, boats carrying goods for St Augustine's from the Continent and even a boat containing Greek and English passengers in the Aegean Sea. The survivors of these incidents enriched St Augustine's with gold, cloth and even a new tower, and they thanked God and Augustine.[101] Other saints who saved their supplicants at sea include Edith, who also helped Cnut and Archbishop Ealdred of York (1061–1069), Swithun, who saved Ealdred when he was Bishop of Worcester (1046–1061), Hadrian, Edmund and John of Beverley.[102]

Saints saved their supplicants from a variety of other problems away from their shrines, including wolf attack, an angry mob and falling from a cliff on an ox-cart.[103] The usual form of a petition for a distance miracle was the invocation of the saint or a short prayer, such as the quarry worker Burchard's invocation of Augustine to save him from bandits.[104] Such invocations and prayers could be supplemented with vows to visit the saint and present gifts. When Swithun saved Ealdred from shipwreck, he was returning from an embassy to Emperor Henry III (1046–1056) in 1054. Caught in a storm, Ealdred prayed to Swithun and promised to donate to him a silver dish he had received from the Emperor and other gifts if he were to make it home. The other people on the boat, having heard Swithun's name, took up the prayer, and the sea calmed. Ealdred made his donation in person at Winchester, and the monks used the proceeds to adorn a statue of Swithun.[105]

Some distance miracles made use of more elaborate petitions, as when Goscelin, or perhaps Goscelin's source, was cured of gout by Ivo through offering thirty Masses and a rendition of the psalter to the saint.[106] The men stranded in the Aegean Sea on Augustine's feast day performed praises and vigils as best they could on a vessel at anchor, waiting out a storm. By the evening of that day, they were sailing easily, and they shouted and sang for joy and thanked Augustine. As soon as they had escaped from the storm, a festive Mass was sung for Augustine. When the ship made harbour for the evening, the bad weather resumed, and a favourable breeze returned upon their setting out again.[107] When a fire spread through Bury, a former servant of Anselm who had moved there was encouraged to recite the Our Father, kneeling and keeping Anselm in mind. The fire was blown away from the servant's house whilst those around it were ravaged.[108] Before her translation to Shrewsbury, Wenefred was responsible for the cure of a monk of Shrewsbury. The subprior of Chester sang the seven penitential psalms, prayed and, after falling asleep, had a vision of Wenefred, in which he was told to send someone to celebrate Mass in a chapel near Wenefred's Well. After a short delay, this was carried out, the monk was cured and the monks of Chester and Shrewsbury became devoted to Wenefred.[109] Some elaborations involved material components other than the saints' relics.

A woman from Antwerp named Maenzindis had visited Rome in hopes of aiding her pregnancy but lay ill and afraid of dying in childbirth. Maenzindis had a vision in her exhausted state, telling her that Augustine would intercede on her behalf due to the tearful petitions of her friends and she was to undo her belt and send it as proof of her healing to England. Maenzindis and her friends wondered at this request but were joyous and gave thanks. Struck with divine inspiration, Maenzindis had a silver girdle made quickly, wrapped it around herself and invoked Augustine. She was healed in this manner and sent the belt on as requested to St Augustine's, where it remained at the time of composition. Another woman of Antwerp, Emma, was also having difficulties with her pregnancy. Emma had a vision instructing her to have a candle made in honour of Augustine, as long as the circumference of her belly, and to offer it in the nearest church. Having done these things, Emma gave birth quickly and easily.[110] A French businessman named William was taken ill in London with a catalepsy-like affliction. William lay in bed for three days until it occurred to one of his compatriots to seek the help of Erkenwald. This Frenchman took a pair of eyes made of wax, touched them to William's eyes and carried them to St Paul's, where they were placed above the altar. Before the Frenchman could leave St Paul's, William stirred in his bed and awoke to tell of Erkenwald visiting him in his sleep and touching his eyes. He proved his sight by taking out and replacing a pin used to hold a cross on a staff, and then rumour spread of the cure.[111]

These stories include an early form of 'measuring' as a part of a petition. In later sources this 'measuring' generally involved making a thin wax taper called a trindle, which was as long as the afflicted body part or person. This trindle was then offered to the saint, usually burnt as a candle, and directly linked the person and their problems to the saint.[112] These practices of measuring and moulding personalised the miracles to the supplicants. These items could only relate to themselves and their bodies, and thus, the miracle would be tailored to their needs. A more abstract connection could also be made to a saint. For example, a monk named Henry was visiting Tynemouth Priory and had been suffering from a severe eye complaint. One of his companions found a book of Oswine's passion, invention and miracles in the priory school. Henry touched the book to his eyes, believing in the power of the saint, and was cured.[113]

Despite these miracles occurring away from the saint's main shrine, they largely conform to the pattern of a shrine cure. The major difference was the performance of the petitionary acts at a distance. They still required knowledge of a saint, which was put to use in the face of a crisis by asking for help. They could include elements of elaboration but could be as simple as a hurried prayer, not unlike that of the man suffering from a wart who went to Modwenna for help. Burning a candle to Swithun at a church in France was much like offering one to the saint in the Old Minster.[114] Both simple and complex petitions were rewarded with miracles by the saints, and people often continued to the shrine eventually in fulfilment of a vow or to present a promised offering. This is not only how these miracles ended up being recorded in a collection; it was also a means of (re)incorporating the supplicant into the saint's community. If you did not report your miracle or attend the shrine, your petition would be between you and the saint, mollifying a potential failed petition but isolating oneself from other supplicants. Such private devotion must have occurred but remains invisible to us. The petition at a distance highlights the two tendencies of a saint's cult, which cause an underlying tension. The tendency towards universality includes the saint within the heavenly choir and sees them approachable anywhere to help with anything. The further away a miracle occurred, the more powerful a saint would seem. The tendency towards specificity sees an individual saint with a home, a body and relics who could be met in person and who formed relationships between and with their communities. The compromise is the miracle petition, a heterodox collection of actions which simply required a knowledge of the saint, a problem to solve and a cry for help.

Making miracles was what the cult of the saints was about. It was why pilgrimages happened beyond Rome and the Holy Land, the reason people fought over saints' bodies and why they conducted translations and relic processions. Altars, statues, chapels and churches could act as miraculous centres, as could old burial places, death sites, wells and springs. The contagious nature of sanctity could infest the basest material: 'charisma [could be] concretized and sedimented in objects'.[115] These items could be monitored and controlled by a saint's custodians to a degree, but our reliance on the 'official discourse' of the custodians may conceal the extent of unofficial miracles and underground trade in holy dust and saint's water. Either way, engagement with a saint had much the same effect at or away from a shrine. Those cured elsewhere often felt compelled to visit the saint in person to offer thanks. Even if you could be helped at a distance, there was some importance to the 'being there of pilgrimage'.[116] Perhaps it was because a shrine, or other cult site, gave an opportunity to perform your misfortune publicly. Through appropriate action, you could demonstrate the life crisis you were embroiled in and your belief that this saint could help you. It was a way to show your piety and an action you could take to solve your particular problem through your relationship with a spiritual patron. Through 'gesture and performance', one could present their 'virtuous self' to others[117] and enjoy the 'tangible benefits' of 'appropriate rituals'.[118] Making miracles relied on all parties to continue: on the saints and their intercession, on the custodians in their facilitation and recording and on the supplicants' petitions. All groups played a role, people moved between groups and all witnessed the miracles of the saints. But without the miracle petition, the whole process fails. There would be far fewer miracles to document, no means to solicit them and, therefore, no need to maintain a relic cult of this sort. If people stopped asking the saints for miraculous help, miracles would not be forthcoming.

This is not to deny the saints agency, and some unsolicited miracles are recorded in the evidence. Lantfred's *Translatio et Miracula S. Swithuni* begins with a vision sent by the saint to a smith. The smith had not prayed for aid, and his role was to tell the cleric Eadsige to inform Bishop Æthelwold that Swithun was a saint and should be translated. The smith worried about being thought insane and so delayed action, and he was urged on by further dreams and threats from Swithun. Eventually word reached Æthelwold, but in the meantime, other supplicants were led to Swithun's grave by visions from the saint.[119] There was a delay of over a century between Swithun's death and the revelation that he was a saint, so such an intervention proved necessary. Swithun was not alone in initiating his own cult. If a saint's remains had been lost, forgotten or otherwise concealed, a miracle could help to locate the body and indicate sainthood.[120] An unexpected or undetected problem could also lead to an unsolicited miracle. The major example would be an unattended candle left burning which when later discovered had caused little or no damage to a shrine and importantly had not caused an inferno.[121] Unsolicited miracles could equally indicate the saint's anger or disapproval at their treatment or the treatment of their community.[122] The unsolicited miracles show the saint as an active agent in a community who could make their presence known and step in to prevent potential disasters when they went unnoticed. Once a cult was established, however, if you wanted help, it seems you generally had to ask for it.

Asking for help from the saints was never a sure thing, but unsuccessful petitions are rare in the source material.[123] An extended petition or one involving promises of gifts and vows of service could become expensive, but a visit to a local shrine or a prayer in extremis was open to anyone. This gave people a set of actions they could call upon to get out of a crisis. A person had to decide to become a supplicant, they had to act like a supplicant and behave in a certain way towards their patron. In cases of property, incarceration and penance, a person could attempt to sway an earthly authority to help them. In cases of health, the same could be said of a doctor or perhaps the sufferer's family and friends. Each person's 'hierarchy of resort' would differ based on their circumstances.[124] Often in miracle collections, the hagiographer describes how appeals to other authorities had been exhausted before the supplicant approached the saint.[125] Other problems were so difficult that medical or legal authorities could not even be consulted. When all seemed lost, a person could engage in the practical action of calling upon a saint and could reasonably expect aid of some kind. They could also show to the community that they were in a state of crisis and knew how best to deal with that crisis. A petition was an opportunity to ask for help and to be seen to be asking for help. Of course, the cult of the saints in medieval England was not only predicated on beneficent miracles. When people misbehaved, the saints acted against them, and these punitive miracles and the reactions to them helped to delimit the cult of the saints.

Notes

1 The best example of an epoch-spanning saint would be Alban, who was martyred in the third or fourth century and seems to have been consistently given cult in medieval England. Another less well-documented example could be Liudhard, who was already in Kent to witness the Augustinian mission and has a cult recorded by Goscelin in the eleventh century.
2 Thacker, '*Loca Sanctorum*', p. 2.
3 'Scio hominem cui forte – ob quam causam nescio – uelut quedam uerruca surrexerit sub oculo, quam cum sensisset cotidie crescere et sepius ostendisset beate uirgini coram feretro eius et dixisset, quasi loquens ad eam, 'Domina mea, potes si uis hoc uicium auferre a me', uerruca eadem miro modo confestim euanuit et, mirantibus cunctis qui ante uiderant, nullo prorsus remanente uestigio, tota simul absque ulla dilatione abcessit.' Geoffrey, *Miracula S. Modwenne*, pp. 210–11.

4. Yarrow, p. 18.
5. Ibid., pp. 18–19.
6. Henry Mayr-Harting, 'Functions of a Twelfth-Century Shrine: The Miracles of St Frideswide', in *Studies in Medieval History: Presented to R. H. C. Davis*, ed. by Henry Mayr-Harting and R. I. Moore (London: Hambledon, 1985), pp. 193–206 (p. 205).
7. Lantfred, *Miracula S. Swithuni*, pp. 270–5.
8. Goscelin, *Miraculis S. Augustini*, p. 406.
9. *Miracula S. Oswini*, pp. 45–6.
10. Lantfred, *Miracula S. Swithuni*, pp. 296–7.
11. William Ketell, *Miracula S. Johannis*, pp. 284–7.
12. Eadmer, *Miracula S. Oswaldi*, pp. 298–9; Herman, *Miracula S. Edmundi*, pp. 80–5; *Miracula S. Yuonis*, p. lxxxii.
13. *Miracula S. Ætheldrethe*, pp. 120–1.
14. Lantfred, *Miracula S. Swithuni*, pp. 306–7, 330–3; Byrhtferth, *Vita S. Ecgwini*, pp. 280–7.
15. Goscelin, *Vita S. Edithe*, p. 293; Goscelin, *Miracula S. Yuonis*, pp. lxvii–lxviii; Goscelin, *Translationis S. Augustini*, p. 437; Osbern, *Miracula S. Dunstani*, pp. 153–4; Eadmer, *Miracula S. Oswaldi*, pp. 294–7; Dominic, *Miracula S. Ecgwini*, pp. 94–7; Arcoid, *Miracula S. Erkenwaldi*, pp. 116–19; Geoffrey, *Miracula S. Modwenne*, pp. 216–19; *Passio S. Edwardi*, p. 15.
16. Love, *Eleventh-Century*, pp. 82–3.
17. Sarah Hamilton, *The Practice of Penance, 900–1050* (Woodbridge: Boydell, 2001), pp. 173–4.
18. B. Thorpe, ed., *Ancient Laws and Institutes of England*, 3 vols (London: Eyre & Spottiswoode, 1840), II, 204–5.
19. Jonathan Sumption, *Pilgrimage: An Image of Mediaeval Religion* (London: Faber, 1975), pp. 153–5.
20. See Matthew 16, pp. 13–20.
21. Early examples can be found in Lantfred. A man was cured by Swithun after a horrifying encounter with furies, and a woman was cured of a dislocated jaw having been possessed, Lantfred, *Miracula S. Swithuni*, pp. 280–3, 322–3. The latest example is of Arkillus, a builder at Tynemouth Priory, who was cured of diabolic visions by Oswine in the mid-twelfth-century collection of the saint's miracles, *Miracula S. Oswini*, pp. 29–30.
22. For an example of a lawsuit see Osbern, *Miracula S. Dunstani*, pp. 158–9. Lost property recovered by the saints could range from the sacristan's keys, Goscelin, *Vita S. Vulfhilde*, pp. 433–4; Goscelin, *Virtutibus S. Adriani*, Vespasian B.xx, fol 240ᵛ, Harley 105, fol 211ᵛ, to a penny intended for donation, Herman, *Miracula S. Edmundi*, pp. 340–1. On issues with livestock, see *Miracula S. Ithamari*, p. 434; Goscelin, *Miraculis S. Augustini*, p. 408.
23. Geoffrey, *Miracula S. Modwenne*, pp. 186–9, 200–5; Goscelin, *Translatione S. Ethelburge*, pp. 435–52; *Miracula S. Guthlaci*, p. 56; Goscelin, *Miracula S. Yuonis*, pp. lxix, lxxx–lxxxi; Goscelin, *Miraculis S. Augustini*, p. 406; *Miracula S. Ithamari*, p. 432; Goscelin, *Miracula S. Mildrethe*, pp. 192–7; Herman, *Miracula S. Edmundi*, pp. 340–1; *Miracula S. Swithuni*, pp. 688–91; Osbern, *Miracula S. Dunstani*, pp. 138–9; Eadmer, *Vita S. Anselmi*, pp. 157–58; Eadmer, *Miracula S. Oswaldi*, pp. 294–95; Dominic, *Miracula S. Ecgwini*, pp. 92–93; Arcoid, *Miracula S. Erkenwaldi*, pp. 102–9; Aelred, *De sanctis Hagustaldensis*, pp. 177–81.
24. Tearful prayer is found in some of the earliest English hagiography as well as the latest. For example, from Wulfstan, *Narratio de S. Swithuno*, pp. 462–3, to the anonymous twelfth-century miracles of Oswine, *Miracula S. Oswini*, p. 31.
25. Michael Winterbottom and Michael Lapidge, eds and trans, *The Early Lives of St Dunstan* (Oxford: Clarendon, 2012), pp. 104–5.
26. Piroska Nagy, 'Religious Weeping as Ritual in the Medieval West', *Social Analysis*, 48.2 (Summer 2004), 119–37 (pp. 126–7).

27 Raymond A. Anselment, 'Mary Rich, Countess of Warwick, and the Gift of Tears', *The Seventeenth Century*, 22 (2007), 336–57 (pp. 336–8).
28 See Julia Barrow, 'Demonstrative Behaviour and Political Communication in Later Anglo-Saxon England', *Anglo-Saxon England*, 36 (2007), 127–50; Levi Roach, *Kingship and Consent in Anglo-Saxon England, 871–978: Assemblies and the State in the Early Middle Ages* (Cambridge: Cambridge University Press, 2013), pp. 187–8.
29 Lantfred, *Miracula S. Swithuni*, pp. 280–3.
30 Those three vigils can be found in Goscelin, *Vita S. Edithe*, pp. 300–2; *Miracula S. Kenelmi*, pp. 86–9; *Miraculis S. Augustini*, p. 398.
31 Dominic, *Miracula S. Ecgwini*, pp. 106–9; Arcoid, *Miracula S. Erkenwaldi*, pp. 144–7; Geoffrey, *Miracula S. Modwenne*, pp. 198–219; Aelred, *De sanctis Hagustaldensis*, pp. 177–87; William Ketell, *Miracula S. Johannis*, pp. 263–4.
32 *Miracula S. Ithamari*, pp. 428–30; *Vita et Passio S. Waltheofi comitis*, in J. A. Giles, ed., *Vita Quorundum Anglo-Saxonum* (London: Smith, 1854), pp. 24–30; *Miracula S. Oswini*, pp. 31–3.
33 Mary Hamilton, *Incubation: The Cure of Disease in Pagan Temples and Christian Churches* (St Andrews: Henderson, 1906), pp. 111–14.
34 Gábor Klaniczay, 'Dream Healing and Visions in Medieval Latin Miracle Accounts', in *The "Vision Thing": Studying Divine Intervention*, ed. by William A. Christian Jr and Gábor Klaniczay, Collegium Budapest Workshop Series, 18 (Budapest: Collegium Budapest, 2009), pp. 37–64 (pp. 37–8).
35 Charles Stewart, 'Ritual Dreams and Historical Orders: Incubation Between Paganism and Christianity', in *Archaeology, Anthropology and Heritage in the Balkans and Anatolia*, ed. by David Shankland, 2 vols (Istanbul: Isis, 2004), I, pp. 31–53 (p. 36).
36 Klaniczay, 'Dream Healing', pp. 40–2.
37 Stewart, pp. 31–2.
38 Goscelin records many visions of the saints as instructors, healers and admonishers. In Goscelin, *Miracula S. Kenelmi*, pp. 68–89, the saint cured three people with daytime visions at his shrine as well as guiding two cases to his shrine with visions. In the *Vita et Miracula S. Yuonis*, Goscelin records many visions of Ivo, including the saint admonishing two monks for their behaviour, Goscelin, *Miracula S. Yuonis*, pp. lxiv–lxvi. In Goscelin, *Miraculis S. Augustini*, pp. 397–8, Leodegar was sent to Canterbury from Westminster at the behest of a vision of St Peter. At Canterbury he was healed in a vision of Augustine, Mellitus and Laurence which occurred on the third night of his vigil.
39 The most important advice given by saints was where a person could go to receive healing. The most obvious physical interaction was the cure of a specific ailment, but in anger saints could beat people or cause their hair to fall out. See Arcoid, *Miracula S. Erkenwaldi*, pp. 158–61; Goscelin, *Miracula S. Mildrethe*, pp. 180–5.
40 Like the man without a tongue who was told to spend a night in vigil at Edith's shrine, Goscelin, *Vita S. Edithe*, pp. 300–2. Also of note is the story of Leodegar, who seems to have been instructed on where to go and what to do before his three nights vigil, Goscelin, *Miraculis S. Augustini*, p. 398.
41 Lantfred, *Miracula S. Swithuni*, pp. 280–3, 298–301.
42 Goscelin, *Miraculis S. Augustini*, p. 398.
43 Arcoid, *Miracula S. Erkenwaldi*, pp. 144–7.
44 Herman, *Miracula S. Edmundi*, pp. 340–3.
45 Goscelin, *Miracula S. Yuonis*, p. lxix.
46 Goscelin, *Virtutibus S. Adriani*, Vespasian B.xx, fols 238^v-39^r, Harley 105, fols 209^v-10^r.
47 Goscelin, *Miracula S. Edmundi*, pp. 276–7.
48 Osbern, *Miracula S. Dunstani*, p. 133.
49 Eadmer, *Miracula S. Oswaldi*, pp. 298–9.

50 *Miracula S. Ithamari*, pp. 432–5.
51 *Miracula S. Swithuni*, pp. 692–3.
52 Aelred, *De sanctis Hagustaldensis*, pp. 186–7.
53 *Miracula S. Oswini*, pp. 32–6.
54 Examples include Wulfhild's former oratory, the site of Kenelm's death and Mildrith's old tomb at Thanet. Goscelin, *Vita S. Vulfhilde*, pp. 430–1; Love, *Eleventh-Century*, pp. cii–cvi, 68; Goscelin, *Miracula S. Mildrethe*, pp. 144–5.
55 For example Swithun's statue at Sherborne, the churches of Augustine and Edmund's altar at Lucca. *Miracula S. Swithuni*, pp. 680–1; Goscelin, *Translationis S. Augustini*, pp. 427–9; Herman, *Miracula S. Edmundi*, pp. 80–5.
56 Lantfred, *Miracula S. Swithuni*, pp. 324–7.
57 Finucane, p. 26.
58 Bede records the blood of saints transmitting miraculous power into dirt, wood and even moss. Bede also shows how such power could pass through water that came into contact with a saint or their relics. See for example Bede, *HE*, I.18, pp. 58–61; III.2, pp. 214–19; III.9, pp. 242–3; III.13, pp. 252–5; III.17, pp. 264–5; V.18, pp. 512–15; III.11, pp. 246–7; IV.3, pp. 346–7.
59 Goscelin, *Vita S. Wlsini*, pp. 84–5.
60 Thacker, 'Making a Saint', pp. 65–6; Gittos, pp. 220–30.
61 James Rattue, *The Living Stream: Holy Wells in Historical Context* (Woodbridge: Boydell, 1995), p. 35.
62 Goscelin, *Miracula S. Yuonis*, pp. lix–lxxv; *Miracula S. Yuonis*, p. lxxxii.
63 Goscelin, *Miracula S. Yuonis*, p. lxxiv.
64 *Miracula S. Mylburge*, pp. 567–8.
65 Goscelin, *Translationis S. Augustini*, pp. 414–17, 435–6.
66 Goscelin, *Virtutibus S. Adriani*, Vespasian B.xx, fols 239r-39v, Harley 105 fols 210r-10v.
67 Eadmer, *Miracula S. Dunstani*, pp. 208–11.
68 Dominic, *Miracula S. Ecgwini*, pp. 114–15.
69 Arcoid, *Miracula S. Erkenwaldi*, pp. 150–5.
70 *Miracula S. Ithamari*, p. 432.
71 Robert, *Translatio S. Wenefrede*, pp. 730–1.
72 Aelred, *De sanctis Hagustaldensis*, pp. 187–8.
73 James Frazer, *The Golden Bough: A Study in Magic and Religion*, abr. edn (London: Macmillan, 1980), p. 1.
74 Matthew 9, pp. 20–2, Mark 5, pp. 25–34, Luke 8, pp. 43–8, Acts 19, pp. 11–12.
75 Bartlett, *Why Can the Dead*, pp. 245–9.
76 Rattue, p. 10.
77 Veronica Strang, *The Meaning of* Water (Oxford: Berg, 2004), pp. 76, 91–6.
78 David Parsons, '*Sacrarium*: Ablution Drains in Early Medieval Churches', in *The Anglo-Saxon Church*, ed. by L. A. S. Butler and R. K. Morris, (London: Council for British Archaeology, 1986), pp. 105–20 (pp. 112–14).
79 Perhaps the most famous example of a saint's water comes from after our period. On the widespread use and importance on St Thomas's water in the cult of Thomas Becket, see Pierre-André Sigal, 'Naissance et Premier Développement d'un Vinage Exceptionnel: L'eau de Saint Thomas', in *Cahiers de Civilisation Médiévale*, 52 (2001), 35–44.
80 Abbo, *Passio S. Eadmundi*, pp. 82–3.
81 Goscelin, *Vita S. Edithe*, p. 277.
82 *Vita S. Erkenwaldi*, in Whatley, *Erkenwald*, pp. 88–9.
83 Herman, *Miracula S. Edmundi*, pp. 88–92.
84 Osbern, *Miracula S. Dunstani*, pp. 144–51.
85 Eadmer, *Miracula S. Dunstani*, pp. 204–7.

86 Eadmer, *Vita S. Anselmi*, pp. 159–65.
87 Eadmer, *Miracula S. Oswaldi*, pp. 308–13.
88 William of Malmesbury, *Saints' Lives*, ed. and trans. by M. Winterbottom and R. Thomson (Oxford: Clarendon, 2002), pp. 450–1.
89 *Miracula S. Yuonis*, pp. lxxix–lxxx.
90 Osbern, *Miracula S. Dunstani*, pp. 144–51.
91 Herman, *Miracula S. Edmundi*, pp. 88–92.
92 Lantfred, *Miracula S. Swithuni*, pp. 288–9.
93 Ibid., pp. 288–91.
94 Ibid., pp. 318–21, 290–1.
95 Ibid., pp. 302–3, 324–5.
96 Ibid., pp. 314–17.
97 Ibid., pp. 308–11.
98 Ibid., pp. 320–3.
99 Wulfstan, *Vita S. Æthelwoldi*, pp. 66–9; Goscelin, *Miraculis S. Augustini*, pp. 405–6, 425; Goscelin, *Miracula S. Mildrethe*, pp. 188–90; *Miracula S. Ithamari*, p. 435; *Miracula S. Bege*, pp. 516–19; Geoffrey, *Miracula S. Modwenne*, pp. 214–15; Aelred, *De sanctis Hagustaldensis*, pp. 176–7; *Miracula S. Oswini*, pp. 33–5; William Ketell, *Miracula S. Johannis*, pp. 276–8.
100 *Miracula S. Swithuni*, pp. 684–5.
101 Goscelin, *Miraculis S. Augustini*, pp. 400–4.
102 Goscelin, *Vita S. Edithe*, pp. 278–80; *Miracula S. Swithuni*, pp. 678–9; Goscelin, *Virtutibus S. Adriani*, Vespasian B.xx, fols 234ᵛ, 235ᵛ-36ʳ, Harley 105, fols 206ʳ-06ᵛ, 207ʳ; Goscelin, *Miracula S. Edmundi*, pp. 300–3; William Ketell, *Miracula S. Johannis*, pp. 287–91.
103 *Miracula S. Swithuni*, pp. 678–9; Goscelin, *Translationis S. Augustini*, p. 424; *Miracula S. Oswini*, p. 38.
104 Goscelin, *Miraculis S. Augustini*, p. 408.
105 *Miracula S. Swithuni*, pp. 678–9.
106 Goscelin, *Miracula S. Yuonis*, p. lxiii.
107 Goscelin, *Miraculis S. Augustini*, pp. 403–4. For the more regular liturgical celebration of a feast day see Appendix I.
108 Eadmer, *Anselm*, pp. 168–70.
109 Robert, *Translatio S. Wenefrede*, p. 727.
110 Goscelin, *Translationis S. Augustini*, pp. 425–6.
111 Arcoid, *Miracula S. Erkenwaldi*, pp. 135–41.
112 C. S. Watkins, *History and the Supernatural in Medieval England*, Cambridge Studies in Medieval Life and Thought: Fourth Series, 66 (Cambridge: Cambridge University Press, 2007), p. 123.
113 *Miracula S. Oswini*, pp. 46–7.
114 Lantfred, *Miracula S. Swithuni*, pp. 320–3.
115 Stanley Jeyaraja Tambiah, *The Buddhist Saints of the Forest and the Cult of Amulets*, Cambridge Studies in Social and Cultural Anthropology, 49 (Cambridge: Cambridge University Press, 1984), p. 335.
116 James F. Hopgood, 'Introduction: Saints and Saints in the Making', in *The Making of Saints: Contesting Sacred Ground*, ed. by James F. Hopgood (Tuscaloosa: University of Alabama Press, 2005), pp. xi–xxi (p. xx).
117 Talal Asad, 'Towards a Genealogy of the Concept of Ritual', in *Vernacular Christianity: Essays in the Social Anthropology of Religion Presented to Godfrey Lienhardt*, ed. by Wendy James and Douglas H. Johnson (Oxford: Journal of the Anthropological Society of Oxford, 1988), pp. 73–87 (pp. 80–4).
118 Carole Rawcliffe, 'Curing Bodies and Healing Souls: Pilgrimage and the Sick in Medieval East Anglia', in *Pilgrimage: The English Experience from Becket to Bunyan*, ed.

by Colin Morris and Peter Roberts (Cambridge: Cambridge University Press, 2002), pp. 108–40 (pp. 139–40).
119 Lantfred, *Miracula S. Swithuni*, pp. 260–85.
120 *Miracula S. Oswini*, pp. 11–17; Goscelin, *Miracula S. Kenelmi*, pp. 60–7; Eadmer, *Miracula S. Oswaldi*, pp. 286–9; Goscelin, *Miracula S. Edmundi*, pp. 134–7.
121 This unattended candle miracle seems to have been a particular concern of Goscelin. See Goscelin, *Miracula S. Kenelmi*, pp. 85–6; Goscelin, *Translationis S. Augustini*, pp. 413, 422–3; Goscelin, *Visio de S. Ethelburge*, in Marvin L. Colker, 'Texts of Jocelyn of Canterbury Which Relate to the History of Barking Abbey', *Studia Monastica*, 7 (1965), 383–460 (p. 454). Byrhtferth records two unsolicited miracles of Ecgwine, the miraculous appearance of a seal and the survival of the relics after the church collapsed. See Byrhtferth, *Vita S. Ecgwini*, pp. 286–91, 296–303. Geoffrey also includes four unsolicited miracles. In two cases, workmen were saved from falling, a bell rope was miraculously strengthened and a child and mother were saved from a collapsing roof beam by Modwenna, Geoffrey, *Miracula S. Modwenne*, pp. 210–13.
122 See chapter IV.
123 Finucane, p. 77. The closest we come in our evidence are two men denied reconciliation following a punitive miracle, Herman, *Miracula S. Edmundi*, pp. 64–7; Goscelin, *Miracula S. Yuonis*, pp. lxix–lxx. Sometimes people were redirected to other saints, for example, Goscelin, *Vita S. Wlsini*, pp. 77–8; Lantfred, *Miracula S. Swithuni*, pp. 276–85, 298–9, 328–31; Goscelin, *Miraculis S. Augustini*, p. 405; Goscelin, *Miracula S. Yuonis*, pp. lxix, lxxix–lxxx; Arcoid, *Miracula S. Erkenwaldi*, pp. 128–33, 160–3.
124 Peregrine Horden, 'Saints and Doctors in the Early Byzantine Empire: The Case of Theodore of Sykeon', in *The Church and Healing*, ed. by W. J. Sheils, Studies in Church History, 19 (Oxford: Blackwell, 1982), pp. 1–13 (pp. 12–13).
125 For examples of medics confounded by illness and injury, see Arcoid, *Miracula S. Erkenwaldi*, pp. 144–7, 162–5; *Miracula S. Yuonis*, pp. lxxx–lxxxi; Goscelin, *Miraculis S. Augustini*, p. 405; Osbern, *Miracula S. Dunstani*, pp. 151–3; Eadmer, *Vita S. Anselmi*, pp. 159–65. On the interaction between saints and legal authorities, see Lantfred, *Miracula S. Swithuni*, pp. 308–11; Herman, *Miracula S. Edmundi*, pp. 14–25, 67–81; Arcoid, *Miracula S. Erkenwaldi*, pp. 116–19; *Miracula S. Ithamari*, p. 435.

4 Retribution and Reconciliation

Tom Lynch

In the previous chapter, we established a basic structure for miracle petitions. A person in crisis with knowledge of a specific saint could ask that saint for help. This could be as simple as a brief prayer but may have involved a great degree of elaboration. The process of petitioning miracles was at the heart of the cult of the saints. The saints were called upon for all sorts of favours, ranging widely in scale and nature. However, not all miracles were as obviously beneficent as cures of the ailing, the freeing of prisoners and the rescue of those in danger. Across England and throughout the period, punitive miracles were recorded in the hagiography as demonstrations of holy power and a guide to expected behaviour. An example of a vengeful saint and a rather foolish man can be found in the anonymous *Miracula S. Swithuni*:

> One time when some men of the same town were, in accordance with popular fashion, attending the funeral rites of some dead man, and were performing the incantations of the funeral games foolishly and wantonly after the manner of the Bacchantes, one of them, possessed by a sudden madness of garrulity and presumption, said, 'I am that St Swithun who is renowned everywhere for his signs and miracles; and I am prepared, if you should wish to placate me with gifts and prayers, to attend to the health both of your bodies and souls, with God acting mercifully through me on you.' Punishment from the Enemy – through whose prompting he had fallen into such audacity of wantonness – straightway follows these words of rashness and lunacy; without any delay at all he is struck down, and once struck down he is ravaged for three whole days by a wretched torment.[1]

Such 'savage little stories' as this help to show us what saints and their custodians found unacceptable.[2] They also show the contested elements of the cult of the saints, where people resisted the saint's influence and how these people enacted their critique. Punitive miracles could come reactively from a saint, but they could be petitioned like a cure. Either way the vengeance of a saint was to be feared, and those foolish enough to provoke a saint did well to reconcile themselves quickly.

The first post-mortem punitive miracles written down in our period are from Ramsey, one each in Abbo's *passio* of Edmund and Byrhtferth's life of Ecgwine.

DOI: 10.4324/9781003205692-5

In Abbo's text, Edmund froze some would-be thieves as they tried to rob his shrine at night. They were found in place the next day, caught and hung for their attempted crime. Edmund also caused a rich man called Leofstan to go insane. Leofstan impiously demanded to inspect the saint's incorrupt body, lost his mind when looking upon it and died a wretched death.[3] Byrhtferth records Ecgwine's wrath on a single occasion. A peasant entered into a property dispute with Evesham. Prior Wigred took up Evesham's part, and it was decided that the truth of the matter would be settled through taking an oath on Ecgwine's relics. Wigred prayed before the relics, sang the seven penitential psalms on bended knee and invoked Ecgwine as his helper. He set out with his companions to the preordained place for the trial, and when they arrived, they set the relics down. The peasant attempted to trick the saint by placing some soil from his home in his shoe, so that when he vowed that he stood on his own land he would be correct. Ecgwine was not fooled, and the peasant decapitated himself with his own scythe. His body was thrown from Ecgwine's land, and he did not receive a proper funeral.[4]

Byrhtferth presents us with the earliest hagiographical depiction of an oath sworn on the relics of a saint. Relic oaths were widespread from the fifth century but began to give way to oaths sworn on the Gospels around 1000, and by the thirteenth century, Gospel oaths were the dominant form.[5] These oaths were usually part of a lawsuit, an oath of office or an oath of loyalty.[6] All relic oaths involved the saint concerned in the process and left the parties open to retribution if they proved false. Alongside the extreme cases found in the hagiography are oaths which have survived from other texts. Relics were required for oaths of fealty in Edmund's laws, for legal oaths in Æthelred's laws and perhaps the English coronation service itself.[7] In a law of Æthelred priests, reeves and hundred-men were required to swear a relic oath promising that they would oversee a special period of almsgiving and fasting, undertaken to try and repel the Viking threat.[8] A relic oath was also at the centre of the events leading up to the Norman Conquest, when Harold Godwinson, who had been shipwrecked in northern France in 1064, supposedly swore a relic oath to support William of Normandy as Edward the Confessor's heir. This event was depicted on the Bayeux Tapestry as well as being noted by several chroniclers following the Norman Conquest.[9] Indeed, in some sources, William wore these same relics around his neck at the Battle of Hastings, reinforcing the broken oath as central to the downfall of Harold.[10]

There is evidence of six other relic oaths in the hagiography. Goscelin records a land dispute between Osgot the Dane and Winchcombe in the reign of King Cnut. The relics of Kenelm were brought out as adjudicator, and the parties were to prove their right to the property by swearing an oath on the relics before twenty-four noble peers. When Osgot went to swear his oath, he was miraculously knocked back. All present prostrated themselves before Kenelm and said the land was his, and Osgot went insane and died not long after. Also in this collection is the story of Godric's cheating of the people by fraud in rent collecting. Godric's crime was revealed when he was called to swear on Kenelm's relics and was subsequently struck dumb.[11] A property dispute involving Sherborne Abbey was settled by using the relics of Wulfsige as arbitrator. Needless to say, the case was found in favour of the monastery.[12] Another land dispute at Evesham was written down by Dominic. Abbot Osweard (c. 970–975) prayed for help, a Mass was said before the relics of Ecgwine and finally the relics were taken to the preordained spot. The tribunal stated that the man must lift the relics from the land he was claiming and swear an oath. The man swore by his beard he would lift relics, but he was unable to do so and plucked off his beard.[13] Bege's bracelet was believed to be effective against perjury if sworn on. When Walter de Spec bore false witness in a land dispute with the mother house of St Bee's, St Mary's, York, the saint's bracelet was brought for him to swear on. Walter maintained his falsehood and was punished by the death of his son Roger, who had been complicit in the lawsuit. Walter, in his grief, returned the land to the monastery and confirmed it with a charter, and now lacking an heir, he left his wealth to religious houses. Another man perjured himself whilst swearing on Bege's bracelet in a property dispute and was afflicted with demonic possession. He remained possessed for ten years until he gave in, went to Bege's shrine and was cured following prayers and vigils.[14]

Saints were involved in lawsuits beyond the use of their relics in oaths. Herman relates that Bishop Herfast of Elmham and Thetford sought to undermine the independence of Bury and brought a lawsuit against them, with an eye to moving his see there and reforming the monastery by introducing canons. A back and forth between the Bishop and Abbot Baldwin ensued. Herfast was seriously injured by a branch hitting him in the eyes while riding in the woods. Normal medicine did not help him, and he was persuaded to set aside his case and go to Edmund. The Bishop confessed his sins and wrongdoings before king's men and disowned those advisers who had been encouraging him in his wrongs. He then approached the high altar weeping and placed his crozier on top. He begged Edmund for absolution and sang the seven penitential psalms prostrate. Then he received medicine from Baldwin, and the monks prayed to Edmund on his behalf. Soon he was healed, and Herfast preached about the merits of the saint on Edmund's feast. However, Herfast went back on his word and resumed the case under the counsel of bad men. The case was found in favour of Bury, its independence was codified in a charter and Herfast had to pay a fine.[15]

In the mid-twelfth-century miracles of Guthlac, the Abbot of Crowland requested the return of a small parcel of land leased to a farmer named Asford. The farmer refused, and this led to a lawsuit. The Abbot and monks of Crowland prayed to God and Guthlac for help in the suit, whereas Asford bribed the judges. Asford died falling from his horse when he left to attend the lawsuit, and his accomplices, fearing divine retribution, went to the Abbot and begged forgiveness from Guthlac. An oath declaring the land to be property of Crowland was taken, and Asford's accomplices were forgiven. On the way to Asford's burial, the procession passed the meadow in question. When the bier reached the meadow, it fell to the floor, demonstrating Guthlac's part in Asford's death.[16]

Modwenna was particularly active in litigation, and Geoffrey of Burton records several instances of the saint's punitive action. Aelfwine, a royal official, had done much harm to Burton. He found against Modwenna's men in a lawsuit and was boasting of it at home. Aelfwine's head slipped in his hand, and he put out his eye with his thumb. The official spent the remainder of his life milder and more conscientious to Burton and Modwenna. Henry, lord of Swadlincote, was overly watchful of his boundaries with the monastery and a bad neighbour who also seized wandering animals. One day he brought a lawsuit against Burton. The monks prayed to Modwenna, and the knight fell ill before the case was heard. Henry realised his situation and performed penance, confessed and begged forgiveness and prayers from the monks and Modwenna. He made arrangements for his household and asked to be buried in the monastery, offering his property in return. This came to pass when he shortly died, but through his actions, he saved his soul. In the brief summaries which end Geoffrey's collection, he mentions that a man brought a lawsuit against Burton over land, but before the day of the trial, he broke his neck hunting. Finally, Geoffrey notes that various perjurers in property disputes were impoverished, killed or driven mad.[17]

Bege was also asked to help in a property lawsuit by the monks of her priory. The monks feared they would be found against prejudicially and prayed to the saint. A heavy snowfall covered Copeland, except for the land properly belonging to the priory, which settled the lawsuit in favour of Bege.[18] There is only one petition to a saint on a matter of law which could be judged to have failed. Abbot Simeon of Ely (1082–1094) was unsatisfied with the military provisions and demands asked of the Abbey by William I. He consulted the monks of Ely who told the Abbot to pray to Æthelthryth and to seek an audience with the King. Simeon obeyed his charges, but William was disinclined to ease the pressure on the monastery. The author goes on to describe the king's death, which occurred soon after the audience, although William's demise was not directly linked to the intercession of Æthelthryth.[19]

Linked to these lawsuit miracles are concerns over land ownership. Edmund, Edith, Ivo, Augustine, Guthlac, Æthelthryth and Bege all took action against those encroaching on their territory. A Norman courtier seized one of Bury's manors and was punished with an eye condition. He attempted to get a cure by offering a candle, but Edmund and God rejected it, and it broke into nine pieces. Also Robert de Curcun and his men were stupefied and driven off by extreme weather after seizing land from Edmund for grazing Robert's horses. Only two of his men escaped, one of whom went insane whilst the other succumbed to frenzy.[20] Agamund, a king's thegn, illegally occupied some of Wilton's land and was struck dead without repenting. The dead man rose from his grave and spoke, asking for help and pity and telling of the power and wrath of Edith. Agamund asked directly for Queen Emma's (1017–1035) aid and said that the land should be restored to Edith. His pleas were repeated until Emma was persuaded to visit the dead man. The Queen calmed Agamund and saw that the land was given back, and after that he rested undisturbed. Another man, Brihtric, also took land from Wilton. He died of illness and refused to return the property. In a vision, Brihtric was shown hiding from Edith, and he asked for prayers to be said for his tormented soul.[21]

A noble of Henry I tried to extort two villages from Ramsey's control. These villages were judged to be Ramsey's property, and the noble was injured falling from his horse and his retinue afflicted with various misfortunes. The noble was taken to the church of Ivo at Slepe and there kept vigil for a few days. The noble gradually got better, then went to Ramsey and begged forgiveness from Abbot Bernard (1102–1107) and Ivo himself and gave thanks for his healing.[22] In Norwich a man named Copman claimed the land on which a church of Augustine had been built. Copman was struck with insanity, and his parents led him around the churches of Norwich, finally coming to the same church of Augustine on the eve of his feast. There Copman's parents brought candles and kept vigil with their son and the other supplicants, praying to Augustine for help, and in the morning, the issue subsided.[23]

A monk of Spalding Priory had a perverse dislike for Guthlac and quibbled over the border with Crowland, the mother house of the priory. The monk was blinded but swiftly recognised the wrongs he had perpetrated and went to Guthlac for forgiveness. He took a votive candle and confessed before the relics of Guthlac, tearfully imploring the saint to aid him. The monks of Crowland took up his cause despite their dislike of the man, and he was cured by the intercession of Guthlac, letting go of all land disputes and reconciling himself to the monks of Crowland.[24] Picot, Sheriff of Cambridge, seized some of Ely's land but claimed ignorance. His fate was unknown, but his disappearance was attributed to Æthelthryth.[25] Godard, a knight of Egremont Castle, pastured his horses on land belonging to St Bee's Priory. He and his followers mocked the saint and left their horses there for some time. When they returned, they found the horses' hooves had been miraculously severed. Crowds gathered to witness the miracle, and Godard, suitably chastened, gave the land over to the priory and provided a charter as proper proof of ownership.[26]

These miracles reveal concerns of the custodians and their saints over the legal process. People may lie, bribe officials and attempt other forms of trickery. There was also always the potential for those judging a case to find against the saint's foundation. It was wise, then, to prepare before an important case in the same manner one would when confronted with any problem, by engaging in a petition. The question of who to approach in these cases had an obvious answer, as the local saint was both a part of and a patron of their religious house. A visit to the shrine was the done thing, with a degree of elaboration, just to make certain of the saint's help as religious houses could lose lawsuits. Of course, as a self-interested agent, a saint could act unilaterally in defence of their home and reputation. Either way the saints could kill, maim, send illness or bad luck against their legal opponents or miraculously ensure their side won a dispute. Bege seems to have been particularly versatile, using the weather and disabling horses as well as killing and allowing someone to become possessed. When those punished survived their fate, they could perform their own petition in turn. In these cases, the saint stood, in some sense, as both the cause of and solution to the life crises afflicting the supplicant.[27] Though, of course, the saint and their custodians would see the supplicant as the source of their own downfall. A punitive miracle could be an occasion for reconciliation, bringing or reintroducing an individual into the saint's community. But the same saint who forgave one perpetrator might kill another outright. Despite all of the consequences, people still brought lawsuits against religious houses and seized their property. The religious houses also relied on the legal system and placed importance on decisions in trials, principles of private property and the use of charters. The communities of the saints remained vulnerable to the law and physical force, and they sought to mitigate this through soliciting and recording miracles of vengeance. Land was not the only asset at risk, and the theft of a saint's movable property, or that of their community, was equally unacceptable.

When Edmund prevented the theft at his shrine by freezing the perpetrators, those thieves were apprehended and put to death. The presiding Bishop, Theodred of London (909/926–951/953), is said to have regretted these executions, fasting for three days and praying for forgiveness.[28] There appears to be a slight disconnect here between the saint and the Bishop. Edmund only froze the perpetrators in place, but Theodred sought further punishment. In such matters, most people left the saint to determine the nature and severity of the penalty. Divine justice could be merciful as well as lethal. Edmund's intervention here is the first miraculous defence against thieves found in the English record. Edmund stopped another thief later in the period, as recorded by Herman. Two ornaments were stolen from Edmund's feretory. When this was discovered, the monks prostrated themselves before Edmund, prayed for vengeance and recited the seven penitential psalms. The thief struck again, but this time he was unable to get rid of his spoils, nor could he leave Bury. He struck a third time, pretending to kiss the shrine but taking a coin with his lips. The sacristan and his servants were watching, and they beat him and recovered the stolen property. The thief confessed and was flogged, branded and banished.[29] This second depiction has the same outcome as the first in that the criminals were intercepted and punished after the saint became involved. Where they differ is that in Herman's account, the monks of Bury engaged in a petition to gain a response from Edmund.

Other saints also took action against thieves. There was a devoted man who would go on pilgrimage to visit Edmund every year, and would also visit Guthlac's shrine on the way, who lost his prize pig. He thought a local official might be responsible, although the official denied any part. After exhausting human recourse, the man prayed to God and Guthlac for help on bended knee and with hands raised to the sky. As he finished his prayer, the leader's barn burst into flames and quickly fell into ashes, and the pig was retrieved from inside untouched by the heat.[30] Another thief stole from a boy employed by the community at Durham Cathedral. In his distress, the boy invoked Cuthbert, and the man went blind. The thief's sight was partially restored after he confessed his crime, returned the stolen goods and went to Cuthbert's shrine.[31] Here we see petitions on both sides of the miracle, with the boy praying to Cuthbert and the thief confessing and visiting Cuthbert in search of a cure. In order for supplicants to enlist a saint in the defence of their property, they had to be aware of the crime or potential for a crime. More often than not, protective miracles were reactive on the part of the saint, with no prompting from supplicants. This is the case for many of the other saints, who prevented theft or punished thieves, including Wulfsige, Edith, Ivo, Modwenna, Bege, Oswine and the saints of Hexham.[32]

Of course, in order to have been recorded as a miracle, the offence had to have eventually become known. This could be through confession, evidence, divine revelation or the behaviour of the guilty party. For example, the Viking raider who stole the covering from Augustine's tomb was far from subtle in his crime. Unfortunately for the raider, the cloth covering stuck to his hands, and he was only freed through tearful prayer and promising to lead a Christian life.[33] A thief tried to rob a man donating to Ecgwine while his relics were on tour in Oxford. On dipping into the man's purse a third time, the thief got his hand stuck. He was spotted and caught. The usual practice was to sentence thieves to death, but the monks prayed to Ecgwine that the man be spared, and the saint saved him. Also in Dominic's collection, a man had gleaned money from servants of Ecgwine by deceit. He had a vision of Ecgwine, but he ignored it. The man subsequently fell off his horse hurt. This sequence of events happened a second and a third time. Finally the man returned the money to Evesham; the owners were recalled, forgave him and had the money donated to Ecgwine.[34] At the end of the twelfth-century life of Osyth, there is another story of a theft. Some sailors were forced to take shelter at a harbour near to Chich, where Osyth was buried. The sailors were stuck for some time and went to the church to pray with the locals. One of the sailors took a small piece of marble from the church. He carried it on board the ship, and shortly the weather improved and they looked to set sail. Whilst other ships could depart, the ship with the marble was stuck, and eventually they figured out the cause. The sailors took the marble back to Osyth, begged forgiveness and offered it up like a votive. This seems to have been acceptable, as when they went back down to their ship, they set sail without incident.[35]

More serious than theft of votives or robbing supplicants was the stealing of relics. Unlike the pious theft of relics in some translations, these thefts were not performed with the saint's consent and are framed very differently in the hagiography. An official of Bishop Flambard of Durham (1099–1128) stole some of Cuthbert's Gospel-book. During the next night, he developed severe pain and swelling in his leg. The man sent for a priest and confessed his crime. The priest prayed, and the man was forgiven and partially healed. He then limped with a stick to Cuthbert's shrine and returned the relic. The official was cured more fully whilst praying at the shrine.[36] Ecgwine treated relic theft just as severely. A woman named Ealdgyth regularly visited the relics of Ecgwine, and the idea came to her to steal some part of them. She recruited some boys to steal for her, with gifts and the promise of more to come. They went at night and got a piece of the saint's arm and one of his teeth. The boys gave these to Ealdgyth, and she put them reverently into a home-made shrine. She was told in three visions to take them back by Ecgwine, but she refused. Ealdgyth was struck blind, one of the boys was drowned and another was crippled, and the monastery eventually got the relics back.[37] Translations provided an opportunity to attempt to steal relics. During Edith's translation at Wilton, a monk tried to cut off some of the saint's clothing. He missed and instead cut the saint, sending out a great torrent of blood. The monk threw down his knife, prostrated himself and wept at what he had done. When he rose up having performed penance, no blood could be seen. Also during the translation, a nun tried to take a piece of Edith's headband, but the saint's head lifted up and frightened the nun into properly revering the saints.[38]

Like the legal miracles, vengeance against thieves supplemented the existing judicial framework. These miracles show us that materiality mattered to the saints, both in terms of cult objects imbued with their power and the mundane belongings of their community. The wealth circulating within the communities of the saints drew in thieves, but wealth was not necessarily bad as long as it was put to good use. Victims of these crimes could call upon the saints in the hopes that their property would be returned or that the perpetrator would be punished. Then these perpetrators, too, could petition the saint for intercession and forgiveness. This redemptive arc again highlights how the cult of the saints could augment the legal system, favouring a change in a person rather than incarceration. Death was only meted out for marauders and certain relic thieves and shrine plunderers.[39] How readily the community accepted these reformed thieves is difficult to say, but the ideal of reincorporation through successful petition is clear in these examples. The grand occasions like feast days and translations seem to have been exploited by thieves. Translations were also prime opportunities to handle and inspect the body of a saint, although this was done with trepidation lest those involved be punished for a lack of reverence. Some people were unable to suppress the desire to investigate the contents of a saint's tomb and, in their rush or ignorance, behaved inappropriately.

The bodies of incorrupt saints were particularly enticing to the curious. Our record for such improper inspection is limited to Edmund and Æthelthryth. In London, whilst the relics of Edmund were in exile, a Dane was blinded for looking under the cover of the bier out of curiosity. He then prayed contritely for forgiveness and was healed by Edmund. Abbot Leofstan (1044–1065) was punished for tugging on Edmund's head during an inspection of the relics, with permanent paralysis of his hands.[40] At the end of Goscelin's miracle collection, there are two punitive miracles concerning Edmund's relics. Toli the sacristan rashly checked the incorruption of Edmund with Prior William, his assistant Spearhavoc and Hereward the goldsmith. All four were killed, although Toli, who was otherwise good, had a chance to confess before dying and received the last rites. Toli appeared to the monk Edwin to proclaim he was not yet in Heaven and to tell him his tale and asked him and the other monks to pray to God and Edmund on his behalf. Before six months had passed, Toli appeared again to tell Edwin he had entered into Heaven. While Herman was preaching at Pentecost, he had the bloody underclothes of Edmund shown to the crowd. This was done in a disorderly and disrespectful fashion, and Herman was killed for his part in it. Toli had appeared a third time to Edwin, asking why they provoked God and Edmund, and thus, all knew the reason for Herman's death. The monks were told to perform penance and must have done so successfully as none of them are reported as having been killed.[41]

The anonymous life of Æthelthryth contains two miracles concerning the saint's body. Firstly a Viking raider tried to break into Æthelthryth's tomb in search of treasure. He made a hole in the marble tomb with his axe, swiftly had both his eyes put out and died. Later a senior priest who led the community and had recently come to Ely sought to investigate Æthelthryth's incorruption by poking around through this hole with sticks and a candle for light, trying to take a piece of the saint's clothing. After this attempt, a plague struck the priest's house, which killed his family and caught up with the priest himself in his hiding place. Following this, two of the priest's helpers were killed, and one was driven insane. Another priest, named Ælfhelm, was paralysed for his part, but he sought forgiveness and was healed by Æthelthryth.[42]

Miracles of vengeance in response to improper inspections emphasise the power of the saints and the need for caution that is represented in many of the translation accounts. There is a sense that the body of the saint in particular was secret, a sight reserved for the specially selected. This group was largely made up of clerics, monks and nuns, and the perpetrators in four of these six miracles were religious. The other two miracles punish a marauding Viking and an overly curious Dane, both foreigners who probably acted out of ignorance. The violence of the Viking was met with a violent death, whereas the Dane was blinded but able to reconcile himself to Edmund through a petition. The religious perpetrators, however, should have known better than to behave in such a manner and were treated with harsh responses from Edmund and Æthelthryth. Only Abbot Leofstan escaped with his life, and only the sacristan Toli was given a chance to save his soul through the intercession of the monks of Bury and Edmund himself. Here we have departed from the legal framework of medieval England and entered into a kind of self-defence by the saints. Incorruption was a rare miracle, and a saint's body and relics were to be respected anyway.[43] Even these taboos, which were so much a part of the cult of the saints, were not enough, and people's curiosity got the better of them. Beyond their property and their bodies, saints were also very concerned with defending the people who made up their communities.

At Hexham a rich man, Aldan, was punished by the local saints for carrying off a girl in lust and killing her brother, who was trying to protect her. Aldan's hand contorted around the offending spear, and this hand was withered for the rest of his life.[44] Bege struck a young man named John dead for raping another man's wife when she was returning home from observing the vigil of Pentecost at St Bee's.[45] The sheriff of Wilton imprisoned two local priests, and Abbess Wulfthryth called on Edith for help. Without delay the priests were released, and the sheriff bit off his own tongue and died.[46] Those who sought sanctuary at a shrine were also protected by the saints. Again Edith defended her people when some guards pursued a thief into the saint's shrine. The thief claimed sanctuary, and the guards were blinded for invading the saint's shrine to take away this newest member of her community.[47]

Edith was not alone in taking punitive action against those who defied a saint's sanctuary. Sheriff Leofstan ordered the sanctuary of Edmund's shrine at Bury to be violated by seizing a woman from there whom he wished to prosecute. The woman was taken, but the monks genuflected, prayed and sang litanies and the seven penitential psalms.[48] Leofstan was driven insane, which distracted the guards, and the woman was freed. Leofstan died still possessed by insanity.[49] One of Earl Tostig's (1055–65) men tried to capture a prisoner who had escaped to Cuthbert. In defying the saint's sanctuary, one of the men fell into a fit and died in three days.[50] During the rebellion in the north of England following the Norman Conquest, people took sanctuary at the shrine of John of Beverley as a last resort.

Soldiers led by their officer, Thurstan, attacked a refugee and followed them into Beverley Minster. Those gathered prayed for help, and Thurstan fell paralysed from his horse. The people praised John as their saviour, and the other soldiers threw down their weapons. William I was informed of this and was sorry for the inappropriate behaviour of his troops. As recompense the King confirmed and enlarged Beverley's holdings and gave the minster gifts. Thurstan himself was taken to John's tomb and prayed. The officer's illness was cured after a few days, and he made a gift every year to John.[51]

Though not representative of formal sanctuary, Ivo's shrine was where a servant fled to in running away from their angry master. The master said he forgave the servant, but he lied and later beat the servant and mocked his faith in Ivo. The master was struck down by illness and finally summoned the servant and asked forgiveness. The servant was sent to Ivo to ask the saint to forgive his master, and following prayer the master was healed. The servant was no longer mistreated by his master, and eventually he was freed.[52] Similarly, students took refuge from angry teachers at the shrines of Eormenhild, Hadrian and Erkenwald, with any attempts to remove the students from their patrons punished.[53] Sanctuary was also claimed at the shrines of Augustine, Ecgwine and Bege.[54] Additionally, Mildrith offered sanctuary to a thief who escaped his captors. The miracle was praised by Abbot Scotland (1070–1087), and he took the case before King William I, accompanied by Archbishop Lanfranc. The King confirmed the validity of claiming sanctuary at St Augustine's.[55]

With these protective miracles, the saints are found working around the fringes of the legal system again. Rapists, murderers and kidnappers were all punished for their crimes against members of a saint's community. Whilst the principle of sanctuary was enshrined in law,[56] there seems to have been some resistance when it came to claiming sanctuary at a saint's shrine. This left the saints to reinforce their role as defenders of all the faithful who sought protection. The case of St Augustine's and the King's proclamation shows how temporal authority could combine with the miraculous spiritual authority of the saints, although, as noted previously, there is no surviving evidence for such a proclamation. The saints' role as protector was particularly used by those who had nobody else to turn to: servants, students and those accused of crimes. Reaching a shrine and petitioning the saint there was the most effective – and perhaps the only – defence against those with more money and power than you.

As well as being concerned with the freedom of their people, saints were also concerned with keeping their people in the right place. Ivo, Mildrith and Dunstan all used punitive measures to encourage wavering religious to remain in their service.[57] At Burton, Modwenna took interest in the fate of the abbey's lay tenants. Two of these tenants moved from the village of Stapenhill to Drakelow without the permission of Abbot Geoffrey but under the protection of Baron Roger the Poitevin. The Abbot responded by confiscating the crops of the offenders. The disloyal tenants then incited Roger to take action against Burton, culminating in armed conflict between the baron's men and knights attached to the abbey. The two tenants were suddenly struck dead and buried in Stapenhill, but they rose from their graves to haunt Drakelow, not only horrifying the inhabitants but also spreading disease and death in the village. Seeing these horrors, Roger repented of his crimes, came with his knights to Burton to beg forgiveness and asked that the monks help to placate God and Modwenna. Roger declared he would reimburse the abbey with double restitution for any damages, and he left calmer for his visit. The baron fulfilled his vow and had the money delivered when the sum had been calculated. The local bishop gave permission to exhume the bodies of the offenders, whose shrouds were found to be covered in blood. The corpses were beheaded, the heads placed between their legs and the hearts burnt. When the two remaining peasants of Drakelow, sick in bed, saw the smoke from this fire, they were immediately healed. They got up, gathered their family and possessions, gave thanks to God and Modwenna and left for nearby Gresley. Drakelow remained abandoned as a site of ill fame.[58] The saints were willing to go to great lengths to keep their people in place. Once a person was a part of a saint's community, it appears it was difficult to leave without permission. Ivo and Mildrith encouraged people with the promise of reincorporation and forgiveness after their indiscretions, whereas Dunstan and Modwenna resorted to killing their disloyal subjects, having exhausted all other options. Whilst these miracles are not very common in the corpus, they highlight the problem of an institution losing control over its members. The saints could be relied upon to help the custodians keep people in their right place when it was necessary, just as the hagiographers could be relied upon to record such miracles.

In the middle of the conflict described by Geoffrey, before the death of the two tenants, the monks of Burton humiliated Modwenna in hopes of gaining her help. According to Geoffrey, '[The] monks entered the church, barefoot and groaning and, in tears, set down on the ground the shrine of the blessed virgin containing her most holy bones. In unison they addressed a desperate appeal to the Lord.'[59] The humiliation of the saints was a phenomenon mainly found in France that occurred between the sixth and the thirteenth centuries.[60] A humiliation could be performed both as a part of the Mass during the *clamor* or as a separate ceremony. Originally the *clamor* was a cry for help which occurred between the *Pater Noster* and the *Pax Domini*. The *clamor* could include a humiliation of the local saint, where the community descended from the choir and perhaps prostrated themselves whilst the major relics and images were placed on the floor.[61] Little has identified three English manuscripts of the *clamor*, which he describes as 'northern French imports'.[62] In addition there is a *clamor* text in the Christ Church, Canterbury pontifical of around 1100, Trinity College, Dublin, MS 98.[63] The English liturgical texts do not contain references to the humiliation of relics. The *clamor* in the Mass was a temporary measure compared to the more elaborate separate ceremony that is recorded in a liturgical text for St Martin's at Tours. At Tours the canons began the humiliation after the hour of prime had been rung. They gathered in the church and sung the seven penitential psalms and a litany whilst seniors placed the reliquaries and a silver crucifix on the ground. The tomb of Martin and a large wooden crucifix were covered in thorns, and all but one of the church doors were blocked with thorns.

The office for the day was conducted in a subdued manner until the *clamor* in the Mass, after which the service was finished in a loud voice.[64]

The humiliation of the saints was not unknown in the British Isles, but it was not widespread. The ceremony was used by Archbishop John Cumin of Dublin (1150–1212) against Norman confiscations of Church land in 1197. This humiliation lasted some days and included the miraculous weeping and bleeding of a crucifix. In Wales, the *Book of Llandaff*, containing material from the sixth to the twelfth century, includes nine uses of the humiliation of relics.[65] There is a description of a *clamor* directed at Cuthbert in Reginald of Coldingham's *Miracula S. Cuthberti*, but it does not contain a full humiliation.[66] The only other English example comes from the Anglo-Norman version of the life of Osyth, unique to the thirteenth-century manuscript, British Library, Additional 70513.[67] That Abbot Geoffrey and the monks of Burton thought it necessary to humiliate the relics of Modwenna indicates the seriousness of the threat from Roger. The situation quickly escalated from a relatively trivial defection of two tenants to a violent impasse with a powerful secular force. The humiliation of the relics and the threat from Roger required an extreme response from the saint. Here Modwenna not only killed the perpetrators, but through their haunting, the saint also rendered Drakelow uninhabitable. Loyalty to a saint was of the utmost import, and once a relationship was entered into, it was best to remain on good terms with a saint. Such proprietary behaviour by a saint over the land, goods and people associated with them is revealing. Acting as 'undying landlords', the saints were important both as guarantors of the rights and properties of a foundation and as owners and defenders of these same foundations.[68] Saints were not passive, and they 'talked (back), owned property, and on occasion fought to protect it'.[69] This talking and fighting back was not limited to offences against the property and people under a saint's protection, however. Some people took it upon themselves to mock the saints and deride their potency as intercessors. Unsurprisingly such behaviour was met with punishment.

Sigal, in his study of miracles in eleventh- and twelfth-century France, divides punitive miracles into those performed in defence of people and things under a saint's protection and those performed in defence of the saint.[70] The cult of the saints in England was fundamental to society and embroiled in structures of spiritual and material power, but it was not immune to critique and mockery. Ivo's cult was questioned by two individuals. First Alwold, a man from Stanton, put a white hen on the altar at Slepe not as a votive but to stir gossip. Alwold bent his leg to pretend to be crippled and asked Ivo for help, looking to make fun of the saint. This faked ailment was made real by Ivo. Alwold begged the saint to restore him but to no avail. Goscelin notes that Alwold was lucky not to have been struck dead for his mockery. On another occasion, a foreign monk was afflicted by weakness for claiming that the taking of Ivo's water was a superstition. The monk was cured after many prayers before Ivo's body at Ramsey.[71]

In London, a drunk silversmith named Eustace entered the workshop in which the wooden frame of a new shrine for Erkenwald was being gilded and made offensive remarks to the workers. Eustace then hid himself in the shrine and cried,

'I am the most holy Erkenwald: bring me gifts; ask for my help; make me a sepulchre of silver!' Following this, Eustace was seized by a severe pain and was borne by his weeping comrades to his bed, where he died several days later. Arcoid explains that the saint was right to react harshly to such provocation.[72] As mentioned previously, in Winchester, a drunk man attending a wake declared himself to be St Swithun and stated that he would cure any ailment in exchange for gifts and prayers. He was struck down on the spot until his family took pity on him and delivered him to Swithun's shrine, where they petitioned the saint. The man was forgiven his blasphemy and healed.[73]

These miracles of vengeance centre on concerns over the petitionary process and the status of the saints. Alwold, Eustace and the drunk at the wake did not merely mock the saints; they impersonated them and portrayed the saints as greedy. Material offerings to the saints were thought of by these men as the primary means of gaining a miracle. Eustace was killed outright for jumping in Erkenwald's new shrine, which he may have understood as another bribe for the saint. In presenting his white hen as a mock offering, Alwold no doubt caused a scene as he had hoped, and this miracle in some ways echoes the declaration by the foreign monk that the taking of Ivo's water was superstition. This implies that some people considered the miracle petitions in the same domain as magic and folk medicine. Alwold's behaviour also brings into question the veracity of supplicants' ailments and injuries, although according to Goscelin, such behaviour would be detected and punished. The drunk man seems to have the measure of Swithun, in that the saint could deal with any problem and that generally this required petitionary action on behalf of the supplicant. It appears that it was his imitation and his bald presentation of the reciprocal character of the cult of the saints which got him into trouble.

The saints were also keen to defend against perceived lapses in proper veneration. Ivo admonished two monks of Ramsey in visions, one for neglecting to say psalms every day and one for not kneeling or bowing to the saint when he passed his tomb.[74] Edith appeared in a vision to comfort and admonish sisters who complained that the saint had not healed them of an epidemic which had hit the nunnery at Wilton.[75] The decline of Seaxburh's community on Sheppey was attributed to a lack of thanksgiving and veneration of the saint and God by the people of the island.[76] Mildrith visited her devotee Ælfwold in a series of visions in order to get her former resting place, the church of Peter and Paul at Thanet, renovated by St Augustine's. Eventually Ælfwold convinced his local priest to go to St Augustine's, where they glorified Mildrith for her miraculous visitations and gave him sixty shillings for repairs.[77] A novice at Ely named Edwin left compline early one night and was possessed by a demon. Although the possession was not directly caused by Æthelthryth, the saint did intercede to help the young man, and the author of the *Liber Eliensis* was keen to point out the ways the Devil takes advantage of those who slip in their duties.[78]

Another way people slighted the saints was to question their efficacy as intercessors. Edith also appeared to Thola, a nun of Wilton, to tell her that Ealdgyth, another nun of Wilton who was at Salisbury, had refuted Edith's power. Ealdgyth claimed that Edith had not protected the monastery's possessions sufficiently.

Thola confronted Ealdgyth on her return, who repented for her sin and begged forgiveness from the community, Thola and Edith.[79] Goscelin records that a woman named Eudochia mocked the icon of Augustine kept in the church, dedicated to Augustine and Nicholas at Constantinople. The icon was dirty, and Eudochia commented on this and asked who this saint was and why he could not even protect his own image. She was informed by her friend that Augustine was the Apostle of the English sent by Gregory the Great and known both in England and Europe and that it was not proper to mock such a saint. That night Eudochia had a vision of Augustine, who sentenced her to an eye complaint that would not respond to medicine. It was so when Eudochia awoke, and her mocking turned to prayers to Augustine. She suffered for some time, and others began to pray on her behalf whilst Eudochia herself made vows and offered gifts. She had a second vision and was told that Augustine had agreed to intercede on account of Eudochia's devout friend and that the icon should be restored. In exchange, not only would Augustine cure Eudochia, but he would also see that her friend's husband would return safely from pilgrimage. The icon was restored, and both miracles came to pass, the friends thanked Augustine and his name became widely known throughout Greece.[80] In the same collection, a soldier named Odo asked why Augustine had not better protected his old see of Canterbury from degradation. For such insolence, Odo was struck down with a severe illness. Bedbound for seven weeks, he kept vigil, flagellated himself and prayed. Finally Odo rose up healed, went on hands and knees to Augustine's tomb, where he gave humble thanks, and vowed to repeat this devotion every year. The monks of St Augustine's heard of this and praised the saint.[81]

People continued to doubt the saints' power and to be punished for it until the end of our period. Bege killed a young Galwegian named Belial for claiming he could not be punished by the saint for the crimes he committed on her land.[82] Some men of Hexham on pilgrimage encountered a cleric who questioned Acca's credentials and mocked the men. This cleric fell into a fit, and the cleric's sister was greatly upset. One of the young men took pity on her and asked if they believed Acca could help them in this crisis. The cleric woke up from his fit and affirmed his new belief, asking to be prayed for. The young man prayed, and when he finished, the cleric was healed. After this no one was more fervent a believer in Acca than the cleric, who invoked the saint's help and sought consolation in the face of many travails.[83] Of course abuse could be more general, and Cuthbert struck Onlafbald dead for abusing the saint in his church and nearly killed a householder who mocked the saint and his followers who were journeying south. The householder was restored to health following the prayers of the monks, and there was much rejoicing.[84] Similarly Æthelthryth and her two sisters appeared to Gervase, who was hostile to the saint and the abbey at Ely. Gervase died screaming, and the abbot spread word of the miracle, causing all who heard it to fear and respect the saints of Ely.[85]

When people neglected veneration or doubted the efficacy of the saints, they were bringing the process of making miracles into question. If the saints could not fulfil their purpose, petitions were useless, and the saints would not fulfil their purpose if they were not accorded the appropriate veneration. These miracles reflect uncertainty, laziness, ignorance and forgetfulness, all of which could be expected within such a pervasive institution as the cult of the saints. A stranger or a foreigner would obviously be less familiar with a saint than a local, but they were still expected to behave with decorum and respect the universal potency of the saints. When such mockery could be corrected, the saints chose to do so through a punitive miracle and ultimate reversal following a petition, thus bringing a new person into a saint's community. However, where the person was judged to have acted too rudely or to be beyond help, saints were willing and able to exact more permanent punishment.

Feast days were also a focus for punitive miracles. The major concern was the proper observance of the feasts of the saints.[86] For Mildrith this meant visiting people who slept when they should be praising her with terrifying dreams which brought them to their senses.[87] For Seaxburh it meant a decent banquet. When the steward Wulfweard refused to distribute alcohol for the banquet of Seaxburh, the following night, his cellar was wrecked and all the contents spilt on the ground. According to the author, this was recompense for not showing the saints due honour and prevented Wulfweard from benefiting from his personal cellar.[88] For other English saints, this meant stopping people working on their feasts.

Feast day punishments were generally related to the work being carried out. Wulfsige and Kenelm both had the tools of offenders adhere to their user's hands until they came to pray at the saints' shrines.[89] Erkenwald caused Vitalis the tanner to be killed by a slip of his scraper after the tanner had been caught working on the saint's feast and had rebuked those who tried to warn him.[90] Kenelm and Dunstan caused ox teams yoked to work on their respective feasts to run wild.[91] A woman was scalded by boiling liquid which she spilt on herself because she refused to honour Augustine's feast day. Badly burnt, she acknowledged her laxity and went to beg forgiveness from Augustine, taking a candle with her. The woman was healed, but she bore the brand of Augustine for the rest of her life.[92] A man was digging up brambles and thorns on Swithun's feast day. He pricked his hand and fell seriously ill, with physicians only making his condition worse. The man was taken to Swithun's statue at Sherborne, where he prayed and was healed.[93] Oswine punished Roger the subdeacon, who collected crops on the saint's feast day. The harvest was placed in a barn, which burst into flames. People who saw this spread word of the miracle and glorified God.[94] There may have been some dispensation for the type of work engaged in, as Erkenwald killed Vitalis the tanner and another labourer but only injured and admonished Teodwin the painter, who was working on the saint's shrine and blocked access to visitors.[95] It was also wrong to force others to work on a saint's day, and a monk of Ely was punished by Ivo with breathing problems for such an offence. The monk admitted to his friends and family what he had done and that he deserved punishment. His loved ones advised him to appease Ivo with prayers and the promise of gifts. The monk was cured and went to Ivo's shrine to give thanks in person.[96]

Feast days were held up as the most important time for a saint, an occasion of devotion and miracles.[97] Evidently not all of these miracles were positive. People were willing to risk the ire of a local saint in order to complete what they saw as necessary work. Dedication to a saint regularly entailed a degree of financial loss, whether in terms of time taken in a visit or the costs of travel and offerings. These miracles show that not all people felt they could afford to take a break from their labours, even if it was in honour of a saint. The fact that the punishments were linked to the perpetrators' tools show a sense of irony seemingly shared by the saints and their hagiographers. The feast of a local saint was a grand occasion which would have been a highlight of the year and well known to inhabitants. Even in this environment, people felt they could ignore the cult of the saints and get on with their lives.

This is an overview of the type of offences which provoked a saint's ire. They are generally concerns related to the saint directly or to their community. Most longer miracle collections contain some punitive material, and many saints performed miracles which eventually led to the death of the perpetrators. These deadly saints included Edmund, Ecgwine, Edith, Kenelm, Augustine, Æthelthryth, Erkenwald, Dunstan, Guthlac, Modwenna, Bege, Cuthbert and Oswine. Those killed by the saints had little recourse beyond confession, the last rites and post-mortem prayers for their soul. In practice most people struck dead by the saints did not even have an opportunity for these ameliorating practices. Often these deadly miracles were prefigured by petitions. Before Ecgwine's relics were used in a property dispute, Prior Wigred prayed before the relics, sang the seven penitential psalms on bended knee and invoked the saint. Likewise the monks of Bury genuflected, prayed and sang litanies and the seven penitential psalms to convince Edmund to stop the disruption of a claim of sanctuary at his shrine. There was a long petitionary process leading up to the death and final internment of the two undead ex-tenants of Burton. Much-simpler petitions could have a similarly devastating effect, as when an old woman invoked Oswine to intercede against the Scottish sailors who raided Tynemouth. The entire fleet was dashed against Coquet Island the next day, and their loot was strewn along the Northumbrian coast.[98]

Whilst a saint could spontaneously respond to a slight, sometimes they had to be 'awakened' with a petition.[99] The sanctions which followed such an awakening were not limited to death, however. A man who had a book stolen prayed for help from Wulfstan of Worcester. After some time and much prayer, the thief was struck down with demonic possession. William of Malmesbury reports that on the day of the saint's vengeance, the supplicant had prayed longer and more determinedly than before.[100] The clergy of Hexham prayed to Eata to stop the removal of the saint's body to York. This prompted the saint to visit Archbishop Thomas (1070–1100) in a dream, as the authority behind the proposed translation. Eata hit the Archbishop twice with his staff, and Thomas was so frightened, he apologised, confessed his guilt and asked the canons of Hexham to pray for him. Thomas suffered from the saint's blow for three days and was healed on the fourth by Eata.[101] Edmund also had to be awakened with prostrate prayer and the seven penitential psalms to encourage him to intercede against a thief.[102] The process of awakening a saint was the same as any other petition, the only difference being that the agents of the crises were human and punitive action was judged to be the best remedy.

Having experienced a problem, the supplicant would petition their saint, often at their shrine and with a degree of elaboration. A person who asked their saint for help appropriately could be confident in the success of their petition.

After a miracle of vengeance, the perpetrator was sometimes given an opportunity to reconcile themselves to the saints. Like awakening a saint, these petitions follow the same structure as those used by supplicants seeking beneficent miracles. For example, when Mazelina hit her child in St Augustine's, the monks sang the penitential psalms on her behalf, and her punishment was reversed.[103] Here we see both the role of the community and the penitential tone of the reconciliatory petition. This penitential tone is also found in the case of Osgod, a former noble of Edward the Confessor, who came to Edmund's shrine drunk and was afflicted with a fit. Because of his noble status, Edward the Confessor asked that Osgod be sprinkled with holy water and have prayers, psalms and litanies performed on his behalf. Aelwine the sacristan offered his help, explaining that, in similar cases, possessed people had been cured through being carried to Edmund's tomb and the monks of Bury praying for them there. Osgod was taken to the tomb and the monks, clothed in albs and kneeling, and sung the seven penitential psalms and a litany. Osgod came to his senses, acknowledged his sin and a hymn and praises were offered up to God and his saint. Osgod was grateful but never fully regained the strength of his hands.[104] As noted previously, Archbishop Thomas of York apologised and confessed the sin of permitting the translation of Eata against the wishes of the saint and the people of Hexham. The Archbishop finally asked for the canons of Hexham to pray for him and was cured.[105] Likewise, Bishop Herfast confessed his crimes before going to Edmund to pray for forgiveness for his lawsuit against Bury.[106] A sacristan of St Augustine's and the monk of Spalding also confessed their wrongs against Augustine and Guthlac respectively.[107]

Such behaviour was not limited to the clergy, with laity from an aristocratic landowner to a thief confessing their indiscretions to the saints.[108] As with the awakening of a saint, we see a tone of humility in these petitions of reconciliation and reincorporation. Some of the forms of humility which were found in the *clamor*, such as prostration and the singing of the penitential psalms,[109] are also found in the petitions surrounding the punitive miracles. Saints could be persuaded to restore those they had punished through correct behaviour and genuine contrition. But the reverse was true: the saints could take away a cure if a supplicant did not fulfil their part of the interaction.

Swithun is shown reversing a miracle when the wealthy woman who vowed to visit the saint with gifts was temporarily healed. Ultimately she neglected her vow and relapsed.[110] Similarly Oswine punished a boy called Henry for shooting one of Tynemouth's doves and chasing it to the saint's shrine, where it had taken refuge. Henry was blinded in one eye and then afflicted with a fever when he had returned to St Albans. The boy was told to repent by the woman who was nursing him in his illness, and Henry agreed to this and promised to return to Tynemouth. Immediately Henry felt better, but he forgot to go to Tynemouth, was struck again with illness and eventually died.[111] In the later anonymous miracle collection, Swithun reverses another cure. A Norman man had been healed of a crippling disfigurement by Swithun at Winchester. He went on his way home, and on the road, he gazed at Swithun's church, perhaps forgetting to ask leave of the saint to depart. The Norman fell, afflicted again with his disfigurement. He was taken back to the church and placed before Swithun's tomb, where he and his companions prayed and he was healed with great rejoicing.[112] This calls to mind the man disapproved of by Lantfred for leaving Swithun without paying due thanks.[113] A foreigner who had been healed by Augustine was blinded by the saint for abusing a devout woman who was visiting St Augustine's. The man was then contrite and spent eight days and nights in prayer, fasting and tearful vigil, after which he was cured again and gave thanks to God, apologised to those he had wronged and refrained from such behaviour in the future.[114] As noted previously, there is also the reversal – and ultimately death – of Ceolwulf found in the miracles of Dunstan, in both Eadmer's and Osbern's versions.[115]

The reversal miracles – and the punitive miracles more generally – emphasise the contingent nature of the cult of the saints. A saint was free to change their mind based on the behaviour of their supplicants, to spare a former enemy or strike down a misbehaving petitioner. As saints were expected to heal the righteous, so, too, were supplicants expected to keep to their vows, behave appropriately and honour the saint. The punitive miracles show us both the limits of a saint's patience and the consequences of engaging a saint inappropriately. In this sense, the stories of the punitive miracles are more overtly pedagogical than those of the beneficent miracles.[116] Indeed, the punitive miracles were often a process of learning from one's mistakes and coming out through the struggles closer and more devoted to the saint and conscious of the correct way to approach them. The monk of Ely who stopped villagers visiting Ivo admitted to his loved ones that he had done wrong, and the cleric who questioned Acca's powers became devoted to the saint.[117] Death was not necessarily a barrier to the learning of these lessons. Toli the sacristan confessed and received the last rites before his death for irreverently handling the body of Edmund. He later appeared to ask for prayers to get himself into Heaven and, within six months, confirmed he had been admitted to paradise.[118] Agamund was killed suddenly by Edith for occupying some of Wilton's land. He had not repented before his death and did not rest easily until the land had been given back to Wilton. It is probable that he feared damnation and did not want to be pursued by Edith in the afterlife: the fate of one Brihtric for a similar offence. Despite his condition, Brihtric, too, asked for prayers for his soul.[119] However, just because a person had learnt from their mistake, that did not mean the saint had to forgive them. The Norman, who had been punished with an eye condition for seizing land from Bury, brought a candle to Edmund and saw it miraculously broken into nine pieces.[120] Alwold, who was stricken with the ailment he faked in mocking Ivo, was also denied healing by the saint.[121] These are the only two examples of a completely failed petition I have found in the evidence.[122] The saints were open to the humble and contrite, and not everyone was deemed worthy of forgiveness.

The punitive material also shows the limits to the cult of the saints. Ubiquitous as saints and their shrines were in medieval England, people still challenged the system. Whether they were motivated by greed, need, anger, laziness or ignorance, people brought lawsuits, seized land, stole, murdered, raped and pillaged all in the face of the saints. Other behaviour was directed at the saints themselves, ignoring their feast days, scrimping on veneration, mocking the saints and mishandling their relics. The cult of the saints was very important to a great number of people, but not to all people all of the time, and it is quite likely that many found their local cult 'a matter for indifference'.[123] Though, as our evidence is almost entirely hagiographical, even these unbelievers are presented as acting against and around the cult of the saints. This behaviour is portrayed as a reaction to the cult of the saints, a set of actions which are presented as invalid by the hagiographers but which we should acknowledge as expressions of concern. We are presented with a world in which a saint could become involved in every aspect of life. In particular the punitive miracles show how a saint's community could supplement and even replace the legal system. This could range from forcing a trial to find in the saint's favour to killing a person outright for a 'crime' against the saint. Saints could act as a corrective, then, for their communities in dealing with what are portrayed as unfair legal structures.[124] But for the subjects of miracles of vengeance, dealings with the saints may well have been perceived as unfair.

Perpetrators normally had some knowledge of the saint, and sometimes they were explicitly warned that their behaviour would lead to trouble.[125] Despite this people still resented the saints and their communities and acted out this resentment. Saints – and by extension their custodians – were given wealth and attention in a manner which could seem close to bribery. Whilst some of the actions of the perpetrators in these stories were obviously unacceptable, the mockery of the saints and questioning of their potency can be seen as an expression of a folk critique of the business of making miracles in medieval England. This is best represented by the speech given by the unnamed man who was killed by Erkenwald for working on his feast day, even after being warned by a canon of St Paul's. The man critiqued the canons, stating they had too much time on their hands if they could come and interrogate him. The man pointed out that the canons were idle and lived off the toil of others. He stated that if they would feed and clothe him, he would spend all his time praising God and Erkenwald. The man then compared the festivities of the workers – marked with food, drink and dancing – with the dour celebrations of the canons. In the end, the man asked to be left to earn his living in peace.[126] Vitalis the pelterer also responded when people asked him not to work on Erkenwald's feast, though the content of his retorts are not recorded.[127] Similarly, the lady who presided over the village of Pailton resented the fact that Kenelm's feast day was celebrated with a break from work. 'Just because of Kenelm', she said, 'I don't know why we should lose a day's profit.' Immediately the lady's eyes fell from her head, and she begged to be forgiven by the saint and stated that his feast should be observed.[128]

This questioning was not limited to the perpetrators. Arcoid describes two debates by onlookers following these punitive miracles. After the killing of the unnamed man, people gathered to find out what had happened. When everything had been explained, some people thought Erkenwald had been right to kill the man. Others questioned the harshness of the miracle and pointed out the weakness and ignorance of humanity.[129] Following Vitalis's death, some felt he got what he deserved whilst others felt only sympathy.[130] Nor was questioning limited to the laity. When the foreign monk questioned the potency of Ivo's water, he compared it to pagan practices. He was also concerned that unproven relics should have been revered like those of an authentic saint. He was struck down for this but restored by Ivo as his crime was rooted in ignorance.[131] During our period, there was a broader criticism of the cult of the saints. Guibert of Nogent was also worried about the authenticity of certain relics and emphasised the need for a clear written record for cults. This can be seen as related to the Anglo-Norman questions over certain earlier English saints.[132] These criticisms seem to have been selective and far from an attempt to topple the cult of the saints or indeed to undermine English saints after the Conquest, although certain relics were tested by fire in an attempt to guarantee their legitimacy.[133] Even some beneficent miracles were investigated thoroughly.[134] Saints and their communities expected respect and could defend themselves with miraculous and secular power. But this did not mean all of England was made up of pious supplicants and loyal custodians or that every aspect of the cult was accepted without question.

What we also glean from the punitive miracles is how well they fit into the petitionary structure. Whether a supplicant was praying for a cure for fever, for an enemy of the community to be reprimanded or for forgiveness after misbehaviour, they followed the same basic pattern. Punitive miracles could be performed without a petition, but in these instances, the offence itself filled the gap. A person knew of the saint in some capacity and behaved in a manner the saint found provocative. The saint then responded with a miracle which addressed the crisis generated by the perpetrator's behaviour. If the perpetrator survived the encounter, a new petition could begin as they became a supplicant. All of this could be carried out at the saint's shrine, in the locality or at a greater distance. The actions of people began the miracle-making process, whether they were asking for aid, insulting a saint or seeking reconciliation. Following this pattern, it is easy to see how a former enemy of a saint could become embroiled in the community. In all cases, the saint reacted to human actions in a predictable, though not inevitable, manner. There is a final key element which we should consider before concluding: the often drawn-out and complex methods of giving thanks to a saint for a miracle.

Notes

1 'Eiusdem ciuitatis hominibus tempore quodam defuncti cuiusdam exequiis pro more uulgari assistentibus ludorumque funebrium nenias stulte et lasciue ritu bachantium celebrantibus, unus ex illis subito garrullitatis et presumptionis furore correptus, 'ego sum', inquit, 'sanctus ille Swithunus qui pro uirtutibus et miraculis suis ubique diffamatur – paratus si cum muneribus et orationibus mihi uolueritis supplicare, tam corporum quam animarum uestrarum salutem Deo per me uobis propitio ministrare.' Quam uocem temeritatis et insanie ilico uindicta subsequitur ab inimico, cuius instinctu in tantam deciderat proteruie audaciam; sine omni dilatione peruaditur, peruasus tribus diebus continuis miserabili tortione colliditur.' *Miracula S. Swithuni*, pp. 676–7.

2. Eamon Duffy, 'St. Erkenwald: London's Cathedral Saint and His Legend', in *The Medieval Cathedral: Papers in Honour of Pamela Tudor-Craig*, ed. by Janet Backhouse (Donington: Tyas, 2003), pp. 150–67 (pp. 151–2).
3. Abbo, *Passio S. Eadmundi*, pp. 83–6.
4. Byrhtferth, *Vita S. Ecgwini*, pp. 290–7.
5. Snoek, p. 132.
6. Bartlett, *Why Can the Dead*, p. 311.
7. David Rollason, 'Relic-Cults as an Instrument of Royal Policy c. 900-c. 1050', *Anglo-Saxon England*, 15 (1986), 91–103 (p. 97).
8. Simon Keynes, 'An Abbot, an Archbishop, and the Viking Raids of 1006–7 and 1009–12', *Anglo-Saxon England*, 36 (2007), 151–220 (pp. 180–1).
9. Frank Stenton, ed., *The Bayeux Tapestry: A Comprehensive Study* (London: Phaidon, 1957), p. 167, plate 20.
10. R. H. C. Davis and Marjorie Chibnall, eds and trans, *The Gesta Guillelmi of William of Poitiers* (Oxford: Clarendon, 1998), pp. 124–5; Marjorie Chibnall, ed. and trans., *The Ecclesiastical History of Orderic Vitalis*, 6 vols (Oxford: Clarendon, 1969–1980), II, pp. 172–3.
11. Goscelin, *Miracula S. Kenelmi*, pp. 72–5.
12. Goscelin, *Vita S. Wlsini*, pp. 83–4.
13. Dominic, *Miracula S. Ecgwini*, pp. 80–3.
14. *Miracula S. Bege*, pp. 513–15.
15. Goscelin, *Miracula S. Edmundi*, pp. 66–81. On preaching and feast days, see chapter I.
16. *Miracula S. Guthlaci*, pp. 57–8.
17. Geoffrey, *Miracula S. Modwenne*, pp. 190–3, 198–211.
18. *Miracula S. Bege*, pp. 510–12.
19. *Liber Eliensis*, pp. 216–17. See also the encounter between the monks of Bury, Edmund and King Swein (1013–1014). Although the embassy to Swein failed, the King was explicitly killed by the saint, who also helped the emissary Aelwine escape. See Herman, *Miracula S. Edmundi*, pp. 14–27.
20. Herman, *Miracula S. Edmundi*, pp. 64–7, 100–3.
21. Goscelin, *Vita S. Edithe*, pp. 281–4.
22. *Miracula S. Yuonis*, pp. lxxvii–lxxviii.
23. Goscelin, *Translationis S. Augustini*, p. 429.
24. *Miracula S. Guthlaci*, p. 59.
25. *Liber Eliensis*, pp. 210–11.
26. *Miracula S. Bege*, pp. 512–13.
27. Generally causation of illness is not covered in the beneficent miracles, except in cases of possession or injuries with obvious natural causes. See Finucane, p. 72.
28. Abbo, *Passio S. Eadmundi*, pp. 83–5.
29. Herman, *Miracula S. Edmundi*, pp. 346–9.
30. *Miracula S. Guthlaci*, pp. 59–60.
31. Bertram Colgrave, 'The Post-Bedan Miracles and Translations of St Cuthbert', in *The Early Cultures of North-West Europe*, ed. by Cyril Fox and Bruce Dickins (Cambridge: Cambridge University Press, 1950), pp. 305–32 (p. 315).
32. Goscelin, *Vita S. Wlsini*, p. 83; Goscelin, *Vita S. Edithe*, pp. 100–1, 268–9; Goscelin, *Miracula S. Yuonis*, pp. lxxii–lxxiii; Geoffrey, *Miracula S. Modwenne*, pp. 182–93; *Miracula S. Bege*, pp. 515–16; *Miracula S. Oswini*, pp. 20–2; Aelred, *De sanctis Hagustaldensis*, pp. 183–4.
33. Goscelin, *Miraculis S. Augustini*, p. 397.
34. Dominic, *Miracula S. Ecgwini*, pp. 104–21.
35. Bethell, 'Osyth', pp. 116–17.
36. Colgrave, 'Post-Bedan', p. 318.

37 Dominic, *Miracula S. Ecgwini*, pp. 86–9.
38 Goscelin, *Vita S. Edithe*, pp. 270–1. Edith also punished three craftsmen with blindness for skimping on the gold that was meant to go into a new shrine for the saint, which had been commissioned by Cnut. Goscelin, *Vita S. Edithe*, pp. 280–1.
39 Goscelin, *Miracula S. Yuonis*, pp. lxxii–lxxiii; Dominic, *Miracula S. Ecgwini*, pp. 86–9; Geoffrey, *Miracula S. Modwenne*, pp. 182–93.
40 Herman, *Miracula S. Edmundi*, pp. 36–7, 50–5.
41 Goscelin, *Miracula S. Edmundi*, pp. 278–99.
42 *Miracula S. Ætheldrethe*, pp. 108–11, 122–9.
43 Bede considered the English saints Cuthbert and Æthelthryth to be incorrupt. When William of Malmesbury was writing in the twelfth century, he still recorded Cuthbert and Æthelthryth as incorrupt and had only added to the list Wihtburh, Edmund of East Anglia and Ælfheah. See Bede, *HE*, IV.19, pp. 392–7; IV.30, pp. 442–5; William of Malmesbury, *Gesta Regum Anglorum*, I, pp. 386–7 (II.207).
44 Aelred, *De sanctis Hagustaldensis*, pp. 181–2.
45 *Miracula S. Bege*, pp. 517–18.
46 Goscelin, *Vita S. Edithe*, pp. 272.
47 Goscelin, *Vita S. Edithe*, pp. 272–3.
48 On litanies see Appendix I.
49 Herman, *Miracula S. Edmundi*, pp. 142–5.
50 Colgrave, 'Post-Bedan', p. 312.
51 William Ketell, *Miracula S. Johannis*, pp. 264–9.
52 Goscelin, *Miracula S. Yuonis*, pp. lxxii.
53 Goscelin, *In Natale Sancte Eormenhilde*, in Love, *Ely*, pp. 20–1; Goscelin, *Virtutibus S. Adriani*, Cotton, Vespasian B.xx, fols 236ᵛ-38ʳ, Harley 105, fols 208ʳ-09ᵛ; Arcoid, *Miracula S. Erkenwaldi*, pp. 102–9.
54 Goscelin, *Translationis S. Augustini*, p. 425; Dominic, *Miracula S. Ecgwini*, pp. 94–7; *Miracula S. Bege*, pp. 516–17.
55 Rollason points out that no such proclamation survives from the reign of William I. Goscelin, *Miracula S. Mildrethe*, pp. 188–90.
56 See chapter II.
57 Goscelin, *Miracula S. Yuonis*, pp. lxviii–lxix, lxxi–lxxii; Goscelin, *Miracula S. Mildrethe*, pp. 207–10; Osbern, *Miracula S. Dunstani*, pp. 155–6; Eadmer, *Miracula S. Dunstani*, pp. 155–6.
58 Geoffrey, *Miracula S. Modwenne*, pp. 192–9.
59 'monachi, nudis pedibus et cum magnis gemitibus, intoierunt ecclesiam et feretrum beate virginis, ubi iacebant sacratissima ossa eius, continuo in magnis fletibus deposuerunt ad terram. Clamauerunt omnes pariter tota intentione ad Dominum', Geoffrey, *Miracula S. Modwenne*, pp. 192–5.
60 Snoek, p. 159.
61 Geary, *Living With the Dead*, p. 98.
62 The three examples are from Rochester, St Germans and Winchester. See Lester K. Little, *Benedictine Maledictions: Liturgical Cursing in Romanesque France* (Ithaca, NY: Cornell University Press, 1993), pp. 48–50.
63 Hartzell, pp. 152–3.
64 Geary, *Living With the Dead*, pp. 98–100.
65 Little, pp. 123–6.
66 Raine, *Reginaldi*, pp. 119–22.
67 D. W. Russel, Jocelyn Wogan-Browne and Jane Zatta, eds and trans, 'La Vie Seinte Osith, Virge et Martire (MS BL Addit. 70513, ff. 134va-146vb)', *Papers on Language & Literature*, 41 (2005), 339–444 (pp. 428–31).
68 Rollason, *Saints and Relics*, pp. 197–208.
69 Little, p. 200.

70 Sigal, *L'homme et le Miracle*, pp. 276–82.
71 Goscelin, *Miracula S. Yuonis*, pp. lxix–lxx, lxxi–lxxii.
72 Arcoid, *Miracula S. Erkenwaldi*, pp. 142–5.
73 *Miracula S. Swithuni*, pp. 676–77.
74 Goscelin, *Miracula S. Yuonis*, pp. lxiv–lxvi.
75 Goscelin, *Vita S. Edithe*, pp. 297–8.
76 *Vita Sexburge*, pp. 184–5.
77 Goscelin, *Miracula S. Mildrethe*, pp. 181–5.
78 *Liber Eliensis*, pp. 208–9.
79 Goscelin, *Vita S. Edithe*, pp. 298–9.
80 Goscelin, *Miraculis S. Augustini*, pp. 410–11.
81 Goscelin, *Translationis S. Augustini*, pp. 426–7.
82 *Miracula S. Bege*, pp. 509–10.
83 Aelred, *De sanctis Hagustaldensis*, pp. 188–9.
84 Colgrave, 'Post-Bedan', pp. 311, 314.
85 *Liber Eliensis*, pp. 212–13.
86 To this end, proclamations seem to have gone out reminding people of the feast and to observe it properly. See Arcoid, *Miracula S. Erkenwaldi*, pp. 108–9; Goscelin, *Miracula S. Kenelmi*, pp. 76–7; *Liber Eliensis*, pp. 370–1.
87 Goscelin, *Miracula S. Mildrethe*, pp. 179–81.
88 *Vita Sexburge*, pp. 184–7.
89 Goscelin, *Vita S. Wlsini*, pp. 81–2; Goscelin, *Miracula S. Kenelmi*, pp. 76–9. See also the serving girl who gardened on the Sabbath and was punished by Æthelthryth, who caused the girl's stake to adhere to her hand. *Miracula S. Ætheldrethe*, pp. 118–23.
90 Arcoid, *Miracula S. Erkenwaldi*, pp. 148–51.
91 Goscelin, *Miracula S. Kenelmi*, pp. 74–7; Eadmer, *Miracula S. Dunstani*, pp. 206–9.
92 Goscelin, *Translationis S. Augustini*, pp. 442–3.
93 *Miracula S. Swithuni*, pp. 676–83.
94 *Miracula S. Oswini*, p. 40.
95 Arcoid, *Miracula S. Erkenwaldi*, pp. 148–51, 108–15, 158–61.
96 Goscelin, *Miracula S. Yuonis*, pp. lxx–lxxi.
97 On liturgical celebration of feasts see Appendix I.
98 *Miracula S. Oswini*, pp. 22–4.
99 Little, pp. 197–8.
100 William of Malmesbury, *Saints*, pp. 148–51.
101 Aelred, *De sanctis Hagustaldensis*, pp. 202–3.
102 Herman, *Miracula S. Edmundi*, pp. 346–9.
103 Goscelin, *Miraculis S. Augustini*, pp. 407–8.
104 Herman, *Miracula S. Edmundi*, pp. 58–9.
105 Aelred, *De sanctis Hagustaldensis*, pp. 202–3.
106 Herman, *Miracula S. Edmundi*, pp. 66–81.
107 Goscelin, *Miraculis S. Augustini*, p. 407; *Miracula S. Guthlaci*, p. 59.
108 Geoffrey, *Miracula S. Modwenne*, pp. 198–211; Herman, *Miracula S. Edmundi*, pp. 346–9.
109 Little, p. 83.
110 Lantfred, *Miracula S. Swithuni*, pp. 292–3.
111 *Miracula S. Oswini*, pp. 40–1.
112 *Miracula S. Swithuni*, pp. 682–3.
113 Lantfred, *Miracula S. Swithuni*, pp. 318–19.
114 Goscelin, *Miraculis S. Augustini*, pp. 409–10.
115 Osbern, *Miracula S. Dunstani*, pp. 131–3; Eadmer, *Miracula S. Dunstani*, pp. 162–3.
116 Klaniczay, 'Certain Conditions', pp. 241–2.

117 Goscelin, *Miracula S. Yuonis*, pp. lxx–lxxi; Aelred, *De sanctis Hagustaldensis*, pp. 188–9.
118 Goscelin, *Miracula S. Edmundi*, pp. 278–86.
119 Goscelin, *Vita S. Edithe*, pp. 281–4.
120 Herman, *Miracula S. Edmundi*, pp. 64–7.
121 Goscelin, *Miracula S. Yuonis*, pp. lxix–lxx.
122 You could perhaps include the failure of the aforementioned embassy to William I by Simeon of Ely after praying to Æthelthryth here as well. Ultimately the King died after rejecting Simeon's petition, but it is unclear if this was Simeon's or indeed the saint's intention. See also Herman, *Miracula S. Edmundi*, pp. 14–27.
123 Yarrow, p. 220.
124 For example against cheating litigants, biased judges and unfair imprisonment, see Byrhtferth, *Vita S. Ecgwini*, pp. 290–7; Geoffrey, *Miracula S. Modwenne*, pp. 182–93; Goscelin, *Vita S. Edithe*, p. 272.
125 Both saints and their communities warned against certain behaviour. For example, see Colgrave, 'Post-Bedan', p. 313; Arcoid, *Miracula S. Erkenwaldi*, pp. 108–15, 148–51 for warnings by humans and Geoffrey, *Miracula S. Modwenne*, pp. 204–7; Herman, *Miracula S. Edmundi*, pp. 14–27 for visions from saints.
126 Arcoid, *Miracula S. Erkenwaldi*, pp. 112–13.
127 Arcoid, *Miracula S. Erkenwaldi*, pp. 148–9.
128 "Pro Kenelmo', inquit, 'nescio quo fructum diei perderemus." Goscelin, *Miracula S. Kenelmi*, pp. 76–7.
129 Arcoid, *Miracula S. Erkenwaldi*, pp. 114–15.
130 Arcoid, *Miracula S. Erkenwaldi*, pp. 150–1.
131 Goscelin, *Miracula S. Yuonis*, pp. lxxi–lxxii. Ivo was not above educating the ignorant, as when he sent a vision to a monk of Ely who claimed not to have heard of the saint. Goscelin, *Miracula S. Yuonis*, pp. lxx–lxxi.
132 Jay Rubenstein, *Guibert of Nogent: Portrait of a Medieval Mind* (London: Routledge, 2002), p. 127. Guibert comments on the case of Lanfranc's questioning of Ælfheah's status, as well as the status of other relics, in his *De Pignoribus Sanctorum*. See *Patrologia Latina*, 156, col. 614–26.
133 Susan J. Ridyard, '"Condigna Veneratio": Post-Conquest Attitudes to the Saints of the Anglo-Saxons', *Anglo-Norman Studies*, 9 (1986), 179–206. Guibert mentions the testing of a relic of Arnulf at Clermont-en-Beauvaisis, Guibert de Nogent, *Autobiographie*, ed. and trans. by Edmond-René Labande, Classiques de l'histoire de France au Moyen Âge, 34 (Paris: Belles Lettres, 1981), pp. 462–3. The only English example from our period is Abbot Walter of Evesham (1077–1104), who tested the relics of the abbey including those of Credan and Wigstan, as recorded by Dominic of Evesham in his *Vita S. Odulfi*. See W. D. Macray, ed., *Chronicon Abbatiae de Evesham, ad Annum 1418*, Rolls Series 29 (London: Longman, 1863), pp. 323–34.
134 See chapter I.

5 Giving Thanks for Miracles

Tom Lynch

Making miracles in the middle ages was a balancing act. One had to express one's piety, humility and devotion whilst still asking for an act of God. The saints had to be kept happy throughout the process, and they would strike back if wronged. The act of thanksgiving is the final element to petitioning a saint for a miracle. There were expectations placed on the saints to intercede on behalf of supplicants and expectations placed on those supplicants to engage the saint appropriately. Between the miracle and the record, there was also an expectation of thanks and praise to the saint and God. In Eadmer's *Miracula S. Oswaldi*, there is a story of a monk of Worcester who was sick with a serious fever that could not be treated by local doctors. Eventually he was taken to the shrine of Oswald, where the following took place:

> When this had been done, he prostrated himself on the ground and began to pray, saying prayers that the magnitude of the sickness afflicting him and his longing to recover especially suggested to him. And there was no delay in this. For no sooner had he risen from prayer than he perceived that he had been restored to the most perfect health . . . And the other brothers, witnessing such a sudden and complete cure in their brother, were overjoyed and coming together they praised God, who had lovingly worked marvels through their own most beloved father; in praising they recommended it, and recommending it they praised him together, with great devotion in their hearts and voices raised on high.[1]

Such thanksgiving is present throughout the evidence. In Lantfred's miracles of Swithun, the paralysed man, cured after three days and nights in prayer and vigil, gave thanks to God and left cured.[2] In fact, Lantfred expected those granted miracles to give thanks appropriately, as he stated that a lame man who left without thanking Swithun as the other supplicants did 'remained spiritually infirm'.[3] Goscelin tells of a crippled boy who was cured by Kenelm as the abbot was beginning the antiphon to the evening Gospel reading. The boy stood up, stretched out his hands and gave thanks to God.[4] In a final miracle appended to Geoffrey of Burton's collection, a French penitent was found outside the monastery and begged to be let in to pray to Modwenna. After he had visited many shrines, he had been released from all of his iron bonds but one, which was cutting off the blood to his arm. Modwenna had twice come to him in a dream, telling him to go to Burton. Hearing this the monks allowed him into the monastery to spend the night in vigil. When Mass was being said the next day, he approached the shrine, his bond came loose and the pain subsided. The man immediately thanked God and Modwenna.[5]

Thanksgiving to God and his saints was a constant feature of the cult of the saints in medieval England. Expressions of individual thanks were directed to God, the saint or both. Whilst thanksgiving generally took the form of unspecified praise, some accounts include a little more detail. In the curing of a mute and lame youth by Dunstan, Osbern noted his thankful cry as 'Glory to God in the highest, Alleluia'.[6] The father of a paralysed boy healed by Ivo at Slepe clapped for joy, as well as thanking the saint and God.[7] When Abbot Scotland was healed by Mildrith at St Augustine's, he knelt before all of the shrines of the saints, one after another.[8] Though thanksgiving was never mandatory, it was definitely encouraged as a coda to the petitionary process, an act which signified a completed successful petition. This indicated the efficacy of the saint and the worthiness of the supplicant. The kind of humble and pious person who would ask the saints for help would also thank them appropriately for their aid. Whilst many people gave thanks for the help the saints had given them or their loved ones, the most elaborate thanksgiving was reserved for those miracles which were picked up on by the saint's custodians.

The practice of corporate thanksgiving is first found in Lantfred's Swithun dossier. Three blind women from the Isle of Wight were led to Swithun's new shrine in the Old Minster by a young mute man. Spending a vigil there, all four were cured, with the young man taking the sacristan outside and explaining to him what had happened and to inform the monks so they could give thanks 'in their usual manner'.[9] What this usual manner was is revealed by the circumstances behind a vision recorded by Lantfred. Bishop Æthelwold had given instruction to the monks of the Old Minster that whenever Swithun effected a miracle, all the brothers were to drop what they were doing and go to church to thank God appropriately. It seems some monks had become remiss in their observation of this practice, annoyed at the regular interruption of their sleep. Æthelwold's instructions were ignored for nearly two weeks when Swithun appeared in a vision to a woman, saying that the lack of thanksgiving was displeasing to God and that, if this was not remedied, the monks would be punished and the miracles would stop. The woman went quickly when she awoke and told the Bishop what had been revealed to her. Upon hearing this, Æthelwold sent out another directive that any monks who did not give thanks as instructed would do penance for seven days on bread and water. This time Æthelwold was heeded, and whenever the sacristan rang the bell indicating a miracle had been performed, the monks went to the church to give thanks.[10]

Therefore, underlying every shrine miracle in Lantfred's collection is a background of corporate thanksgiving by the monks of the Old Minster. Wulfstan also comments on the countless wonders of Swithun produced night and day. These miracles often interrupted the monks eating, learning and even their thanksgiving for previous miracles, but they would gladly stop what they were doing in favour of going to church and chanting hymns to God.[11] Kenelm's miracles at Winchcombe were met with thanks, praises and hymns led by the abbot and monks.[12] Osbern claims to have witnessed the cure of a blind girl by Dunstan whilst she was keeping vigil. Those present shed tears and thanked God. The next day, the boys of Christ Church were to be beaten but were let off on account of the miracle. The bells were rung, and the whole city praised Dunstan.[13]

It is unsurprising that miracles which benefited the whole community of a saint resulted in corporate thanksgiving as well. For example, during Abbot Ingulf's (1085/86–1109) leadership, the monks of Crowland had run out of food and could not easily resupply with winter setting in. The Abbot led all the monks in prayer on bended knee before the shrine of Guthlac, where they spent the night in vigil. When the monks assembled in the morning for the office, they heard angelic voices reporting the success of Guthlac's intercession and, upon investigation, found four sacks of grain and flour in the cellars. All of the monks gave heartfelt thanks to God and Guthlac and marvelled at the miracle. The Abbot also decreed that in memory of such a miracle, the Mass on that day of the week, Thursday, would be in honour of Guthlac and celebrated in copes and dalmatics.[14] Similarly, under Abbot Elfstan of St Augustine's (1016/19–1045/46), there was a lack of fish for the banquet associated with the feast of Augustine. Following vespers on the eve of the feast, Elfstan prostrated himself in prayer, asking the saint for help. Overnight a fourteen-foot sturgeon was washed up on the shore some seven leagues from the monastery. This fish was brought to Elfstan, who accepted it with eagerness and thanks, and the feast was held.[15]

Provisions and feasts were not the only concerns of monasteries, and occasionally their saints were invoked against existential threats. Aelred records how the people and buildings of Hexham were saved from marauding Scots, under King Malcolm III (1031–1093). Upon hearing of the imminent attack, the people of Hexham had assembled in the abbey and prayed prostrate before the saints. The clergy sang psalms and prayed. People invoked Wilfrid, Cuthbert, Acca and Alchmund. A priest had a vision of Cuthbert and Wilfrid coming from the south on horseback to save Hexham. This priest interrupted the people to tell them of his vision and reassure them that they had been heard. Following this, those present continued their prayers and psalms, and in the morning, a fog so dense rose that the Scots ended up getting lost and eventually found their way back to their own territory. The river also flooded, and the Scots gave up their intention after three days. The gathered people tearfully exclaimed their thanks and praises, and the monks celebrated Mass.[16] Two elements are common to these corporate displays of thanksgiving. The first is the singing of hymns, and the hymn of choice was *Te Deum Laudamus*.

The *Te Deum* is now attributed to Bishop Nicetas of Remesiana (c. 400), and sections of the hymn can be found in the *Musica Enchiriadis* of c. 900. The *Te Deum* was performed both as an occasional hymn of praise and as a regular but not constant feature of matins.[17] The singing of the *Te Deum* in response to a miracle is included in the work of Byrhtferth, Goscelin, Herman, Symeon of Durham, Dominic of Evesham and Arcoid.[18] Other hymns of praise seem to have been sung in response to a miracle, but these go unnamed in the source material.[19] Sometimes other chants and songs are indicated in the hagiography, but this was for context rather than in response to a miracle. For example, Goscelin describes the healing of two girls on the feast of Augustine. The first girl was cured during the hymns sung for Augustine during the vigil of his feast. The second girl was healed as the *Benedictus* was sung at lauds on the feast.[20] Hymns were usually sung in the office, with Proper material for feast days confined to matins, lauds and vespers.[21] Milfull has examined the relevant liturgical material and has found hymns for saints Andrew, Stephen, Cuthbert, Benedict, Dunstan, Augustine of Canterbury, John the Baptist, Peter and Paul, Laurence, Archangel Michael, All Saints, Martin of Tours, the Apostles, Barnabas, Gregory, Edmund the Martyr and Oswald of Worcester as well as a stock of hymns for the common of the saints.[22] Thus, it was conceivable to sing other hymns of thanksgiving to saints, and it appears there was a stock of hymns for the liturgy which could be repurposed. But the *Te Deum* reoccurs in the hagiography throughout our period, and it is worth considering why this was the case. The *Te Deum* would be well known to the monks, nuns and regular clerics with its place in the liturgy. Indeed it seems the hymn was also associated with the cult of the saints somewhat, and it was used on occasions like translations and feast days.[23] The content of the hymn was also appropriate for thanks and praise to God. When something miraculous was witnessed or reported the *Te Deum* would be an obvious choice of hymn with which to glorify God and the wonders of his creation.

The second element common to corporate thanksgiving was the use of bells. Bells and bell towers were found in most larger churches and monastic centres in England by around 800.[24] Their major liturgical use was to ring the hours of the office, but bells were also used to summon those within earshot to the church.[25] Like hymns, the ringing of bells is sometimes used in the hagiography to contextualise a miracle, particularly to mark the liturgical hour.[26] But for us, the more interesting use of bells was when they were rung in pronouncement and celebration of a miracle. The use of bells to draw attention to a miracle is recorded by Lantfred in his description of the corporate thanksgiving, which was required by Swithun at the Old Minster.[27] Bells were rung in thanksgiving for miracles performed by Ecgwine, Edmund, Ivo, Hadrian, Dunstan, Mildburh and Erkenwald as well.[28] Here bells both mark an event and draw others into that event; the noise of the celebration of a miracle would spread news of that miracle further and encourage others into thanksgiving. In this way, the sound of bells was an appeal to the community of a saint to join together in specific acts or to at least acknowledge the active role of the saint in the community. Each ringing of the bells was an example of the 'auditory performances of community', implicating all who heard the bells in a commonality even if they could ultimately ignore them.[29]

According to Lanfranc, the person in charge of the bells in a religious house was the sacristan, both in terms of their physical upkeep and in terms of ringing the hours and other occasions.[30] Therefore, the sacristan was usually the person to decide if a miracle warranted the attention of the whole community.[31] The ringing of bells could draw great crowds, even the whole city of Canterbury according to Osbern.³² Bell ringing was regularly combined with the singing of hymns and general celebrations.³³ Such a 'performance of community' would only have been matched by the celebration of major feasts, the consecration of a church or the translation of a saint. Corporate thanksgiving helped to involve the whole community in a miracle, even if they had not witnessed the miracle themselves. This was often in celebration of the reversal of communal troubles, but it could be to mark something as simple as the cure of a sick child. What was important was that the saint had made a miracle, the community had acknowledged this intercession and they then engaged in public thanksgiving.

Whilst a thanksgiving of devotional acts, whether corporate or individual, was the most common response to a successful intercession at a shrine, there is a great deal of evidence for material reciprocity in medieval England. These acts saw the donation of a gift dedicated to the saint in relation to a miracle. Lantfred details several examples of material reciprocity. A blind woman promised she would give gifts to Swithun in exchange for her eyesight. When she was taken to Swithun's shrine, she placed her gift of cloth on the altar, was instantly healed and gave thanks.³⁴ Here the fulfilled promise appears to be as significant as the material gift. This is emphasised by Lantfred's next entry, where another wealthy woman promised Swithun she would spend a vigil at his tomb and come with gifts if only he would help her with what seemed to be a mortal illness. As she made this promise, she was healed and, forgetting her commitment, rode to a wedding with her husband. At the wedding, she was struck down by the same illness, realised her fault and ordered that she be taken to Swithun's shrine. There she was cured, gave thanks and returned the next day to the same wedding.³⁵ Also demonstrated here is the conditional nature of such gifts, commonly referred to as ex-votos as they were given in the fulfilment of a vow.³⁶

Lantfred includes the deposit of mementos at Swithun's shrine without a vow as well. Some of the chains and bonds miraculously fell from a foreign penitent's body, who had come from across the sea to Winchester having heard of Swithun's power. The miracle was effected after the man had prayed at the shrine and the metal bonds that flew off were kept as a reminder.³⁷ Similarly, a woman bound in iron for having allowed her master's clothes to be stolen fled to Swithun's tomb. Whilst she prayed there her manacles fell off, which were only big enough to fit three fingers in. These manacles were kept as a token of the miracle.³⁸ The ungrateful foreigner cured of lameness, who left without thanks, did also leave behind his crutches which were retained.³⁹

Here we have two classes of gifts to the saint, votives and mementos directly linked to the miracle received. The most common votive offered to the saints was a candle. Candles were given to Augustine, Mildrith, Hadrian, Edmund, Ecgwine and Ithamar.⁴⁰ Unspecified gifts abound and other items given included a gold coin, a necklace and a chunk of marble.⁴¹ Offerings did not have to be expensive, however, and the gifts of the poor worked just as well.⁴² Mementos of miracles were largely the crutches of the disabled and chains of the penitent. Such signs were displayed at the shrines of Bege, Modwenna, Ecgwine and Edith.⁴³ Other more unique tokens were left after some miracles. Raven of Tutbury, a blind man cured at Burton by Modwenna, left his head wrap behind.⁴⁴ The cart which had carried two French boys to be cured at Bege's tomb was kept as a reminder of the miracle.⁴⁵ The author of the *Miracula S. Mylburge* notes the deposition of a large worm in a purpose built wooden box at Mildburh's shrine at Much Wenlock. The worm was vomited up by a woman and her husband fashioned the box himself so that it could be given to the saint.⁴⁶ Unique to the corpus is the wax model of a hand, given by an Italian woman named Benedicta who was finally healed after many visits to the Erkenwald.⁴⁷

Benedicta's wax hand is the first record I have found of a wax votive in England. This form of offering, relating perhaps to ideas of imprinting as well as the practical applications of wax in a church, provided a link between the saint and their supplicant.⁴⁸ This link is also demonstrated by the use of a pair of wax eyes to cure a Frenchman after they had been placed above Erkenwald's altar at St Paul's.⁴⁹ Wax votives seem to have been used in Europe from the eleventh century and only became widespread in the thirteenth and fourteenth centuries.⁵⁰ For our period, then, we lack evidence of a large number of such ex-votos, as we lack the pilgrim badges which first appeared in the second half of the twelfth century at Compostela and became popular in England with the cult of Thomas Becket.⁵¹ The two most common forms of offering deposited at saints' shrines, as depicted in the hagiography, were the candle and the memento of the miracle, both of which make sense as predecessors of the wax ex-voto. These material offerings were a representation of the devotion of individuals and a way that supplicants could add to and alter the appearance of a shrine.⁵² In England the dedication of a memento of a miracle is first found in the Swithun material and the offering of a candle after a miracle originates in the post-Conquest collections. More extravagant offerings were presented by those who could afford them, including Æthelwine building a new tower at St Augustine's and Emma of Normandy giving twenty silver coins in thanks to Mildrith.⁵³

Material offerings seem to have been a weak point for saints cults in terms of critique. As noted previously, people drew attention to the relationship between miracles and material gain, with predictably dire consequences for the critics.⁵⁴ What was a pious donation to some appeared to be a bribe to others. Such base exchange over a spiritual matter could strike one as incongruous, but it appears to have functioned more like a collection plate. People did not have to engage in material exchange in order to be granted miraculous aid or in response to a miracle already given. They had to behave in a certain manner, but they did not have to make a financial contribution. Nor was there a fixed tariff for a miracle, or indeed a scale depending on the degree of help delivered. A person could give whatever they could afford as a sign of thanks to God and his saint and, by extension, to the role played by the saint's custodians.

Exact revenues from pilgrimage are not recorded for our period and even where they are recorded expenditure on pilgrims and related services could be complex. The split between maintenance of the shrine and building, pilgrim services and profit for the custodians seems to have varied between institutions. Perhaps the most amicable solution was laid out in a bull of 1212 stating that the money left at the main altar of St Peter at Rome was to be divided equally between the canons, maintenance and the poor.[55] The cult of Thomas Becket saw an average of £426 3s. 7d. per year in offerings between 1198 and 1213, out of total average receipts of £1406 1s. 8d. and total average expenditure of £1314 19s. 2d. A famous cult could generate a lot of money, but a centre of pilgrimage could spend a lot of money.[56] According to our evidence, a wealthy supplicant could finance a whole rebuilding programme, and even small tokens could add up. In terms of supplicant behaviour, though, a material gift was as much a part of thanksgiving as a cry of praise or a hymn. One could not buy miracles, but that did not mean that wealthy people were not afforded better treatment and superior access to a saint. And evidently in some peoples' minds, a gift or a bribe was seen as an essential part of making a miracle. Whilst harder to quantify, perhaps the greatest act of thanksgiving was to dedicate your life to the saint in question.

John of Vermandois had a vision of Edward the Martyr telling him to come to Shaftesbury to be cured of his contorted body. John obeyed, travelled to England and was healed after praying to God and Edward for some time. He spent the rest of his days in service to Shaftesbury Abbey.[57] Likewise, a slave was given to the service of Swithun after the saint saved him from a judicial ordeal.[58] A deaf, dumb and lame woman was cured by Augustine at his tomb, where the woman prayed on bended knees and was struck down in a fit. When she came to her senses, the woman cried the name of Augustine aloud three times and then fell back down. Those present marvelled at the miraculous cure of the woman, who woke again and recited the names of the all the translated saints of St Augustine's, as if saying a litany, followed by the Our Father. When the brothers and the Abbot discovered the cure, they sprinkled her with holy water. The woman then dedicated her life to the service of Augustine, emphasising that she had not learnt the words she said but was told them by Augustine himself in a vision. Similarly an East Saxon man and a dying infant were saved by being vowed into Augustine's service.[59] Ranulf, a Norman courtier of William I, was cured in a dream of a sickness of the mind by Edmund. He then awoke, gave thanks to the saint, received the tonsure as he had once vowed and took up service at Bury.[60] Finally, after the bondsman named Raven had been cured by Acca of his blindness, his master gave him over with his possessions to serve at Hexham.[61]

Here we have two different categories of people being given over to the service of the saint, the bonded and the nominally free. Although the slaves would have been pleased at their miracles, this act of thanksgiving was essentially a transfer of ownership between masters; the saint's intervention in their lives was tantamount to a claim of possession. In the case of the slave saved by Swithun, his owner promised him to Swithun if the saint interceded on his behalf.[62] As the slave had committed a crime, saving him from punishment was also saving the owner's embarrassment and potentially culpability. The slave acted as an ex-voto of sorts in a reciprocal relationship established between the owner and Swithun. In Raven's case, his master was not personally put at risk by the bondsman's blindness. However, Aelred states that the master was looking to gain favour with Acca in delivering Raven into the service of Hexham.[63] The free people who dedicated their lives to the saints were generally cured of life-changing or life-threatening ailments, the exception being Ranulf, who had previously vowed to enter into Edmund's service. These people owed their lives to the saints, and their dedication was the most all-encompassing way of giving thanks to their patron. By giving themselves over to the saints, these people also became custodians and could become more intimate with their patrons and involved in the day-to-day life of their new homes.

People gave thanks for miracles no matter how they were petitioned. This includes relic miracles: whether it was Anselm's belt, Oswald's cup or relic water from St Augustine's, supplicants were demonstrably grateful for the intercession of the saints.[64] When these miracles occurred at a distance, thanksgiving could be combined with a visit to the shrine to recount the story. This was the case with Humphrey, the knight who was cured by Anselm's belt and went to Christ Church to inform the monks and to ask them to help him in giving thanks.[65] Distance miracles were often based on vows and promises, which required an eventual visit to the saint's shrine. This could range from a simple visit, like the blind man on his way to Swithun,[66] to a construction project, like the tower which Abbot Æthelwine promised to Augustine if he saved him at sea.[67] Reciprocity could be as simple or elaborate as that found in shrine cures. The criminal saved from execution in France simply praised God for Swithun's intercession.[68] Distance miracles reported at the shrine could be picked up and result in corporate thanksgiving, including bell ringing, sermons and the singing of hymns, again favouring the *Te Deum*.[69] Visiting or revisiting a shrine after a distance miracle meant that the miracle could be noted and properly acknowledged by the community. This would appease the saint and allow the supplicant to feel that their life crisis was complete, satisfying the social pressure to give thanks appropriately. It would also implicate the supplicant in the saint's community in a way that was impossible from a distance.

Thanksgiving was not limited to beneficent miracles. Whenever a saint interceded, there was an expectation of thanks and praise no matter what the saint had done. Thanks was given by the saints' communities for the vengeance miracles they had successfully petitioned. As with the beneficent miracles, the *Te Deum* was sung in response to the death of the peasant, who tried to trick Ecgwine and Evesham in a property dispute.[70] The community of Bury praised Edmund and God for exacting the asked-for vengeance on a thief.[71] Bege's community gave thanks for her legal help which they had petitioned her for.[72] Thanksgiving was also performed for more spontaneous punitive miracles, as when the monks of St Augustine's praised Mildrith's miraculous awakening of Hunfrith, who slept on her feast and fled after being awoken by the saint.[73]

Thanksgiving could also follow the forgiveness of a saint. Odo crawled to Augustine's tomb to give thanks after being cured of the serious illness that the saint punished him with for questioning his protection of the see of Canterbury. Odo promised to repeat this act of gratitude every year. The monks of St Augustine's heard of this and thanked the saint as well.[74] When Eudochia was healed in Constantinople, Augustine was thanked, and this episode encouraged his reputation as an intercessor in Greece.[75] Osgod was grateful to Edmund and the monks of Bury for curing him of the fit he fell into for entering the saint's sanctuary drunk.[76] The Dane who was punished for looking at Edmund's body was cured, gave the saint his golden bracelets and venerated Edmund from that day on.[77] A perjurer who had been afflicted with possession thanked God and Bege and publicly repented his perjury after being released by the saint.[78] A noble struck down by Ivo gradually got better after prayers and vigils; he then went to Ramsey and begged forgiveness from Abbot Bernard (1102–1107) and Ivo himself and gave thanks for his healing.[79] Even the last two peasants at Drakelow, who were bedridden following Modwenna's ravaging of the village and who seem to have been otherwise innocent, gave thanks for their healing by the saint once the perpetrators had been dealt with.[80]

Having considered thanksgiving as the final element in the making of a miracle, the reciprocal nature of the cult of the saints really comes into focus. It appears that most supplicants 'were inclined to expect some material benefit in exchange for fasts, pilgrimages and prayers'.[81] The whole system of pilgrimage and miracle petitions in return for material benefit can be understood as a process of exchange.[82] This is similar to the *do ut des* interpretation of pagan sacrifice in pre-Christian Rome, that in giving something to the gods, one should get something in return.[83] Such an attitude can be seen reflected in the deposition of votives, the making of vows and the petitions of supplicants at saints' shrines.[84] Ultimately this theory of exchange is based on the work of Mauss, particularly his ideas about gifts and reciprocity. Mauss notes the development of obligation and expectation in gift exchange. Such exchanges need not be limited to material goods and can include rituals, services and festivals, amongst other things. From this exchange, bonds are developed that have the appearance of being voluntary but are socially obligatory.[85] The gift then is not free at all but the beginning of a social relationship. A 'pure gift', given with no expectation of reciprocity, is rare, and even in cases like almsgiving, evidence suggests that givers are often looking for something with 'the benefits of the socially entangling Maussian gift'.[86]

When it comes to the cult of the saints, it is important to bear in mind that these social entanglements were not between social equals. There is a human intimacy between saint and supplicant, but it is the intimacy of the patron and the client.[87] Hierarchy and social norms are not undone by gift exchange, and the reciprocity at the heart of the cult of the saints is uneven. Such a structure means that the miracles are essentially 'favours from superiors' which reinforce the social position of saints and their custodians.[88] Saints freely chose who they engaged with initially, could defer or redirect supplicants and punished those who disrupted a reciprocal arrangement. The 'gift' of intercession was of such an order of magnitude greater than even the most lavish votive that a supplicant could never truly repay it. A supplicant always remained inferior to their saint, unable to gain parity let alone to overtake the saint in a system of 'fragile, competitive equality between actors'.[89] In a sense, something like a 'feudal bond' was initiated between a saint and a supplicant in the petitionary process.[90] The saints did not need anything from their supplicants, but the social interaction of the miracle petition required that the supplicants should do something in exchange for intercession. Therefore, we see the petition before the miracle and the thanksgiving afterwards. The action of a supplicant required a reaction from the saint, which triggered another action from the supplicant. This could lead to a lifetime of cyclical interactions between an individual and a saint.[91] Whilst people did give coins and other easily alienable portable wealth to saints, the most popular votive deposits seem to have been candles and mementos of miracles. A person who could never repay a saint could at least donate a sign of their personal experience of an intercession. Heaped up, these items would reinforce the saint's reputation as an intercessor and demonstrate the swathes of people indebted to the saint in perpetuity.

It seems that thanksgiving was a part of a being a good supplicant. These devotional acts helped to solidify a place within the saint's community and helped to ensure that a saint did not reverse their intercession. The power of the saints was awesome, and they did not shy away from collective punishment and collateral damage, so it was best to keep them content as an individual and as a community. Even if they did not directly punish people, the saints could always withhold future intercession, a disaster for an institution which was centred around the production of miracles. If the petition allowed a person to perform their misfortune in a pious manner, so thanksgiving allowed a person to perform their gratitude publicly. Giving thanks showed you were recovered from your personal crisis and able to take a full part in communal life again. It also showed that you were willing and able to solicit a miracle through your correct behaviour. People did not have to thank a saint and God for their aid, but if you had resorted to a saint for help, it was likely that you would want to thank them if they had listened to your pleas. Thus, thanksgiving fits into our structure of the petitionary process as the final action, an optional though highly recommended end to that specific ordeal. Thanksgiving could bring people into a closer relationship with the saint and their community; it gave people another reason to visit a saint at their main shrine and brought in stories of the saint's deeds throughout the country and beyond. Following thanksgiving, a supplicant could return to their old life physically and spiritually whole, in contrast to the man who left Swithun without thanking him properly.[92]

Notes

1 'Quod ubi factum est, solo prostratus, precibus incubuit, iis uidelicet quas sibi dictabat magnitudo doloris quo uexabatur, et desiderium sanitatis recuperandae quo raptabatur. Nec mora. Nam non prius ab oratione surrexit, quam se integerrimae sanitati restitutum intellexit . . . Ast alii fratres, intuentes in illo fratre tam subitam et integram curationem, ualde laetati sunt, et pium Deum per carissimum patrem suum mira operatum conuenientes magnificant, magnificantes praedicant, praedicantes multa cordis deuotione ac sullimi uocis exultatione collaudant.' Eadmer, *Miracula S. Oswaldi*, pp. 292–5.
2 Lantfred, *Miracula S. Swithuni*, pp. 298–301.
3 'mente permansit debilis', Lantfred, *Miracula S. Swithuni*, pp. 318–19.
4 Goscelin, *Miracula S. Kenelmi*, pp. 84–5.
5 Geoffrey, *Miracula S. Modwenne*, pp. 216–19.
6 'Gloria in excelsis Deo, Alleluia.' Osbern, *Miracula S. Dunstani*, p. 133.
7 *Miracula S. Yuonis*, pp. lxxx–lxxxi.

8 Goscelin, *Miracula S. Mildrethe*, p. 207.
9 '... ut solito more Deo reddant grates!' Lantfred, *Miracula S. Swithuni*, pp. 288–9.
10 Lantfred, *Miracula S. Swithuni*, pp. 292–7.
11 Wulfstan, *Narratio de S. Swithuno*, pp. 504–7.
12 Goscelin, *Miracula S. Kenelmi*, pp. 78–81.
13 Osbern, *Miracula S. Dunstani*, pp. 136–7.
14 *Miracula S. Guthlaci*, pp. 57–8. See also Appendix I on the elaborations used for certain feast days.
15 Goscelin, *Miraculis S. Augustini*, p. 406.
16 Aelred, *De sanctis Hagustaldensis*, pp. 177–81.
17 John Caldwell, 'The "Te Deum" in Late Medieval England', *Early Music*, 6 (1978), 188–94 (p. 188).
18 Byrhtferth, *Vita S. Ecgwini*, pp. 280–7; Goscelin, *Miracula S. Yuonis*, p. lx; Goscelin, *Translationis S. Augustini*, p. 418; Goscelin, *Virtutibus S. Adriani*, Cotton Vespasian B.xx, fols 239^v-40^v, Harley 105, fols 210^v-11^v; Herman, *Miracula S. Edmundi*, pp. 108–11; Symeon, *Libellus*, pp. 150–1; Dominic, *Miracula S. Ecgwini*, pp. 90–1; Arcoid, *Miracula S. Erkenwaldi*, pp. 135–41, 160–3.
19 Examples of non-specific hymnody include Lantfred, *Miracula S. Swithuni*, pp. 318–19; Herman, *Miracula S. Edmundi*, pp. 58–9; *Passio S. Edwardi*, pp. 14–15; *Miracula S. Ætheldrethe*, pp. 114–15; Geoffrey, *Miracula S. Modwenne*, pp. 198–201; Aelred, *De sanctis Hagustaldensis*, pp. 186–7; Goscelin, *Miracula S. Yuonis*, pp. lxxiii–lxxiv; Goscelin, *Virtutibus S. Adriani*, Cotton, Vespasian B.xx, fol. 236^r, Harley 105, fols 207^r-207^v.
20 Goscelin, *Miraculis S. Augustini*, pp. 404–5. The *Benedictus*, or *Canticle of Zachary*, is found at Luke 1. 68–79.
21 John Harper, *The Forms and Orders of Western Liturgy from the Tenth to the Eighteenth Century: A Historical Introduction and Guide for Students and Musicians* (Oxford: Clarendon, 1991), p. 80.
22 Inge B. Milfull, ed. and trans., *The Hymns of the Anglo-Saxon Church: A Study and Edition of the 'Durham Hymnal'*, Cambridge Studies in Anglo-Saxon England, 17 (Cambridge: Cambridge University Press, 1996), pp. 107–472. On other elements of festal observance see Appendix I.
23 Wulfstan, *Narratio de S. Swithuno*, pp. 458–9; Goscelin, *Translationis S. Augustini*, p. 423. The *Te Deum* was also chanted by Kenelm during his execution, Goscelin, *Miracula S. Kenelmi*, pp. 60–1.
24 Neil Christie, *On Bells and Bell-Towers: Origins and Evolutions in Italy and Britain, AD 700–1200*, Brixworth Lecture: Second Series, 4 (Brixworth: The Friends of All Saints' Church, 2004), p. 8.
25 John H. Arnold and Caroline Goodson, 'Resounding Community: The History and Meaning of Medieval Church Bells', *Viator*, 43 (2012), 99–130 (p. 100).
26 Eadmer, *Miracula S. Dunstani*, pp. 180–1; Herman, *Miracula S. Edmundi*, pp. 104–9; Wulfstan, *Narratio de S. Swithuno*, pp. 452–5.
27 Lantfred, *Miracula S. Swithuni*, pp. 292–7.
28 Byrhtferth, *Vita S. Ecgwini*, pp. 280–7; Herman, *Miracula S. Edmundi*, pp. 104–9; Goscelin, *Miracula S. Yuonis*, pp. lxvii–lxviii; Goscelin, *Virtutibus S. Adriani*, Cotton, Vespasian B.xx, fol. 236^r, Harley 105, fols 207^r-207^v; Osbern, *Miracula S. Dunstani*, pp. 136–8; *Miracula S. Mylburge*, pp. 568–70; Dominic, *Miracula S. Ecgwini*, pp. 92–3; Arcoid, *Miracula S. Erkenwaldi*, pp. 135–41.
29 Arnold and Goodson, pp. 127–8.
30 Knowles and Brooke, pp. 122–7.
31 As noted above, this did not mean they were the final authority in an investigation into a miracle; this seems to have been the role of the abbot or bishop. However, the sacristan would have been the person on the ground, and they seem to have had a major role in

witnessing and celebrating miracles. See Lantfred, *Miracula S. Swithuni*, pp. 292–7; *Miracula S. Mylburge*, pp. 568–70; Herman, *Miracula S. Edmundi*, pp. 104–9 for the use of bells and the sacristan. For the role of the sacristan more generally see Lantfred, *Miracula S. Swithuni*, pp. 288–9; Herman, *Miracula S. Edmundi*, pp. 28–39, 58–9, 346–9; Goscelin, *Vita S. Vulfhilde*, pp. 415–16.
32 Osbern, *Miracula S. Dunstani*, pp. 136–8.
33 Herman, *Miracula S. Edmundi*, pp. 104–9; Goscelin, *Virtutibus S. Adriani*, Cotton, Vespasian B.xx, fol. 236^r, Harley 105, fols 207^r-207^v; Osbern, *Miracula S. Dunstani*, pp. 136–8; Dominic, *Miracula S. Ecgwini*, pp. 92–3; Arcoid, *Miracula S. Erkenwaldi*, pp. 135–41.
34 Lantfred, *Miracula S. Swithuni*, pp. 290–1.
35 Ibid., pp. 292–3.
36 G. W. Bowersock, and others, eds, *Late Antiquity: A Guide to the Postclassical World* (Cambridge, MA: Harvard University Press, 1999), pp. 440–1.
37 Lantfred, *Miracula S. Swithuni*, pp. 306–7.
38 Ibid., pp. 330–3.
39 Ibid., pp. 318–19.
40 Goscelin, *Miraculis S. Augustini*, p. 404; Goscelin, *Translationis S. Augustini*, p. 437; Goscelin, *Miracula S. Mildrethe*, pp. 194–7; Goscelin, *Virtutibus S. Adriani*, Cotton Vespasian B.xx, fols 235^r-35^v, Harley 105, fols 206^r-07^v; Herman, *Miracula S. Edmundi*, pp. 340–1; Dominic, *Miracula S. Ecgwini*, pp. 90–1, 106–9; *Miracula S. Ithamari*, pp. 430–1, 434–5.
41 Goscelin, *Translationis S. Augustini*, p. 437; Goscelin, *Virtutibus S. Adriani*, Vespasian B.xx, fols 234^v-235^r, Harley 105, fol. 206^v; Herman, *Miracula S. Edmundi*, pp. 104–5.
42 *Miracula S. Ithamari*, pp. 433–6; Herman, *Miracula S. Edmundi*, pp. 340–1.
43 *Miracula S. Bege*, pp. 516–17; Geoffrey, *Miracula S. Modwenne*, pp. 186–7, 198–201; Dominic, *Miracula S. Ecgwini*, pp. 92–3; Goscelin, *Vita S. Edithe*, p. 293.
44 Geoffrey, *Miracula S. Modwenne*, pp. 186–9.
45 *Miracula S. Bege*, pp. 518–19.
46 *Miracula S. Mylburge*, pp. 567–8.
47 Arcoid, *Miracula S. Erkenwaldi*, pp. 128–33.
48 Megan Holmes, 'Ex-votos: Materiality, Memory, and Cult', in *The Idol in the Age of Art: Objects, Devotions and the Early Modern World*, ed. by Michael Cole and Rebecca Zorach (Aldershot: Ashgate, 2009), pp. 165–88 (pp. 160–3).
49 Arcoid, *Miracula S. Erkenwaldi*, pp. 135–41.
50 Holmes, p. 161.
51 Brian North Lee, 'The Expert and the Collector', in *Beyond Pilgrim Souvenirs and Secular Badges: Essays in Honour of Brian Spencer*, ed. by Sarah Blick (Oxford: Oxbow, 2007), pp. 4–16 (p. 8).
52 Sarah Blick, 'Votives, Images, Interaction and Pilgrimage to the Tomb and Shrine of St. Thomas Becket, Canterbury Cathedral', in *Push Me, Pull You: Art and Devotional Interaction in Late Medieval and Renaissance Art*, ed. by Sarah Blick and Laura D. Gelfand (Leiden: Brill, 2011), pp. 21–58 (p. 58).
53 Goscelin, *Miraculis S. Augustini*, pp. 400–1; Goscelin, *Miracula S. Mildrethe*, pp. 176–8.
54 *Miracula S. Swithuni*, pp. 676–7; Arcoid, *Miracula S. Erkenwaldi*, pp. 142–5; Goscelin, *Miracula S. Yuonis*, pp. lxix–lxx.
55 Adrian R. Bell and Richard S. Dale, 'The Medieval Pilgrimage Business', *Enterprise & Society*, 12 (2011), 601–27 (pp. 616–18).
56 Charles Eveleigh Woodruff, 'The Financial Aspect of the Cult of St. Thomas of Canterbury', *Archaeologia Cantiana*, 44 (1932), 13–32 (p. 16).
57 *Passio S. Edwardi*, pp. 13–14.
58 Lantfred, *Miracula S. Swithuni*, pp. 308–11.

59 Goscelin, *Translationis S. Augustini*, pp. 418, 428–9.
60 Herman, *Miracula S. Edmundi*, pp. 94–8.
61 Aelred, *De sanctis Hagustaldensis*, pp. 186–7.
62 Lantfred, *Miracula S. Swithuni*, pp. 308–11.
63 Aelred, *De sanctis Hagustaldensis*, pp. 186–7.
64 Eadmer, *Vita S. Anselmi*, pp. 159–65; Eadmer, *Miracula S. Oswaldi*, pp. 308–13; Goscelin, *Translationis S. Augustini*, pp. 414–17, 435–6.
65 Eadmer, *Vita S. Anselmi*, pp. 159–60.
66 Lantfred, *Miracula S. Swithuni*, pp. 318–19.
67 Goscelin, *Miraculis S. Augustini*, pp. 400–1.
68 Lantfred, *Miracula S. Swithuni*, pp. 324–5.
69 Lantfred, *Miracula S. Swithuni*, pp. 318–19; Arcoid, *Miracula S. Erkenwaldi*, pp. 135–41; Herman, *Miracula S. Edmundi*, pp. 104–9.
70 Byrhtferth, *Vita S. Ecgwini*, pp. 290–7.
71 Herman, *Miracula S. Edmundi*, pp. 346–9.
72 *Miracula S. Bege*, pp. 510–12.
73 Goscelin, *Miracula S. Mildrethe*, pp. 179–81.
74 Goscelin, *Translationis S. Augustini*, pp. 426–7.
75 Goscelin, *Miraculis S. Augustini*, pp. 410–11.
76 Herman, *Miracula S. Edmundi*, pp. 58–9.
77 Herman, *Miracula S. Edmundi*, pp. 36–7.
78 *Miracula S. Bege*, pp. 513–15.
79 *Miracula S. Yuonis*, pp. lxxvii–lxxviii.
80 Geoffrey, *Miracula S. Modwenne*, pp. 192–9.
81 Donald Weinstein and Rudolph M. Bell, *Saints and Society: The Two Worlds of Western Christianity, 1000–1700* (Chicago, IL: University of Chicago Press, 1982), p. 5.
82 Dee Dyas, 'To Be A Pilgrim: Tactile Piety, Virtual Pilgrimage and the Experience of Place in Christian Pilgrimage', in *Matter of Faith: An Interdisciplinary Study of Relics and Relic Veneration in the Medieval Period*, ed. by James Robinson, and others, Research Publication, 195 (London: British Museum, 2014), pp. 1–7 (pp. 4–5).
83 Jörg Rüpke, *The Religion of the Romans*, trans. by Richard Gordon (Cambridge: Polity, 2007), p. 149.
84 Klaniczay, 'Certain Conditions', p. 238.
85 Mauss, *The Gift*, pp. 3–6.
86 James Laidlaw, 'A Free Gift Makes No Friends', *The Journal of the Royal Anthropological Institute*, 6 (2000), 617–34 (p. 632).
87 Brown, *Saints*, p. 61.
88 Yunxiang Yan, 'Unbalanced Reciprocity: Asymmetrical Gift Giving and Social Hierarchy in Rural China', in *The Question of the Gift*, ed. by Mark Osteen (London: Routledge, 2002), pp. 67–84 (pp. 80–1).
89 Graeber, p. 221.
90 Blick, p. 25.
91 For example, Odo who promised to repeat his thanksgiving yearly, Goscelin, *Translationis S. Augustini*, pp. 426–7, and the young man who went back to Hadrian for a cure having remembered his previous one, Goscelin, *Virtutibus S. Adriani*, Vespasian B.xx, fols 238^v-39^r, Harley 105, fols 209^v-10^r.
92 Lantfred, *Miracula S. Swithuni*, pp. 318–19.

6 Conclusions

Tom Lynch

To revisit the question posed in the introduction, it is worth considering how miracles were made in medieval England in light of the evidence presented previously. Take the example of a boy cured of a deformity during Swithun's translation as recorded by Wulfstan:

> Meanwhile a woman brought her own son; she was moaning with spasmodic sobs because of this same child. It chanced that his fingers were twisted back across his palm; thus afflicted in each hand he had come forth from his mother's womb. With burning faith she cast him upon the tomb from which the saint had been translated. By chance she was holding in her hands that variety of fruit which an Englishman calls *cyresan* ('cherries'). She continued in prayer, suddenly (it was wonderful to see!) the boy jumped up wholly sound; he snatched the cherries away from the hands of his mother and ate them. When she saw this she joyously poured forth devout tears and said: 'Glory be to You, bountiful Christ, Who desert no-one who hopes in You, but in Your kindness bestow unexpected gifts on the wretched. Glory be to you through the Lord, St Swithun, who in your compassion for me, a poor woman, have from heaven relieved this boy from so great an illness, and have restored him to me sound by your prayer alone.' The miracle becomes known as its report flies through the town. Those who shortly before had withdrawn come together again; the countless people all around behold these mighty events. The bells sound as usual; all things praise Christ and at the same time the holy praise echoes their patron Swithun, through whom God granted such mighty miracles to the world.[1]

First came the moment of crisis, the point when a person could not endure their problem anymore and resorted to a saint for help. In this case, the suffering of a son caused his mother to act. Generally such crises were either chronic conditions which had become too much to bear or more immediate and unexpected emergencies. People's tolerance for pain and misfortune must have varied a great deal, and whilst most supplicants had a serious problem, the saints were open to dealing with less extreme issues.[2] These crises could be caused by anything, including the supplicants own misdeeds. Indeed, the whole process could be started by a crime against a saint. For the crisis to change into a miracle, the instigator had to have a knowledge of a saint.

In order to know of a saint, that saint first had to be recognised as such. For our purposes, there was no saint without an attendant community. In the previous example, the action takes place in the midst of the translation of Swithun. Saints could be discovered, rediscovered or have been subject to cult since time immemorial. All of the saints whose cults we have considered came to be enshrined within a church through a translation, but this was not necessary for miracles to be made. The invention of a saint and translating them involved the whole community. For instance the invention of Swithun involved the laity and the clergy of Winchester as well as the saint's future custodians, supplicants and the saint himself.[3] Likewise the 1136 translation of Guthlac at Crowland was requested by the monks of the abbey, permitted by Abbot Waltheof and confirmed by miraculous signs from Guthlac. Bishop Alexander of Lincoln helped to complete the ceremony, and throughout the translation, a crowd of lay and religious folk watched the proceedings and successfully petitioned miracles.[4] A saint had to be known to a person for a miracle to be made, and this usually meant that a religious community looked after the relics and that stories about the saint, whether oral or written, were circulating. The first step in making a miracle was to have knowledge of the relevant saint.

Next came the action which triggered the miracle. This included everything from a quick prayer, as in the previous example, to an extended pilgrimage with attendant vigils and fasts. It also included everything from insulting a saint to attacking a saint's shrine. This is the point when the contingency of a person's life coincided with the structures of the cult of the saints. As such these actions were heterodox but not entirely unpredictable. For a miracle petition, a person had only to ask for help. If this did not result in a miracle, various degrees of elaboration could be included, resulting either in divine intervention or the end of a supplicant's patience.[5] If a person had committed an offence against a saint, they could spur the saint into a reactive miracle. If not, the saint's community could petition the saint for revenge or to otherwise solve the problem induced by the offence. Either way, a person punished by the saints could then petition the saint to reverse or alleviate their punishment. All of these actions had a communal expectation of intercession behind them. Saints rewarded the righteous, punished their enemies and reconciled with the contrite. This expectation could be fulfilled anywhere.

The English saints interceded at their shrines and away from them. They cured people as far away as Greece and Italy; they saved people at sea and liberated the incarcerated. They even cured people on their way to visit them. In the same way, they could punish people regardless of where they were located. Even after death, a saint could exact their revenge. Despite this there remained a preference for the shrine as the locus of intercession. I believe this ties into the intimate relationship between saint and supplicant. Supplicants chose their saint, knew about them and connected with them on a human level. They knew, or found out, where the saint's home was and wanted to visit them there. Where people asked for help at a distance, they usually had a compelling reason not to attend the saint in person. Usually this was due to the extremity or immediacy of their problem. There is something of a tension here between the universal and the local, between the spiritual potency of the saint and their embodied earthly form. Even when miracles were performed at a distance, people were often brought back to the shrine, finally, to give thanks.

Thanksgiving was pervasive and expected, if not strictly mandatory, much like the translation of the saints. Thanksgiving allowed people to address their debt to the saint, a debt which could never be fully repaid. For some it was enough to admit their debt to the saints, say thank you as best they could and move on with their lives. Others felt compelled to visit and revisit the shrine, donate huge fortunes or dedicate their whole lives to the saints. In the previous example, the mother immediately gave thanks for Swithun's intercession, and this was picked up by the community of Winchester, almost becoming an element of the translation festivities. No matter the reaction, an act of thanksgiving would begin the person's life after their crisis and the miracle which solved it. Like a miracle petition, thanksgiving could be enacted anywhere, but people were drawn to the shrine to meet with the saint personally. These visits could also fulfil vows, be accompanied by gifts and bring new stories to the attention of the saints' custodians. As in the example of the woman and her son above, sometimes a miracle was picked up on by the custodians and the act of thanks spiralled into a quasi-liturgical event with hymns and bells and crowds in tow.

At the end of all of this, some miracle stories would resonate and be retold. Fewer still would be written down for later recitation or against the ravages of time. The previous vignette shows a miracle performed before a crowd and then circulating through the community and drawing people in. Saints built reputations through their thaumaturgy, but they needed supplicants to petition them, enemies to threaten them, custodians to run their shrines and hagiographers to record select events. The writing down of a miracle story helped to fix these events. Written miracle stories are satisfyingly complete narratives that show how things should, and sometimes did, work. These stories could be copied and distributed, added to the liturgical texts of a house, recited on feast days and paraphrased in sermons and discussions. Writing miracles was a part of making miracles; the hagiographer took from and added to the community of the saint. In fact, the hagiographers were a part of that community, whether they collected their stories at a remove or they lived with the saint and their custodians for their entire life. But without the hagiography, the cult could have survived. The central pillar of the cult of the saints was the structure of the petition. A person had a problem, they knew of a saint, they asked that saint for help and the saint responded. This is how miracles were made in medieval England.

Each step in the making of miracles saw the interaction of different elements of the saint's community. Miracle petitions were initiated by supplicants, who made decisions as to the nature and length of the petition. As the person petitioned, the saint responded to this request. This response did not have to be immediate and could lead to other shrines and new petitions. The whole process was moderated by the custodians of the saint through access to the saint's shrine and relics.

Miracles of vengeance saw the saint reacting to the actions of their enemies. This was often in defence of the accepted norms of the custodians regarding issues of property, sanctuary and service. The saint could also defend the community more generally from all manner of offences. When giving thanks for a miracle, the supplicant would declare they had received successful intercession. This could then be investigated and picked up by the custodians of the saint and the other people gathered at the shrine. Stories of the saints' power would reverberate within and between their communities. Miracle collections were made through an interaction with these stories, taking into account the supplicants, custodians and saints as well as the influences and inclinations of the hagiographers. The hagiography would then feed into the liturgical observation of the cult and augment the tales of the prowess of the saint.

Having looked at how miracles were made, it is worthwhile to consider why they were made in this way. Saints were Christlike both in their ability to perform miracles and in their dual nature. The humanity of the saints made them more easily approachable than the Trinity. The physical bonds of the body and relics of a saint made them more obviously present in the world than God. Relationships could be formed with a saint as with any powerful human being, although the favours requested were of a different magnitude.[6] People visited saints as they would do any other patron, and they often came to pay homage when a saint interceded in their lives away from the shrine. People knew of the saints because there were stories of their power written and spoken, rumours of the punishment of the unworthy and the deliverance of the worthy. They also knew of saints because it was personally useful. Knowing where a saint rested, when their feast day was and who acted as custodians of their relics gave you the option to call upon that saint in the most favourable manner. Of course supplicants had to maintain their piety, promises had to be kept and the saints propitiated. If the saints were capable of miracles, they were capable of exposing the cynical and withholding support or even punishing them. Equally miracles could be used to strengthen faith and bring outsiders into a saint's community. The devout would visit and revisit a saint regardless of their intercessory potential, but miracle-seeking behaviour could easily be reconciled with genuine belief.

Therefore, a saint's cult was a way for a person to take action against their own misfortune. Through dealing with the saint, you could change your lot for the better. The vicissitudes of life could be counteracted by performing a petition successfully and dealing appropriately with a near omnipotent – if still human – patron. The agency of the supplicant was magnified by the cult of the saints. Ultimately they chose whether to engage a saint, which saint to go to and how to approach the petition. At any stage, the saint could interpose themselves and alter the course of the petition as the custodians could bar access to a shrine or impose additional requirements. But the supplicant still had the choice to take up the petition, the choice to give thanks and the choice of when to go home. This choice also existed for the subjects of the punitive miracles. They chose to commit these offences, more often than not with some knowledge of the saint and their reputation. Saints reacted to people's actions, and these people in turn reacted to the saints.

Petitioning the saints gave people an opportunity to exert agency in an uncertain world, but a petition said something about the supplicant as well. When a person resorted to the saints for help, they were humbled, admitting that whatever other means they had to deal with their problem had failed. This demonstrated a faith in the petitionary process. We cannot access people's understanding of the powers behind miracles, of the exact nature of the saints or of their relationship to God. What we can see is that 'appropriate participation' seems to have been required for intercession[7] and was favoured by the custodians and hagiographers. We are shown that people who petitioned the saints were pious and that those who behaved poorly were sinful and could be damned. By petitioning a saint, a person was expressing that they had a problem and that they knew how to deal with it appropriately. The supplicant performed their misfortune publicly, demonstrating relationships with the saint, the custodians and other supplicants. At the end, a person was nominally back where they were before their crisis, but they had shown they were worthy individuals. The whole ordeal would also have been cathartic, a way of putting misfortune behind you and beginning your life in a different phase. The great noise and joy of corporate thanksgiving, of bells and shouts and group singing, was a fine way to end a crisis, as was a quiet prayer of thanks.

To take into account all of these people and their sometimes conflicting needs, the cult of the saints had to be flexible. People were more or less able to travel, to spend time away from home or to visit a shrine. The contingent nature of each individual's life had to be encompassed by the structure of the cult of the saints. This is shown not only by the diversity of the problems brought to the saints and of the methods of supplication but also by the incorporation of distance miracles, unlooked-for miracles and reconciliation. Of course there were failures, reversals, collateral damage and people who acted in such a manner that they could not be reincorporated. The hagiographers portray perpetrators as enemies of God, the saints and their communities. This helps to explain the lack of failed petitions in the miracle collections. A person is either good and gets a beneficent miracle or is bad and gets a negative miracle. Supplicants could be sent on to another saint, healed conditionally on the fulfilment of a vow or forced to wait for days for intercession. Perpetrators could transition into supplicants in the right situations, as well. But an outright failure is unsatisfying, both in terms of the narrative of a miracle story and in terms of the structure of the cult of the saints. Where hagiographers allow for failure, it serves a purpose within a story and does not reflect poorly on the power of the saint.[8] In reality every petition to a saint cannot have succeeded, just as every enemy of a saint cannot have been all bad. Whilst many perpetrators were self-serving and some were violent, they were reacting against an institution which they felt unfairly curtailed their behaviour or encouraged unscrupulous actions in others. People seem to have thought that it was unfair that the saint was enriched while they were impoverished, that the invocation of a saint in a legal case prejudiced the outcome or that the local religious house had a monopoly on usable land. If they acted on these feelings, they could well be the subject of a miracle of vengeance, and the only record we have of many of them is in this context.

Another tension that is evident from the hagiography is over access to the saints, particularly at their shrines. Custodians – and sometimes the saints themselves – kept certain people excluded at certain times, often for unclear reasons. It is likely that leading a religious life in a foundation with a major cult was difficult. Interruptions could come at all hours of the day, during the performance of the divine office and Mass and especially at irregular or seasonal occasions like processions, translations and feast days. Custodians wanted their saint to be popular and hagiographers wanted to represent them as such, but popularity brought issues of overcrowding, access and comportment to the fore. The difference between a mob and a crowd was largely how the people behaved, whether they pushed and shoved and tore doors from their hinges or they followed along taking a small part in the celebrations of their saint. Some of these pressures may have led to changes in the cult of the saints, but these are difficult to track.

The cult of the saints in 1170 was very similar to the cult in 970, or indeed in 770. Change comes slowly to large, complex and enduring systems like the cult of the saints, often through an 'accumulation of incalculable little glitches'.[9] Any changes would come by living and reproducing the cult of the saints. By engaging in and observing the cult, the lived experience of the cult of the saints, the community developed their understanding of appropriate behaviour. This is what Mauss termed *habitus*, the total education that all people must go through in order to know how to behave in any given situation. This is an embodied experience which may include mistakes, errors and even deliberate misbehaviour but that goes beyond mere instruction.[10] Mauss' idea of *habitus* has been much developed by Bourdieu. For Bourdieu each person in a society produces and reproduces their society through their *habitus*. Through this process, individuals become culturally competent, are able to cope with most social situations and are also able to improvise appropriately when they have to. Practices can change over time and include individual variation, but people always start from a point of observation and imitation as children. Behaviour is not taken from abstract models of how things should work but from actions actually working in the world.[11] Thus, every petition, reconciliation and thanksgiving was an imitative and an original act. This collision of a social structure and a contingent event could change the way the cult worked. There was no great crisis in the cult of the saints in England during this time, but there are traces of a few 'glitches'.

Perhaps the potential disruption caused by miracle seekers in processions led to the later practice of holding or fixing a feretory aloft at the end of a procession, which allowed people to pass underneath.[12] We see a development in the later evidence of the deposit of wax votives and measuring to a saint, both precursors to large trindles donated to saints after 1170. The use of saints' water was popular in earlier medieval England and then is absent from the evidence until after the Conquest. As our only sizeable collections from late-tenth-century England concern Swithun at the Old Minster this could be due to some local issue. According to Wulfstan, Swithun's remains were washed during his translation, and it can be presumed that dust would have gathered on the saint's tomb and dirt was available at his original grave site.[13] Distance miracles were recorded in Lantfred's work and continued to be throughout the period. Such petitions are a common feature of the later material, but they were always in the minority compared to shrine cures. Largely the cult remained the same, the saints being reliable patrons in times of change and conflict: probably never as hegemonic or ubiquitous as the hagiographers described them, with tension within and from outside the saint's community, but weathering the trials of the Conquest and the Anarchy.

Making miracles in medieval England was a communal affair. It required people to interact, to make space for one another and to communicate. None of this was a given, and people fell into conflict with the saints. They fell into conflict amongst themselves as well over the possession of relics and access to the shrines. A miracle could change the course of someone's life, and a good relationship with a saint could be proof against misfortune. All of this relied upon the actions of the community to keep the saints happy and to facilitate their cults. Saints grew in reputation and had their intercessions documented and their deeds read and recited. Translations were conducted, saints were carried out in processions and elaborate feast day celebrations were performed. Churches were dedicated to English saints, fairs coalesced around their feasts and places were named for them. But none of this would have happened if not for the miracles. At the heart of the cult of the saints was a suffering person petitioning their saint for help.

Notes

1 'Adtulit interea proprium muliercula natum, singultu quatiente gemens pro pignore eodem. Cuius erant digiti trans palmam forte retorti, sic in utraque manu matris progressus ab aluo. Proicit hunc tumulo sanctus fuit unde leuatus ardescente fide. Casu manibusque tenebat id genus uuarum 'cyresan' quod nuncupat Anglus. Prestitit in precibus; subito (mirabile uisu!) prosilit incolomis totus puer, abripit uuas e manibus matris comedens. Quod uidit ut illa laeta pias fundit lacrimas, 'sit gloria', dicens, 'O bone Christe, tibi, nullum qui deseris umquam in te sperantem, miseris sed munera prestas insperata pius. Tibi sit, Suuithuneque sancte, gloria per Dominum, mihi qui miserendo misellae caelitus hunc puerum tanta de clade leuasti huncque mihi incolomem sola prece restituisti.' Fit notum signum fama uolitante per urbem. Rursum conueniunt qui illinc paulo ante recedunt; innumeri circum populi magnalia cernunt. Signa sonant solito, conlaudant omnia Christum, Suuiðhunumque simul reboat laus sancta patronum per quem tanta Deus tribuit magnalia saeclo.' Wulfstan, *Narratio de S. Swithuno*, pp. 462–3.
2 For example, the three miracles concerning spending money, the sacristan's keys and a new curtain for Æthelburh's shrine, the lost penny of a supplicant visiting Edmund and the lack of fish for the banquet on the feast of St Augustine at Canterbury. See Goscelin, *Vita S. Vulfhilde*, pp. 433–4; Herman, *Miracula S. Edmundi*, pp. 340–1; Goscelin, *Miraculis S. Augustini*, p. 406. On the other hand, a woman put up with an agonising and untreatable paralysis for six years before going to Æthelthryth's shrine for a cure. *Miracula S. Ætheldrethe*, pp. 110–13.
3 Lantfred, *Miracula S. Swithuni*, pp. 260–85.
4 *Miracula S. Guthlaci*, pp. 55–7.
5 Unsurprisingly the impatient are not generally included in the miracle accounts. However, see Goscelin, *Translationis S. Augustini*, pp. 423–4 for a woman who lost patience in her initial petition for the healing of her son but who returned nine months later and succeeded in her petition on the saint's feast.

6 Mia Di Tota, 'Saint Cults and Political Alignments in Southern Italy', *Dialectical Anthropology*, 5.4 (1981), 317–29 (pp. 327–8).
7 Roger M. Keesing, 'On Not Understanding Symbols: Towards an Anthropology of Incomprehension', *HAU: Journal of Ethnographic Theory*, 2 (2012), 406–30 (p. 422).
8 See Herman, *Miracula S. Edmundi*, pp. 14–27, 64–7; Goscelin, *Miracula S. Yuonis*, pp. lxix–lxx; *Liber Eliensis*, pp. 216–17.
9 Kleinberg, p. 289.
10 Mauss, *Sociology and Psychology*, pp. 120–2.
11 Bourdieu, pp. 79–89.
12 See William of Malmesbury, *Gesta Pontificum*, I, pp. 642–43 (V.270); William Ketell, *Miracula S. Johannis*, pp. 278–80. Examples of potential disruption in a procession can be found in *Passio S. Edwardi*, pp. 9–10; *Miracula S. Guthlaci*, pp. 55–7; Goscelin, *Translationis S. Augustini*, p. 443.
13 Wulfstan, *Narratio de S. Swithuno*, pp. 452–61.

Appendix I
Saints in the Liturgy

Tom Lynch

The liturgy refers to 'the whole body and practice of corporate worship' of the Christian tradition.[1] The liturgy was focused on clerics and religious, with the laity left as observers or minor participants. In medieval England, some form of liturgical commemoration was a common aspect of the cult of the saints. Communities in possession of a saint's relics were particularly likely to work their saint into the yearly round of feasts and to invoke them in other parts of the liturgy. The liturgy was not necessarily about making miracles, but it could be seen as a part of thanksgiving for previous miracles or as a means to help secure future miracles. The saints cared how they were treated by their community, and they could stop interceding altogether if they were not appeased. They could even punish people for a lack of proper observance.[2] Incorporating a saint into the Mass and divine office was a way to honour the saint and also a means of 'assuring the successful prosecution of the vital activities of the group'.[3] Liturgical elements could be used in translations, corporate petitions, corporate thanksgiving and ad hoc processions to lend those occasions a sense of ceremony and to authenticate them as official acts of the custodians of the saints.[4] The liturgy was one of the most important tasks of the religious, and placing a local saint at the centre of the work of God showed how highly the custodians of the saints held their patrons.

The liturgy can be broadly divided into the divine office, the Mass and the celebration of less regular occasions such as church consecration, ordination and processions. Although most of the Mass and office was sung from memory, liturgical books were used to help. The parts of the Mass and office which varied through the year, known as the Proper, featured prominently in liturgical books.[5] Included in the Proper were those sections specially selected or composed for the feast days of the saints. One of the major features required for the celebration of a saint's feast was the Mass dedicated to them. A full Mass-set for a saint would include a series of specified prayers: the collect, secret, preface and post-communion.[6] These could be new compositions, though sometimes they were copied from another saint. If a saint was not locally significant, the religious may have used the common of the saints, a series of prayers based on the type of saint. These categories were generally confessor, martyr and virgin, occasionally including further subcategories.[7] There was a conscious grading of feast days, often with more elaboration for those saints who had a shrine nearby or who had a special association for a community.[8]

There are several Mass-books surviving from our period and containing Proper material for English saints. Kenelm receives a full Mass-set in the *Winchcombe Sacramentary*, with the addition of a prayer for vespers.[9] This Mass-set is copied, including the vespers prayer – although it is marked as *alia* – in the *Missal of Robert of Jumièges*. It accompanies five other Masses for English saints, one each for Guthlac, Botulf and Alban and two for Edward the Martyr, found at the beginning of the text.[10] Masses for the following feasts of English saints are found in the *sanctorale* of the *Missal of Robert of Jumièges:* Eormenhild, Cuthbert, Dunstan, Augustine of Canterbury, Æthelthryth, the translation of Swithun, Æthelwold of Winchester, Oswald of Northumbria, the translation of Æthelwold, Edmund the Martyr and Birinus.[11] The eleventh-century *Giso Sacramentary*, another bishop's book traditionally linked to Bishop Giso of Wells (1060–1088), contains Masses for the feasts of the English saints: Patrick, Edward the Martyr, Cuthbert, Guthlac, Ælfheah, Dunstan, Aldhelm, Augustine of Canterbury, Eadburh, Alban, Æthelthryth, Swithun, Grimbald, the translation of Swithun, the deposition of Alban, the translation of Cuthbert, the translation of Birinus, translation of Æthelwold, the feast of Æthelwold and Oswald of Northumbria.[12]

The late-eleventh-century *Missal of the New Minster* is a remarkably thorough though fragmentary Mass-book. It contains Masses for the translation of Judoc, Eormenhild, Edward the Martyr, Cuthbert, Ælfheah, Dunstan, Æthelberht the Martyr, Augustine of Canterbury, Eadburh, Alban, Æthelthryth, the vigil of the feast of Swithun, the feast of Swithun, Seaxburh, Grimbald, the translation of Swithun, Æthelwold, Oswald of Northumbria, the translation of Cuthbert, the translation of Birinus, the translation of Æthelwold, Edmund the Martyr, the second translation of Birinus, the feast of Birinus and two Masses for the feast of Judoc.[13] The *Missal of St Augustine's Abbey* dates from the late eleventh century and must have been composed later than the 1091 corporate translation at St Augustine's as it contains a Mass to honour the occasion.[14] The other English saints honoured with Masses in this book are Hadrian (Mass erased from manuscript), Laurence of Canterbury, Cuthbert, Mellitus, Liudhard, the translation of Mildrith, Dunstan, in vigil of the feast of Augustine, the feast of Augustine, Alban, Mildrith, Deusdedit, Theodore, Justus, the consecration of Augustine (added in the margin), Edmund the Martyr and Ælfheah.[15] An early-twelfth-century missal from Bury contains Masses for the translation of Jurmin, Eormenhild, Oswald of Worcester, Cuthbert, Dunstan, Augustine of Canterbury, Botulf, Alban, Æthelthryth, Kenelm, Æthelwold, Oswald of Northumbria, Osyth, Edmund of East Anglia and Birinus.[16] The fragmentary sacramentary of St Albans – dated to c. 1160, making it our latest Mass-book – includes Mas-sets for Cuthbert, Ælfheah, Dunstan, Swithun, the invention of Alban, Oswald, the octave of Alban, Augustine of Canterbury and Edmund of East Anglia.[17]

Patterns emerge from the saints honoured with feast day Masses in these texts. Cuthbert and Alban receive Masses in six out of seven Mass-books. Augustine of Canterbury has a Mass in all of the six later Mass-books, as do Dunstan and Oswald of Northumbria.[18] Edmund of East Anglia has a Mass in five of the books whilst Ælfheah, Æthelthryth, Æthelwold, Birinus and Swithun feature in four. There are also a number of saints unique to certain books. Patrick is found only in the *Giso Sacramentary*, perhaps linking it to Glastonbury.[19] Judoc receives three Masses for two occasions in the *Missal of the New Minster* but does not have a dedicated Mass in any of the other Mass-books. Similarly the locally important figures of Canterbury, Hadrian, Laurence, Mellitus, Liudhard, Mildrith, Deusdedit, Theodore and Justus, are unique to the *Missal of St Augustine's Abbey*. The twelfth-century missal from Bury also contains saints of more local interest in Osyth and Jurmin. Greater elaboration was afforded to patrons and local saints. The New Minster apparently celebrated Masses to Swithun in vigil of his feast, on the day of his feast and on the day of his translation. Not to be outdone, St Augustine's celebrated their founder on four occasions including a Mass marking his consecration as bishop. The inclusion of English saints within the *sanctorale* seems to have been established by the tenth century, but real incorporation became standard in the eleventh century. The liturgical sources do not show any concerted effort to exclude English saints following the Norman Conquest, although there was perhaps an increased localism.

Other forms of Mass also included mention of or dedication to English saints. Masses for the relics of the church at St Augustine's and Winchcombe include their respective patrons, Augustine and Kenelm.[20] The *Red Book of Darley* does not contain a feast day Mass for an English saint, but it does include a daily votive Mass in honour of Swithun.[21] An individual Mass text was not required, however, to mark the feast of a saint as one could use a Mass-set from the common of the saints. The seven Mass-books discussed previously, as well as the *Red Book of Darley*, all contain common material for saints. English saints were also included in the text of the canon of the mass in a few cases.[22] The beginning of the canon does not survive in the late tenth-century *Winchcombe Sacramentary*, but it does contain the text from the end of the first intercession. The saints clearly listed there are Augustine, Gregory, Jerome, Benedict and Florentius. Additions to the second intercession consist of Kenelm, Genevieve and Eulalia. All of these unorthodox entries have been struck out, perhaps as a result of the movement of the book from England, probably Winchcombe, to Fleury in the eleventh century.[23] The canon is similarly added to in the *Missal of Robert of Jumièges*, with the first intercession ending with the additional names of George, Benedict, Martin and Gregory. Æthelthryth and Gertrude are also appended to the list in the second intercession.[24] This early eleventh-century Mass-book appears to have been either written at or for one of the great houses of East Anglia, Pfaff suggests Ely or Peterborough.[25] The eleventh-century *Red Book of Darley* also contains an unusual list of saints in the first intercession, adding Hilary, Martin, Benedict, Gregory, Augustine, Amand and an otherwise unknown Caurentius.[26] Some of these additions may be explained by the use of exemplars which included them, especially the more unusual ones. There is a clear case, however, for the deliberate inclusion of certain saints in the canon where they reflect local patrons, as with Kenelm and Æthelthryth, or are important figures in English Christianity, such as Augustine, Benedict, Gregory and perhaps Martin.

The office consisted of the corporate prayer sung at eight points throughout the day and night: the hours of matins, lauds, prime, terce, sext, none, vespers and compline. The liturgy of the hours was 'dominated by the recitation of the psalms', but on a feast day, short collects could be interspersed.[27] These collects were often borrowed from the Mass-sets in use and a total of four were usually required for a feast day.[28] There are fewer surviving texts from medieval England for the office than the Mass. We have four pre-Conquest and two post-Conquest collectars. The *Durham Collectar*, *Ælfwine's Prayerbook*, the *Wulfstan Portiforium* and the *Leofric Collectar* make up the pre-Conquest examples and have all been edited. Of these only the *Wulfstan Portiforium* contains offices for English saints, and these are mostly entries of a single prayer. One prayer is provided for Wærburh, Eormenhild, Oswald of Worcester, Edward the Martyr, Cuthbert, Dunstan, Æthelberht the Martyr, Augustine of Canterbury, Aldhelm and Bede, Botulf, Seaxburh, Oswald of Northumbria, Cuthburh, Wilfrid and Edmund the Martyr. Two prayers are provided for Eadburh and Headda and three for Alban, Grimbald, Kenelm, Beornstan and Judoc. A functionally full set of prayers was provided for Æthelthryth, the translation of Swithun, Æthelwold and Justus. On his feast, Swithun is provided with six prayers whilst Birinus has five for his feast as well as one for his octave.[29] All four books contain a common of the saints which could be used to fill any gaps. The post-Conquest books are the *Winchcombe Breviary* and the *Sherborne Cartulary*. The *Sherborne Cartulary* dates to c. 1146 and combines forty-one charter items relating to Sherborne Abbey, with liturgical material including Gospel readings and collects. The collect and reading for fifteen feasts survive, one of which is for Wulfsige.[30] The *Winchcombe Breviary*, dating to the 1170s, contains office material for Kenelm, Cuthbert and Oswald of Northumbria.[31] The material for Kenelm is a full twelve lessons to be read at matins, which have here been drawn from the eleventh-century *Vita* of Kenelm, as well as the collects, chapters, psalms and other chant required to celebrate the office on the saint's feast day.[32]

The calendar of a church facilitated not only the tracking of the feasts of the year but also provided help in deciding what form the celebration of those feasts took. Feast days could be ranked by importance to the religious foundation. The most basic division was whether a feast was simple or double – that is, whether they celebrated the vespers before the feast or both the vespers before and the vespers on the day itself. Various other degrees of elaboration could differentiate the feasts, including the wearing of copes or albs and the number of lections read at matins.[33] A feast could be marked as important in the calendar through the use of colour, majuscule, crosses and other indicative marks or additional annotation. Importance could also be indicated through the inclusion of a vigil or octave for a feast.[34]

For example, the feast of Oswald of Northumbria (5 August), recorded in the mid-twelfth-century calendar from Durham, Cambridge, Jesus College MS. Q B 6, is written in green ink and marked *cappis*, meaning it was to be celebrated by the choir wearing copes as was appropriate for a solemn feast. This calendar includes an octave of the feast, this time written in normal ink but marked as *xii*.

lc. – that is, twelve lessons to be read at matins.[35] The connection between Oswald and Durham was one of locality and relics. The feast of a church's patron could likewise be marked, as found in the St Peter's, Gloucester calendar in Oxford, Jesus College, MS., 10. Here the feast of Peter and Paul (29 June) is written in blue capitals and is to be celebrated in copes with a vigil the day before and an octave celebrated in copes as well.[36] As long as a foundation had a calendar and a common of the saints, any feast could feasibly be observed. For instance, the apparent fading of Guthlac's popularity when looking at Mass-sets is countered somewhat by his presence in the calendars from our period. An eleventh-century calendar from Crowland includes a unique pre-1100 witness for the feast of Pega, Guthlac's sister, as well as including Guthlac in blue capitals to emphasise his importance.[37] Guthlac's feast day is recorded in both of the later calendars mentioned previously, as well as in twenty of the twenty-four early-English calendars which contain an entry for April, as tabulated by Rushforth.[38]

For English saints the most commonly observed feasts were the death of the saint. Occasions such as inventions, consecrations or translations could also be commemorated, usually at a saint's main shrine or at a church particularly associated with them.[39] However, the feasts of the translation of ten English saints were often recorded in calendars beyond their main shrine: the feasts of Ælfheah, Æthelthryth, Æthelwold, Edith, Edmund the Martyr, Edward the Confessor, Edward the Martyr, Swithun, Cuthbert and Oswald of Worcester.[40] It is impossible to know which of these recorded feasts were actually kept as represented in the English calendars. It seems plausible that feasts added in later hands were observed at least for a time following their notation and that the feasts of patrons and saints with local relics were kept. Calendars were not only products of the moment of their creation but were also cumulative documents that were sometimes used for centuries and which shed light on the 'current of devotion' at specific religious foundations.[41]

The calendar was not the only place where saints were listed en masse. The litany of the saints was both a written repository of potential intercessors and a propitiatory element deployed in various parts of the liturgy and elsewhere. The litany of the saints was a list of saints which most often began with the threefold *Kyrie Eleison*, 'Lord, have mercy', followed by an invocation of the Trinity and each of the individual persons of the Trinity. What followed was an invocation of the saints by category beginning with the Virgin Mary and then the archangels, patriarchs, apostles, martyrs, confessors and virgins with a petition to 'pray for us' (*ora pro nobis*) after each name. The invocations were followed by supplications to God to be delivered from evil and to aid the Church and its people. Then followed invocations of *Agnus Dei* and the litany was closed with a repetition of the threefold *Kyrie*.[42]

The litany was not something performed in isolation but was generally a part of a ceremonial occasion or a response to a specific event. Bede records that the Augustinian missionaries chanted litanies and said prayers, in procession to the meeting with Æthelberht of Kent.[43] Litanies were also chanted in the procession of Oswald's relics against plague in Worcester.[44] From the manuscript context,

Lapidge has deduced that litanies were used in the dedication of a church, as a part of the office, as a part of the visitation of the sick or dying and in the service for Holy Saturday or potentially as a part of the ordination of a monk.[45] Litanies formed a part of most processions, including those in Lent and on the Rogation Days, the dedication of cemeteries and the consecration of bishops.[46] The litany generally had a propitiatory tone, deployed as it was to secure the success of an occasion or to avert or overcome a crisis.[47]

As with the calendar, the saints in the litany could be marked out for distinction. For example, the mid-eleventh-century litany in the Bury Psalter calls for the petitions to Peter, Edmund of East Anglia, Benedict, Botulf and Jurmin to be repeated.[48] This would emphasise two foundational figures of the Church as well as the saints whose bodies rested at Bury whenever a litany was called for. An early-twelfth-century litany from Ely also marks Peter out for repetition as the patron of the abbey church, but Æthelthryth is marked in capitals, and the English saints Alban, Edmund of East Anglia, Ælfheah, Birinus, Swithun, Æthelwold, Wilfrid, Cuthbert, Botulf, Neot, Seaxburh, Wihtburh and Eormenhild were included.[49]

Similar in form to the litany though different in tone is the hymn referred to as the *Laudes Regiae*. This hymn of praise, originally from Francia, invokes the conquering God in 'jubilant acclamations' in praise of a ruler or rulers.[50] As a form, it was unknown to pre-Conquest England, but the Normans in England wrote their own and developed a unique style.[51] There are two *Laudes Regiae* texts which survive from our period in British Library, Cotton, Vitellius, E.XII and in the *Cosin Gradual*, both of which are late eleventh century. The Vitellius, E.XII text has become associated with the coronation of Queen Matilda at Pentecost, 1068.[52] The structure of the Vitellius, E.XII text is similar to a litany, with help being asked for specifically for Pope Alexander II (1061–1073), King William I, Queen Matilda and Ealdred, Archbishop of York. These named benefactors were followed by more general requests for aid for the bishops, for the abbots and for the English leaders and their armies.[53] The *Cosin Gradual* text is similar in structure, although it does not include names for the individuals, places the Archbishop between the King and Queen and does not include the bishops and abbots at all. Also, the Cosin text introduces the king-saints Edmund of East Anglia and Oswald of Northumbria to the king's section and the Archbishops Augustine, Dunstan (in capitals) and Ælfheah to the archbishop's section.[54]

Notes

1 Harper, p. 12.
2 On punishment for lack of proper observance see Goscelin, *Miracula S. Yuonis*, pp. lxiv–lxvi; *Liber Eliensis*, pp. 208–9; Goscelin, *Miracula S. Mildrethe*, pp. 179–81. On miracles being stopped see Lantfred, *Miracula S. Swithuni*, pp. 292–7.
3 William Christian, *Person and God in a Spanish Valley* (New York, NY: Seminar, 1972), p. 44.
4 See chapters II and V.
5 Harper, pp. 58–64.
6 Nicholas Orchard, 'An Anglo-Saxon Mass for St Willibrord and Its Later Liturgical Use', *Anglo-Saxon England*, 24 (1995), 1–10 (p. 1).

7 Bartlett, *Why Can the Dead*, p. 117.
8 Ibid., pp. 120–8.
9 Davril, p. 170.
10 H. A. Wilson, ed., *The Missal of Robert of Jumièges*, Henry Bradshaw Society, 11 (London: Harrison, 1896), pp. 3–7.
11 Ibid., p. xxviii.
12 F. E. Warren, ed., *The Leofric Missal, as Used in the Cathedral of Exeter during the Episcopate of Its First Bishop, A.D. 1050–1072* (Oxford: Clarendon, 1883), pp. 303–7.
13 D. H. Turner, ed., *The Missal of the New Minster, Winchester: Le Havre, Bibliothèque Municipale, MS.330*, Henry Bradshaw Society, 93 (Leighton Buzzard: Faith, 1962).
14 Pfaff, *Liturgy*, p. 113; Martin Rule, ed., *The Missal of St Augustine's Abbey: With Excerpts from the Antiphonary and Lectionary of the Same Monastery* (Cambridge: Cambridge University Press, 1896), p. 110.
15 Rule, pp. 72–157.
16 Victor Leroquais, *Les Sacramentaires et les Missels Manuscrits des Bibliothèques Publiques de France*, 4 vols (Paris: Leroquais, 1925), I, pp. 219–22.
17 Rodney M. Thomson, *Manuscripts from St Albans Abbey, 1066–1235*, 2 vols (Woodbridge: Brewer, 1982), I, p. 110.
18 Presuming the Oswald from the St Albans sacramentary is in fact Oswald of Northumbria, as Thomson does not indicate.
19 Pfaff, *Liturgy*, pp. 124–6.
20 Rule, pp. 139–40; Pfaff, *Liturgy*, p. 175.
21 Pfaff, *Liturgy*, p. 95.
22 That is the intercessory prayers asking the listed saints – as well as Christ, the Virgin Mary and Joseph – to aid those taking part in the Mass. The list is usually made up of universal saints from the early Christian period.
23 Davril, pp. 9, 33–36.
24 Wilson, *Jumièges*, pp. 45–7.
25 Pfaff, *Liturgy*, pp. 88–91.
26 Ibid., pp. 94–6.
27 Harper, pp. 74–7.
28 Alice Corrêa, ed., *The Durham Collectar*, Henry Bradshaw Society, 107 (Woodbridge: Boydell, 1992), pp. 3–4.
29 Anselm Hughes, ed., *The Portiforium of Saint Wulstan: Corpus Christi College, Cambridge, MS.391*, Henry Bradshaw Society, 89–90, 2 vols (Leighton Buzzard: Faith, 1958), I, pp. 93–151.
30 Pfaff, *Liturgy*, pp. 176–9.
31 Leroquais, *Les Bréviaires*, IV, pp. 283–5.
32 Love, *Eleventh-Century*, pp. 130–4.
33 Harper, pp. 53–7; Lapidge, *Swithun*, pp. 104–5.
34 Rebecca Rushforth, ed., *Saints in English Kalendars Before A.D. 1100*, Henry Bradshaw Society, 117 (London: Boydell, 2008), p. 3.
35 Francis Wormald, ed., *English Benedictine Kalendars After A.D. 1100*, Henry Bradshaw Society, 77 & 82, 2 vols (London: Harrison, 1939 & 1946), I, p. 175.
36 Ibid., II, pp. 49–50.
37 Francis Wormald, ed., *English Kalendars Before A.D. 1100*, Henry Bradshaw Society, 72 (London: Harrison, 1934), pp. 254–65.
38 Rushforth, Table IV.
39 Rule, pp. 90, 110, 121.
40 Richard W. Pfaff, 'Telling Liturgical Times in the Middle Ages', in *Procession, Performance, Liturgy, and Ritual: Essays in Honour of Bryan R. Gillingham*, ed. by Nancy van Deusen, Musicological Studies, 62/8 (Ottawa: Institute of Mediaeval Music, 2007), pp. 43–64 (pp. 53–7).

41 Richard W. Pfaff, 'The Calendar', in *The Eadwine Psalter: Text, Image and Monastic Culture in Twelfth-Century Canterbury*, ed. by Margaret Gibson, and others, Publications of the Modern Humanities Research Association, 14 (University Park, PA: Pennsylvania State University Press, 1992), pp. 53–87 (p. 62).
42 Michael Lapidge, ed., *Anglo-Saxon Litanies of the Saints*, Henry Bradshaw Society, 106 (Woodbridge: Boydell, 1991), p. 1.
43 Bede, *HE*, I.25, pp. 74–7.
44 Eadmer, *Miracula S. Oswaldi*, pp. 318–19. For other uses of the litany in miracle petitions, see Herman, *Miracula S. Edmundi*, pp. 58–9, 142–5.
45 Lapidge, *Litanies*, pp. 43–9.
46 For processions, see Lapidge, *Litanies*, pp. 48–9. On the dedication of cemeteries, see Gittos, pp. 46–48. For an example of a litany used in the consecration of a bishop, see H. A. Wilson, ed., *The Pontifical of Magdalen College: With an Appendix of Extracts from Other English MSS. of the Twelfth Century*, Henry Bradshaw Society, 39 (London: Harrison, 1910), pp. 97–8.
47 Michael McCormick, 'The Liturgy of War in the Early Middle Ages', *Viator*, 15 (1984), 1–24 (pp. 7–8).
48 Lapidge, *Litanies*, pp. 296–9.
49 Nigel J. Morgan, ed., *English Monastic Litanies of the Saints After 1100*, Henry Bradshaw Society, 119–120, 2 vols (Woodbridge: Boydell, 2012–2013), I, pp. 30, 104–7.
50 Ernst H. Kantorowicz, *Laudes Regiae: A Study in Liturgical Acclamations and Mediaeval Ruler Worship*, University of California Publications in History, 33 (Berkeley, CA: University of California Press, 1958), pp. 13–14.
51 Herbert Edward John Cowdrey, 'The Anglo-Norman Laudes Regiae', *Viator*, 12 (1981), 37–78 (p. 67).
52 Kantorowicz, p. 171.
53 Cowdrey, pp. 70–1.
54 Ibid., pp. 72–3.

Bibliography

Primary Sources

Arnold, Thomas, ed., *Symeonis Monachi Opera Omnia*, Rolls Series, 75, 2 vols (London: Longman, 1882–1885)

Barrow, Julia, ed., *English Episcopal Acta: Hereford 1079–1234*, English Episcopal Acta, 7 (Oxford: Oxford University Press, 1993)

Bartlett, Robert, ed. and trans., *The Miracles of St Æbbe of Coldingham and St Margaret of Scotland* (Oxford: Clarendon, 2003)

Bethell, D., ed., 'The Lives of St Osyth of Essex and St Osyth of Aylesbury', *Analecta Bollandiana*, 88 (1970), 75–127

——, ed., 'The Miracles of St Ithamar', *Analecta Bollandiana*, 89 (1971), 421–37

Birch, Walter de Grey, ed., *Liber Vitae: Register and Martyrology of New Minster and Hyde Abbey* (London: Simpkin, 1892)

Blake, E. O., *Liber Eliensis*, Camden Third Series, 92 (London: Royal Historical Society, 1962)

Bolland, John, and others, eds, *Acta Sanctorum*, 68 vols (Antwerp: Société des Bollandistes, 1643–1940)

Byrhtferth of Ramsey, *The Lives of St Oswald and St Ecgwine*, ed. and trans. by Michael Lapidge (Oxford: Clarendon, 2009)

Cheney, C. R. and Bridgett E. A. Jones, eds, *English Episcopal Acta: Canterbury 1162–1190*, English Episcopal Acta, 2 (Oxford: Oxford University Press, 1986)

Chibnall, Marjorie, ed. and trans., *The Ecclesiastical History of Orderic Vitalis*, 6 vols (Oxford: Clarendon, 1969–1980)

Colgrave, Bertram, ed. and trans., *The Earliest Life of Gregory the Great, by an Anonymous Monk of Whitby* (Cambridge: Cambridge University Press, 1985)

——, ed. and trans., *Felix's Life of Saint Guthlac* (Cambridge: Cambridge University Press, 1956)

——, ed. and trans., *The Life of Bishop Wilfrid by Eddius Stephanus* (Cambridge: Cambridge University Press, 1985)

——, 'The Post-Bedan Miracles and Translations of St Cuthbert', in *The Early Cultures of North-West Europe*, ed. by Cyril Fox and Bruce Dickins (Cambridge: Cambridge University Press, 1950), pp. 305–32

——, ed. and trans., *Two Lives of St Cuthbert: A Life by an Anonymous Monk of Lindisfarne and Bede's Prose Life* (Cambridge: Cambridge University Press, 1985)

Colgrave, Bertram and R. A. B. Mynors, eds and trans, *Bede's Ecclesiastical History of the English People* (Oxford: Oxford University Press, 1969)

Colker, Marvin L., ed., 'A Hagiographic Polemic', *Mediaeval Studies*, 39 (1977), 60–108
———, ed., 'Texts of Jocelyn of Canterbury Which Relate to the History of Barking Abbey', *Studia Monastica*, 7 (1965), 383–460
Corrêa, Alice, ed., *The Durham Collectar*, Henry Bradshaw Society, 107 (Woodbridge: Boydell, 1992)
Davis, R. H. C., and Marjorie Chibnall, eds and trans, *The Gesta Guillelmi of William of Poitiers* (Oxford: Clarendon, 1998)
Davril, Anselme, ed., *The Winchcombe Sacramentary*, Henry Bradshaw Society, 109 (London: Boydell, 1995)
Eadmer of Canterbury, *The Life of St Anselm*, ed. and trans. by R. W. Southern (Oxford: Clarendon, 1962)
———, *Lives and Miracles of Saints Oda, Dunstan, and Oswald*, ed. and trans. by Andrew J. Turner and Bernard J. Muir (Oxford: Clarendon, 2006)
Ewald, Paul and Ludovic M. Hartmann, eds, *Gregorii I Papae Registrum Epistolorum*, Monumenta Germaniae Historica; Epistolae 1–2, 2 vols (Berlin: Weidmann, 1891–1899)
Fell, Christine E., ed., *Edward, King and Martyr* (Leeds: University of Leeds, 1971)
Geoffrey of Burton, *Life and Miracles of St Modwenna*, ed. and trans. by Robert Bartlett (Oxford: Clarendon, 2002)
Giles, J. A., ed., *Vita Quorundum Anglo-Saxonum* (London: Smith, 1854)
Goscelin of Saint-Bertin, *The Hagiography of the Female Saints of Ely*, ed. and trans. by Rosalind C. Love (Oxford: Clarendon, 2004)
Guibert de Nogent, *Autobiographie*, ed. and trans. by Edmond-René Labande, Classiques de l'histoire de France au Moyen Âge, 34 (Paris: Belles Lettres, 1981)
Haddan, Arthur West and William Stubbs, eds, *Councils and Ecclesiastical Documents Relating to Great Britain and Ireland*, 3 vols (Oxford: Clarendon, 1869–78)
Harper-Bill, Christopher, ed., *English Episcopal Acta: Norwich 1070–1214*, English Episcopal Acta, 6 (Oxford: Oxford University Press, 1990)
Hayward, Paul Antony, ed., 'The *Miracula Inventionis Beate Mylburge Virginis* Attributed to the Lord Ato, Cardinal Bishop of Ostia', *English Historical Review*, 114 (1999), 543–73
Herman the Archdeacon and Goscelin of Saint-Bertin, *The Miracles of St Edmund*, ed. and trans. by Tom Licence with Lynda Lockyer (Oxford: Clarendon, 2014)
Hudson, John, ed. and trans., *Historia Ecclesie Abbendonensis*, 2 vols (Oxford: Clarendon, 2002–2007)
Hughes, Anselm, ed., *The Portiforium of Saint Wulstan: Corpus Christi College, Cambridge, MS.391*, Henry Bradshaw Society, 89–90, 2 vols (Leighton Buzzard: Faith, 1958)
Jaager, Werner, ed., *Bedas Metrische Vita Sancti Cuthberti*, Palaestra, 198 (Leipzig: Mayer & Müller, 1935)
Kaniecka, Mary Simplicia, ed. and trans., *Vita Sancti Ambrosii, Mediolanensis Episcopi, a Paulino eius Notario ad Beatum Augustinum Conscripta*, Catholic University of America Patristic Studies, 16 (Washington, DC: Catholic University of America, 1928)
Kemp, Brian, ed., *English Episcopal Acta: Salisbury 1078–1217*, English Episcopal Acta, 18 (Oxford: Oxford University Press, 1999)
———, trans., 'The Miracles of the Hand of St James: Translated with an Introduction', *Berkshire Archaeological Journal*, 65 (1970), 1–19
Knowles, David and Christopher L. Brooke, eds and trans, *The Monastic Constitutions of Lanfranc* (Oxford: Clarendon, 2002)

Lapidge, Michael, ed., *Anglo-Saxon Litanies of the Saints*, Henry Bradshaw Society, 106 (Woodbridge: Boydell, 1991)

Lapidge, Michael and others, *The Cult of St Swithun*, Winchester Studies, 4.II (Oxford: Clarendon, 2003)

Leroquais, Victor, *Les Bréviaires Manuscrits des Bibliothèques Publiques de France*, 6 vols (Paris: Leroquais, 1934)

——, *Les Sacramentaires et les Missels Manuscrits des Bibliothèques Publiques de France*, 4 vols (Paris: Leroquais, 1925)

Love, Rosalind C., trans., 'The Life of St Wulfsige of Sherborne by Goscelin of Saint-Bertin', in *St Wulfsige and Sherborne: Essays to Celebrate the Millennium of the Benedictine Abbey, 998–1998*, ed. by K. Barker and others (Oxford: Oxbow, 2005), pp. 98–123

——, ed. and trans., *Three Eleventh-Century Saints' Lives: Vita S. Birini, Vita et Miracula S. Kenelmi, and Vita S. Rumwoldi* (Oxford: Clarendon, 1996)

Luard, Henry Richards, ed., *Annales Monastici*, Rolls Series, 36, 5 vols (London: Longman, 1864–1869)

Macray, W. D., ed., *Chronicon Abbatiae de Evesham, ad Annum 1418*, Rolls Series, 29 (London: Longman, 1863)

——, ed., *Chronicon Abbatiae Rameseiensis*, Rolls Series, 83 (London: Longman, 1886)

Mellows, W. T. and Alexander Bell, eds, *The Chronicle of Hugh Candidus, a Monk of Peterborough with La Geste De Burch* (London: Oxford University Press, 1949)

Migne, Jacques-Paul and others, eds, *Patrologia Latina*, 221 vols (Paris: Garnier, 1863–1891)

Milfull, Inge B., ed. and trans., *The Hymns of the Anglo-Saxon Church: A Study and Edition of the 'Durham Hymnal'*, Cambridge Studies in Anglo-Saxon England, 17 (Cambridge: Cambridge University Press, 1996)

Morgan, Nigel J., ed., *English Monastic Litanies of the Saints After 1100*, Henry Bradshaw Society, 119–120, 2 vols (Woodbridge: Boydell, 2012–2013)

Neininger, Falko, ed., *English Episcopal Acta: London 1076–1187*, English Episcopal Acta, 15 (Oxford: Oxford University Press, 1999)

Osbern, '*Translatio Sancti Ælfegi Cantuariensis Archiepiscopi et Martiris*', ed. and trans. by Alexander R. Rumble and Rosemary Morris, in *The Reign of Cnut: King of England, Denmark and Norway*, ed. by Alexander R. Rumble (London: Leicester University Press, 1994), pp. 283–315

Raine, James, ed., *The Historians of the Church of York and Its Archbishops*, Rolls Series, 71, 3 vols (London: Longman, 1879–1894)

——, ed., *Miscellanea Biographica: Oswinus, Rex Northumbriae, Cuthbertus, Episcopus Lindisfariensis, Eata, Episcopus Haugustaldensis*, Publications of the Surtees Society, 8 (London: Nichols, 1838)

——, ed., *The Priory of Hexham*, Publications of the Surtees Society, 44 & 46, 2 vols (Durham: Andrews, 1864–1865)

——, ed., *Reginaldi Monachi Dunelmensis Libellus de Admirandis Beati Cuthberti Virtutibus quae Novellis Patratae sunt Temporibus*, Publications of the Surtees Society, 1 (London: Nichols, 1835)

Ramsey, Francis M. R., ed., *English Episcopal Acta: Bath and Wells 1061–1205*, English Episcopal Acta, 10 (Oxford: Oxford University Press, 1995)

Riley, Henry Thomas, ed., *Gesta Abbatum Monasterii Sancti Albani a Thoma Walsingham, Regnante Ricardo Secundo*, Rolls Series, 28, 3 vols (London: Longman, 1867–1869)

Rollason, David, ed., 'Goscelin of Canterbury's Account of the Translation and Miracles of St Mildrith: An Edition with Notes', *Mediaeval Studies*, 48 (1986), 139–210

———, *The Mildrith Legend: A Study in Early Medieval Hagiography in England* (Leicester: Leicestershire University Press, 1982)

Rule, Martin, ed., *The Missal of St Augustine's Abbey: With Excerpts from the Antiphonary and Lectionary of the Same Monastery* (Cambridge: Cambridge University Press, 1896)

Rushforth, Rebecca, ed., *Saints in English Kalendars Before A.D. 1100*, Henry Bradshaw Society, 117 (London: Boydell, 2008)

Russel, D. W., and others, eds and trans, 'La Vie Seinte Osith, Virge et Martire (MS BL Addit. 70513, ff. 134va–146vb)', *Papers on Language & Literature*, 41 (2005), 339–444

Scott, John, ed. and trans., *The Early History of Glastonbury: An Edition, Translation and Study of William of Malmesbury's De Antiquitate Glastonie Ecclesie* (Woodbridge: Boydell, 1981)

Scragg, D. G., ed., *The Vercelli Homilies and Related Texts*, Early English Text Society, 300 (Oxford: Oxford University Press, 1992)

Smith, David M., ed., *English Episcopal Acta: Lincoln 1067–1185*, English Episcopal Acta, 1 (Oxford: Oxford University Press, 1980)

———, ed., *English Episcopal Acta: Lincoln 1186–1206*, English Episcopal Acta, 4 (Oxford: Oxford University Press, 1986)

Snape, M. G., ed., *English Episcopal Acta: Durham 1153–1195*, English Episcopal Acta, 24 (Oxford: Oxford University Press, 2002)

Stubbs, William, ed., *The Memorials of St Dunstan*, Rolls Series, 63 (London: Longman, 1874)

Symeon of Durham, *Libellus De Exordio Atque Procursu Istius, Hoc Est Dunhelmensis, Ecclesie*, ed. and trans. by David Rollason (Oxford: Clarendon, 2000)

Symons, Thomas, ed. and trans., *Regularis Concordia Anglicae Nationis Monachorum Sanctimonialiumque* (London: Nelson, 1953)

Talbot, C. H., ed., 'The Life of St Wulsin of Sherborne by Goscelin', *Revue Bénédictine*, 49 (1959), 68–85

Thomas of Marlborough, *History of the Abbey of Evesham*, ed. and trans. by Jane Sayers and Leslie Watkiss (Oxford: Clarendon, 2003)

Thomas of Monmouth, *The Life and Miracles of William of Norwich*, ed. and trans. by M. R. James and Augustus Jessopp (Cambridge: Cambridge University Press, 1896)

Thomson, Rodney M., *Manuscripts from St Albans Abbey, 1066–1235*, 2 vols (Woodbridge: Brewer, 1982)

Thorpe, B., ed., *Ancient Laws and Institutes of England*, 3 vols (London: Eyre & Spottiswoode, 1840)

Turner, D. H., ed., *The Missal of the New Minster, Winchester: Le Havre, Bibliothèque Municipale, MS.330*, Henry Bradshaw Society, 93 (Leighton Buzzard: Faith, 1962)

Walford, Edward, trans., *The Ecclesiastical History of Sozomen* (London: Bohn, 1855)

Warren, F. E., ed., *The Leofric Missal, as Used in the Cathedral of Exeter during the Episcopate of Its First Bishop, A.D. 1050–1072* (Oxford: Clarendon, 1883)

Whatley, E. Gordon, ed. and trans., *The Saint of London: The Life and Miracles of St Erkenwald*, Medieval & Renaissance Texts & Studies, 58 (Binghamton, NY: Medieval & Renaissance Texts & Studies, 1989)

William of Malmesbury, *Gesta Pontificum Anglorum*, ed. and trans. by M. Winterbottom, 2 vols (Oxford: Clarendon, 2007)

———, *Gesta Regum Anglorum*, ed. and trans. by R. Mynors, and others, 2 vols (Oxford: Clarendon, 1998–1999)

———, *Saints' Lives*, ed. and trans. by M. Winterbottom and R. Thomson (Oxford: Clarendon, 2002)

Wilmart, A., ed., 'La légend de Ste Édith en Prose et Vers par le Moine Goscelin', *Analecta Bollandiana*, 56 (1938), 5–101, 265–307

Wilson, H. A., ed., *The Missal of Robert of Jumièges*, Henry Bradshaw Society, 11 (London: Harrison, 1896)

———, ed., *The Pontifical of Magdalen College: With an Appendix of Extracts from Other English MSS. of the Twelfth Century*, Henry Bradshaw Society, 39 (London: Harrison, 1910)

Wilson, James, ed., *The Register of the Priory of St Bees*, Publications of the Surtees Society, 126 (Durham: Surtees Society, 1915)

Winterbottom, Michael, ed., *Three Lives of English Saints* (Toronto: Pontifical Institute of Mediaeval Studies for the Centre for Medieval Studies, 1972)

Winterbottom, Michael and Michael Lapidge, eds and trans, *The Early Lives of St Dunstan* (Oxford: Clarendon, 2012)

Woodcock, Audrey M., ed., *The Cartulary of the Priory of St Gregory, Canterbury*, Camden Third Series, 88 (London: Royal Historical Society, 1956)

Wormald, Francis, ed., *English Benedictine Kalendars After A.D. 1100*, Henry Bradshaw Society, 77 & 82, 2 vols (London: Harrison, 1939 & 1946)

———, ed., *English Kalendars Before A.D. 1100*, Henry Bradshaw Society, 72 (London: Harrison, 1934)

Wulfstan of Winchester, *The Life of St Æthelwold*, ed. and trans. by Michael Lapidge and Michael Winterbottom (Oxford: Clarendon, 1991)

Secondary Sources

Ambrose, Shannon, 'The Social Context and Political Complexities of Goscelin's Sermon for the Feast of Saint Augustine of Canterbury, the "Apostle of the English"', *Studies in Philology*, 109 (2012), 364–80

Anselment, Raymond A., 'Mary Rich, Countess of Warwick, and the Gift of Tears', *The Seventeenth Century*, 22 (2007), 336–57

Arnold, John, *Belief and Unbelief in Medieval Europe* (London: Hodder Arnold, 2005)

Arnold, John and Caroline Goodson, 'Resounding Community: The History and Meaning of Medieval Church Bells', *Viator*, 43 (2012), 99–130

Asad, Talal, 'Towards a Genealogy of the Concept of Ritual', in *Vernacular Christianity: Essays in the Social Anthropology of Religion Presented to Godfrey Lienhardt*, ed. by Wendy James and Douglas H. Johnson (Oxford: Journal of the Anthropological Society of Oxford, 1988), pp. 73–87

Ashley, Kathleen, 'Introduction: The Moving Subjects of Processional Performance', in *Moving Subjects: Processional Performance in the Middle Ages and the Renaissance*, ed. by Kathleen Ashley and Wim Hüsken, Ludus, 5 (Amsterdam: Rodopi, 2001), pp. 7–34

Bailey, Anne E., 'Modern and Medieval Approaches to Pilgrimage, Gender and Sacred Space', *History and Anthropology*, 24 (2013), 493–512

———, 'Peter Brown and Victor Turner Revisited: Anthropological Approaches to Latin Miracle Narratives in the Medieval West', in *Contextualizing Miracles in the Christian West, 1100–1500: New Historical Approaches*, ed. by Matthew M. Mesley and Louise E. Wilson, Medium Aevum Monographs, 32 (Oxford: The Society for the Study of Medieval Languages and Literature, 2014), pp. 17–39

———, 'The Rich and the Poor, the Lesser and the Great', *Cultural and Social History*, 11 (2014), 9–29

———, 'Wives, Mothers and Widows on Pilgrimage: Categories of "Woman" Recorded at English Healing Shrines in the High Middle Ages', *Journal of Medieval History*, 39 (2013), 197–219

Barlow, Frank, *Edward the Confessor* (London: Eyre & Spottiswoode, 1970)

Barrow, Julia, 'Demonstrative Behaviour and Political Communication in Later Anglo-Saxon England', *Anglo-Saxon England*, 36 (2007), 127–50

Bartlett, Robert, *England Under the Norman and Angevin Kings, 1075–1225* (Oxford: Clarendon, 2000)

———, 'The Hagiography of Angevin England', *Thirteenth-Century England*, 5 (1995), 37–52

———, *The Natural and the Supernatural in the Middle Ages: The Wiles Lecture Given at the Queen's University of Belfast, 2006* (Cambridge: Cambridge University Press, 2008)

———, *Why Can the Dead Do Such Great Things?: Saints and Worshippers from the Martyrs to the Reformation* (Princeton, NJ: Princeton University Press, 2013)

Bell, Adrian R. and Richard S. Dale, 'The Medieval Pilgrimage Business', *Enterprise & Society*, 12 (2011), 601–27

Biddle, Martin, 'Archaeology, Architecture, and the Cult of Saints in Anglo-Saxon England', in *The Anglo-Saxon Church: Papers on History, Architecture, and Archaeology in Honour of Dr. H. M. Taylor*, ed. by L. A. S. Butler and R. K. Morris (London: Council for British Archaeology, 1986), pp. 1–31

Blair, John, *The Church in Anglo-Saxon Society* (Oxford: Oxford University Press, 2005)

———, 'A Handlist of Anglo-Saxon Saints', in *Local Saints and Local Churches in the Early Medieval West*, ed. by Alan Thacker and Richard Sharpe (Oxford: Oxford University Press, 2002), pp. 495–565

———, 'A Saint for Every Minster? Local Cults in Anglo-Saxon England', in *Local Saints and Local Churches in the Early Medieval West*, ed. by Alan Thacker and Richard Sharpe (Oxford: Oxford University Press, 2002), pp. 455–94

Blick, Sarah, 'Votives, Images, Interaction and Pilgrimage to the Tomb and Shrine of St. Thomas Becket, Canterbury Cathedral', in *Push Me, Pull You: Art and Devotional Interaction in Late Medieval and Renaissance Art*, ed. by Sarah Blick and Laura D. Gelfand (Leiden: Brill, 2011), pp. 21–58

Bourdieu, Pierre, *Outline of a Theory of Practice*, trans. by Richard Nice (Cambridge: Cambridge University Press, 1977)

Bowersock, G. W., and others, eds, *Late Antiquity: A Guide to the Postclassical World* (Cambridge, MA: Harvard University Press, 1999)

Boyer, Régis, 'An Attempt to Define the Typology of Medieval Hagiography', in *Hagiography and Medieval Literature: A Symposium*, ed. by Hans Bekker-Nielsen and others (Odense: Odense University Press, 1981), pp. 27–37

Brown, Peter, *The Cult of the Saints: Its Rise and Function in Latin Christianity* (London: SCM, 1981)

———, 'The Rise and Function of the Holy Man in Late Antiquity', *Journal of Roman Studies*, 61 (1971), 80–101

———, *The Rise of Western Christendom*, 2nd edn (Oxford: Blackwell, 2003)

Bussell, Donna Alfano and Jennifer N. Brown, 'Introduction: Barking's Lives, the Abbey and its Abbesses', in *Barking Abbey and Medieval Literary Culture: Authorship and Authority in a Female Community*, ed. by Jennifer N. Brown and Donna Alfano Bussell (Woodbridge: Boydell, 2012), pp. 1–30

Caldwell, John, 'The "Te Deum" in Late Medieval England', *Early Music*, 6 (1978), 188–94

Caraher, William R., 'Abandonment, Authority, and Religious Continuity in Post-Classical Greece', *International Journal of Historical Archaeology*, 14 (2010), 241–54

Christian, William, *Local Religion in Sixteenth-Century Spain* (Princeton, NJ: Princeton University Press, 1981)

——, *Person and God in a Spanish Valley* (New York, NY: Seminar, 1972)

Christie, Neil, *On Bells and Bell-Towers: Origins and Evolutions in Italy and Britain, AD 700–1200*, Brixworth Lecture: Second Series, 4 (Brixworth: The Friends of All Saints' Church, 2004)

Clanchy, M. T., *From Memory to Written Record: England 1066–1307*, 2nd edn (Oxford: Blackwell, 1993)

Cowdrey, Herbert Edward John, 'The Anglo-Norman Laudes Regiae', *Viator*, 12 (1981), 37–78

Cox, J. Charles, *The Sanctuaries and Sanctuary Seekers of Mediaeval England* (London: Allen, 1911)

Crook, John, *The Architectural Setting of the Cult of the Saints in the Early Christian West c. 300–c. 1200* (Oxford: Clarendon, 2000)

——, *English Medieval Shrines* (Woodbridge: Boydell, 2011)

Cross, J. E., 'English Vernacular Saints' Lives before 1000 A.D.', in *Hagiographies: histoire internationale de la littérature hagiographique latine et vernaculaire, en Occident, des origines à 1500*, ed. by G. Philippart and M. Goullet, 7 vols (Turnhout: Brepols, 1994–2018), II, 413–28

Davies, John Reuben, 'Cathedrals and the Cult of Saints in Eleventh and Twelfth Century Wales', in *Cathedrals, Communities and Conflict in the Anglo-Norman World*, ed. by Paul Dalton and others, Studies in the History of Medieval Religion, 38 (Woodbridge: Boydell, 2011), pp. 99–115

d'Avray, David, 'Popular and Elite Religion: Feastdays and Preaching', in *Elite and Popular Religion*, ed. by Kate Cooper and Jeremy Gregory, Studies in Church History, 42 (Woodbridge: Boydell, 2006), pp. 162–79

Di Tota, Mia, 'Saint Cults and Political Alignments in Southern Italy', *Dialectical Anthropology*, 5.4 (1981), 317–29

Duffy, Eamon, 'St. Erkenwald: London's Cathedral Saint and His Legend', in *The Medieval Cathedral: Papers in Honour of Pamela Tudor-Craig*, ed. by Janet Backhouse (Donington: Tyas, 2003), pp. 150–67

Dyas, Dee, 'To Be A Pilgrim: Tactile Piety, Virtual Pilgrimage and the Experience of Place in Christian Pilgrimage', in *Matter of Faith: An Interdisciplinary Study of Relics and Relic Veneration in the Medieval Period*, ed. by James Robinson and others, Research Publication, 195 (London: British Museum, 2014), pp. 1–7

Eade, John, 'Order and Power at Lourdes: Lay Helpers and the Organisation of a Pilgrimage Shrine', in *Contesting the Sacred: The Anthropology of Christian Pilgrimage*, ed. by John Eade and Michael J. Sallnow (London: Routledge, 1991), pp. 51–76

Eade, John and Michael J. Sallnow, 'Introduction', in *Contesting the Sacred: The Anthropology of Christian Pilgrimage*, ed. by John Eade and Michael J. Sallnow (London: Routledge, 1991), pp. 1–29

Egmond, Wolfert S. van, 'The Audience of Early Medieval Hagiographical Texts', in *New Approaches to Medieval Communication*, ed. by Marco Mostert, Utrecht Studies in Medieval Literacy, 1 (Turnhout: Brepols, 1999), pp. 41–67

Finucane, Ronald C., *Miracles and Pilgrims: Popular Beliefs in Medieval England* (London: Dent, 1977)

Flanigan, C. Clifford, 'The Moving Subject: Medieval Liturgical Processions in Semiotic and Cultural Perspective', in *Moving Subjects: Processional Performance in the Middle*

Ages and the Renaissance, ed. by Kathleen Ashley and Wim Hüsken, Ludus, 5 (Amsterdam: Rodopi, 2001), pp. 35–51

Frazer, James, *The Golden Bough: A Study in Magic and Religion*, abr. edn (London: Macmillan, 1980)

Geary, Patrick J., *Furta Sacra: Thefts of Relics in the Central Middle Ages*, rev. edn (Princeton, NJ: Princeton University Press, 1990)

——, *Living With the Dead in the Middle Ages* (Ithaca, NY: Cornell University Press, 1994)

Gennep, Arnold van, *The Rites of Passage*, trans. by Monika B. Vizedom and Gabrielle L. Caffee (Chicago, IL: University of Chicago Press, 1960)

Gittos, Helen, *Liturgy, Architecture, and Sacred Spaces in Anglo-Saxon England* (Oxford: Oxford University Press, 2013)

Goodich, Michael, '*Mirabilis Deus in Sanctis Suis*: Social History and Medieval Miracles', in *Signs, Wonders, Miracles: Representations of Divine Power in the Life of the Church*, ed. by Kate Cooper and Jeremy Gregory, Studies in Church History, 41 (Woodbridge: Boydell, 2005), pp. 135–56

Graeber, David, *Toward an Anthropological Theory of Value: The False Coin of Our Own Dreams* (Basingstoke: Palgrave, 2001)

Gransden, Antonia, *Historical Writing in England c. 550 to c. 1307* (London: Keegan & Paul, 1974)

Gregory-Abbott, Candace, 'Sacred Outlaws: Outlawry and the Medieval Church', in *Outlaws in Medieval and Early Modern England: Crime, Government and Society, c.1066–c.1600*, ed. by John C. Appleby and Paul Dalton (Farnham: Ashgate, 2009), pp. 75–90

Grindal, Bruce, 'Into the Heart of Sisala Experience: Witnessing Death Divination', *Journal of Anthropological Research*, 39 (1983), 60–80

Gurevich, Aron, *Medieval Popular Culture: Problems of Belief and Perception*, trans. by János M. Bak and Paul A. Hollingsworth, Cambridge Studies in Oral and Literate Culture, 14 (Cambridge: Cambridge University Press, 1988)

Hagger, Mark, 'The *Gesta Abbatum Monasterii Sancti Albani*: Litigation and History at St Alban's', *Historical Review*, 81 (2008), 373–98

Hamilton, Mary, *Incubation: The Cure of Disease in Pagan Temples and Christian Churches* (St Andrews: Henderson, 1906)

Hamilton, Sarah, *The Practice of Penance, 900–1050* (Woodbridge: Boydell, 2001)

Hamilton, Sarah and Andrew Spicer, 'Defining the Holy: The Delineation of Sacred Space', in *Defining the Holy: Sacred Space in Medieval and Early Modern Europe*, ed. by Sarah Hamilton and Andrew Spicer (Aldershot: Ashgate, 2005), pp. 1–23

Harper, John, *The Forms and Orders of Western Liturgy from the Tenth to the Eighteenth Century: A Historical Introduction and Guide for Students and Musicians* (Oxford: Clarendon, 1991)

Hartzell, K. D., *Catalogue of Manuscripts Written or Owned in England up to 1200 Containing Music* (Woodbridge: Boydell, 2006)

Hayward, Paul Antony, 'De-Mystifying the Role of Sanctity in Western Christendom', in *The Cult of Saints in Late Antiquity and the Middle Ages: Essays on the Contribution of Peter Brown*, ed. by James Howard-Johnston and Paul Antony Hayward (Oxford: Oxford University Press, 1999), pp. 115–42

——, 'Translation-Narratives in Post-Conquest Hagiography and English Resistance to the Norman Conquest', *Anglo-Norman Studies*, 21 (1999), 67–93

Head, Thomas, *Hagiography and the Cult of the Saints: the Diocese of Orléans, 800–1200*, Cambridge Studies in Medieval Life and Thought: Fourth Series, 14 (Cambridge: Cambridge University Press, 1990)

Heffernan, Thomas J., *Sacred Biography: Saints and Their Biographers in the Middle Ages* (Oxford: Oxford University Press, 1988)

Hill, Joyce, 'The Litaniae Maiores and Minores in Rome, Francia and Anglo-Saxon England: Terminology, Texts and Traditions', *Early Medieval Europe*, 9 (2000), 211–46

Hill, Thomas D., '*Imago Dei*: Genre, Symbolism and Anglo-Saxon Hagiography', in *Holy Men and Holy Women: Old English Prose Saints' Lives and Their Contexts*, ed. by Paul E. Szarmach (Albany: State University of New York Press, 1996), pp. 35–50

Holmes, Megan, 'Ex-Votos: Materiality, Memory, and Cult', in *The Idol in the Age of Art: Objects, Devotions and the Early Modern World*, ed. by Michael Cole and Rebecca Zorach (Aldershot: Ashgate, 2009), pp. 165–88

Hopgood, James F., 'Introduction: Saints and Saints in the Making', in *The Making of Saints: Contesting Sacred Ground*, ed. by James F. Hopgood (Tuscaloosa: University of Alabama Press, 2005), pp. xi–xxi

Horden, Peregrine, 'Saints and Doctors in the Early Byzantine Empire: The Case of Theodore of Sykeon', in *The Church and Healing*, ed. by W. J. Sheils, Studies in Church History, 19 (Oxford: Blackwell, 1982), pp. 1–13

——, 'What's Wrong with Early Medieval Medicine?', *Social History of Medicine*, 24 (2009), 5–25

Howard-Johnston, James, 'Introduction', in *The Cult of Saints in Late Antiquity and the Middle Ages: Essays on the Contribution of Peter Brown*, ed. by James Howard-Johnston and Paul Antony Hayward (Oxford: Oxford University Press, 1999), pp. 1–24

Howe, John, 'Creating Symbolic Landscapes: Medieval Development of Sacred Space', in *Inventing Medieval Landscapes: Senses of Place in Western Europe*, ed. by John Howe and Michael Wolfe (Gainesville: University Press of Florida, 2002), pp. 208–23

Ivakhiv, Adrian, 'Orchestrating Sacred Space: Beyond the "Social Construction" of Nature', *Ecotheology*, 8 (2003), 11–29

Jones, Graham, 'Introduction: Diverse Expressions, Shared Meanings: Surveying Saints across Cultural Boundaries', in Graham Jones, ed., *Saints of Europe: Studies Towards a Survey of Cults and Culture* (Donington: Tyas, 2003), pp. 1–28

Kantorowicz, Ernst H., *Laudes Regiae: A Study in Liturgical Acclamations and Mediaeval Ruler Worship*, University of California Publications in History, 33 (Berkeley, CA: University of California Press, 1958)

Keesing, Roger M., 'On Not Understanding Symbols: Towards an Anthropology of Incomprehension', *HAU: Journal of Ethnographic Theory*, 2 (2012), 406–30

Kemp, E. W., *Canonization and Authority in the Western Church* (Oxford: Oxford University Press, 1948)

Kent, Alexandra, 'Divinity, Miracles and Charity in the Sathya Sai Baba Movement of Malaysia', *Ethnos*, 69 (2004), 43–62

Keynes, Simon, 'An Abbot, an Archbishop, and the Viking Raids of 1006–7 and 1009–12', *Anglo-Saxon England*, 36 (2007), 151–220

King'oo, Clare Costley, *Miserere Mei: The Penitential Psalms in Late Medieval and Early Modern England* (Notre Dame, IN: University of Notre Dame Press, 2012)

Klaniczay, Gábor, 'Dream Healing and Visions in Medieval Latin Miracle Accounts', in *The "Vision Thing": Studying Divine Intervention*, ed. by William A. Christian Jr and

Gábor Klaniczay, Collegium Budapest Workshop Series, 18 (Budapest: Collegium Budapest, 2009), pp. 37–64

———, 'Healing with Certain Conditions: The Pedagogy of Medieval Miracles', *Cahiers de Recherches Médiévales et Humanistes*, 19 (2010), 237–48

Kleinberg, Aviad M., *Flesh Made Word: Saints' Stories and the Western Imagination*, trans. by Jane Marie Todd (Cambridge, MA: Harvard University Press, 2008)

Koopmans, Rachel, *Wonderful to Relate: Miracle Stories and Miracle Collecting in High Medieval England* (Philadelphia: University of Pennsylvania Press, 2011)

Laidlaw, James, 'A Free Gift Makes No Friends', *The Journal of the Royal Anthropological Institute*, 6 (2000), 617–34

Lapidge, Michael, *Anglo-Latin Literature, 900–1066* (London: Hambledon, 1993)

Lapidge, Michael and Rosalind C. Love, 'England and Wales (600–1550)', in *Hagiographies: histoire internationale de la littérature hagiographique latine et vernaculaire, en Occident, des origines à 1500*, ed. by G. Philippart and M. Goullet, 7 vols (Turnhout: Brepols, 1994–2018), III, 203–325

Little, Lester K., *Benedictine Maledictions: Liturgical Cursing in Romanesque France* (Ithaca, NY: Cornell University Press, 1993)

MacCormack, Sabine, *Art and Ceremony in Late Antiquity* (Berkeley: University of California Press, 1981)

Mauss, Marcel, *The Gift: The Form and Reason for Exchange in Archaic Societies*, trans. by W. D. Halls (London: Routledge, 1990)

———, *Sociology and Psychology: Essays*, trans. by Ben Brewster (London: Routledge, 1979)

Mayr-Harting, Henry, 'Functions of a Twelfth-Century Shrine: The Miracles of St Frideswide', in *Studies in Medieval History: Presented to R. H. C. Davis*, ed. by Henry Mayr-Harting and R. I. Moore (London: Hambledon, 1985), pp. 193–206

McCormick, Michael, 'The Liturgy of War in the Early Middle Ages', *Viator*, 15 (1984), 1–24

Morris, Lawrence P., 'Did Columba's Tunic Bring Rain? Early Medieval Typological Action and Modern Historical Method', *Quaestio*, 1 (2000), 45–65

Nagy, Piroska, 'Religious Weeping as Ritual in the Medieval West', *Social Analysis*, 48.2 (Summer 2004), 119–37

Newman, Barbara, 'Possessed by the Spirit: Devout Women, Demoniacs, and the Apostolic Life in the Thirteenth Century', *Speculum*, 73 (1998), 733–70

Nilson, Ben, *Cathedral Shrines of Medieval England* (Woodbridge: Boydell, 1998)

———, 'The Medieval Experience at the Shrine', in *Pilgrimage Explored*, ed. by J. Stopford (Woodbridge: York Medieval Press, 1999), pp. 95–122

North Lee, Brian, 'The Expert and the Collector', in *Beyond Pilgrim Souvenirs and Secular Badges: Essays in Honour of Brian Spencer*, ed. by Sarah Blick (Oxford: Oxbow, 2007), pp. 4–16

Orchard, Nicholas, 'An Anglo-Saxon Mass for St Willibrord and Its Later Liturgical Use', *Anglo-Saxon England*, 24 (1995), 1–10

Parsons, David, '*Sacrarium*: Ablution Drains in Early Medieval Churches', in *The Anglo-Saxon Church*, ed. by L. A. S. Butler and R. K. Morris, Council for British Archaeology Research Report, 60 (London: Council for British Archaeology, 1986), pp. 105–20

Pfaff, Richard W., 'The Calendar', in *The Eadwine Psalter: Text, Image and Monastic Culture in Twelfth-Century Canterbury*, ed. by Margaret Gibson, and others, Publications of the Modern Humanities Research Association, 14 (University Park, PA: Pennsylvania State University Press, 1992), pp. 53–87

——, *The Liturgy in Medieval England: A History* (Cambridge: Cambridge University Press, 2009)

——, 'Telling Liturgical Times in the Middle Ages', in *Procession, Performance, Liturgy, and Ritual: Essays in Honour of Bryan R. Gillingham*, ed. by Nancy van Deusen, Musicological Studies, 62/8 (Ottawa: Institute of Mediaeval Music, 2007), pp. 43–64

Phelpstead, Carl, 'King, Martyr and Virgin: Imitatio Christi in Ælfric's *Life of St Edmund*', in *St Edmund, King and Martyr: Changing Images of a Medieval Saint*, ed. by Anthony Bale (Woodbridge: York Medieval Press, 2009), pp. 27–44

Powell, Hilary, '"Once Upon a Time There Was a Saint . . .": Re-evaluating Folklore in Anglo-Latin Hagiography', *Folklore*, 121 (2010), 171–89

Rattue, James, *The Living Stream: Holy Wells in Historical Context* (Woodbridge: Boydell, 1995)

Rawcliffe, Carole, 'Curing Bodies and Healing Souls: Pilgrimage and the Sick in Medieval East Anglia', in *Pilgrimage: The English Experience from Becket to Bunyan*, ed. by Colin Morris and Peter Roberts (Cambridge: Cambridge University Press, 2002), pp. 108–40

Ridyard, Susan J., '"Condigna Veneratio": Post-Conquest Attitudes to the Saints of the Anglo-Saxons', *Anglo-Norman Studies*, 9 (1986), 179–206

——, *The Royal Saints of Anglo-Saxon England: A Study of West Saxon and East Anglian Cults*, Cambridge Studies in Medieval Life and Thought: Fourth Series, 9 (Cambridge: Cambridge University Press, 1988)

Roach, Levi, *Kingship and Consent in Anglo-Saxon England, 871–978: Assemblies and the State in the Early Middle Ages* (Cambridge: Cambridge University Press, 2013)

Rollason, David, 'List of Saints Resting-Places in Anglo-Saxon England', *Anglo-Saxon England*, 7 (1978), 61–93

——, *Northumbria, 500–1100: Creation and Destruction of a Kingdom* (Cambridge: Cambridge University Press, 2003)

——, 'Relic-Cults as an Instrument of Royal Policy c. 900–c. 1050', *Anglo-Saxon England*, 15 (1986), 91–103

——, *Saints and Relics in Anglo-Saxon England* (Oxford: Blackwell, 1989)

Rosenthal, Joel T., 'Bede's Use of Miracles in "The Ecclesiastical History"', *Traditio*, 31 (1975), 328–35

Rosser, Gervase, 'Sanctuary and Social Negotiation', in *The Cloister and the World: Essays in Medieval History in Honour of Barbara Harvey*, ed. by John Blair and Brian Golding (Oxford: Clarendon, 1996), pp. 57–79

Rubenstein, Jay, *Guibert of Nogent: Portrait of a Medieval Mind* (London: Routledge, 2002)

Rüpke, Jörg, *The Religion of the Romans*, trans. by Richard Gordon (Cambridge: Polity, 2007)

Sahlins, Marshall, *Historical Metaphors and Mythic Realities: Structure in the Early History of the Sandwich Islands Kingdom* (Ann Arbor: University of Michigan Press, 1981)

——, *Islands of History* (Chicago, IL: University of Chicago Press, 1985)

Sallnow, Michael J., 'Communitas Reconsidered: The Sociology of Andean Pilgrimage', *Man*, New Series, 16 (1981), 163–82

Sexton, John P., 'Saint's Law: Anglo-Saxon Sanctuary Protection in the Translatio et Miracula S. Swithuni', *Florilegium*, 23.2 (2006), 61–80

Shaffern, Robert W., 'The Medieval Theology of Indulgences', in R. N. Swanson, ed., *Promissory Notes on the Treasury of Merits: Indulgences in Late Medieval Europe*, Brill's Companions to the Christian Tradition, 5 (Leiden: Brill, 2006), pp. 11–36

Sharpe, Richard, *Medieval Irish Saints' Lives: An Introduction to Vitae Sanctorum Hiberniae* (Oxford: Clarendon, 1991)

——, 'Words and Music by Goscelin of Canterbury', *Early Music*, 19 (1991), 94–97

Shenoda, Anthony, 'The Politics of Faith: On Faith, Skepticism, and Miracles among Coptic Christians in Egypt', *Ethnos*, 77 (2004), 477–95

Sigal, Pierre-André, *L'homme et le Miracle dans la France Médiévale, XIe-XIIe Siècle* (Paris: Cerf, 1985)

——, 'Naissance et Premier Développement d'un Vinage Exceptionnel: L'eau de Saint Thomas', *Cahiers de Civilisation Médiévale*, 52 (2001), 35–44

Slocum, Kay, 'Goscelin of Saint-Bertin and the Translation Ceremony for Saints Ethelburg, Hildelith and Wulfhild', in *Barking Abbey and Medieval Literary Culture: Authorship and Authority in a Female Community*, ed. by Jennifer N. Brown and Donna Alfano Bussell (Woodbridge: Boydell & Brewer, 2012)

Snoek, G. J. C., *Medieval Piety from Relics to the Eucharist: A Process of Mutual Interaction*, Studies in the History of Christian Thought, 63 (Leiden: Brill, 1995)

Stenton, Frank, ed., *The Bayeux Tapestry: A Comprehensive Study* (London: Phaidon, 1957)

Stewart, Charles, 'Ritual Dreams and Historical Orders: Incubation Between Paganism and Christianity', in *Archaeology, Anthropology and Heritage in the Balkans and Anatolia*, ed. by David Shankland, 2 vols (Istanbul: Isis, 2004), I, 31–53

Strang, Veronica, *The Meaning of Water* (Oxford: Berg, 2004)

Sumption, Jonathan, *Pilgrimage: An Image of Mediaeval Religion* (London: Faber, 1975)

Swanson, R. N., *Indulgences in Late Medieval England: Passports to Paradise?* (Cambridge: Cambridge University Press, 2007)

Tambiah, Stanley Jeyaraja, *The Buddhist Saints of the Forest and the Cult of Amulets*, Cambridge Studies in Social and Cultural Anthropology, 49 (Cambridge: Cambridge University Press, 1984)

Thacker, Alan, '*Loca Sanctorum*: The Significance of Place in the Study of the Saints', in *Local Saints and Local Churches in the Early Medieval West*, ed. by Alan Thacker and Richard Sharpe (Oxford: Oxford University Press, 2002), pp. 1–43

——, 'The Making of a Local Saint', in *Local Saints and Local Churches in the Early Medieval West*, ed. by Alan Thacker and Richard Sharpe (Oxford: Oxford University Press, 2002), pp. 45–73

——, 'Monks, Preaching and Pastoral Care in Early Anglo-Saxon England', in *Pastoral Care Before the Parish*, ed. by John Blair and Richard Sharpe (Leicester: Leicester University Press, 1992), pp. 137–70

Thiry-Stassin, M., 'L'hagiographie en Anglo-Normand', in *Hagiographies: histoire internationale de la littérature hagiographique latine et vernaculaire, en Occident, des origines à 1500*, ed. by G. Philippart and M. Goullet, 7 vols (Turnhout: Brepols, 1994–2018), I, 407–28

Thomson, Rodney M., *William of Malmesbury*, rev. edn (Woodbridge: Boydell, 2003)

Tudor, Victoria, 'The Misogyny of Saint Cuthbert', *Archaeologia Aeliana*, Fifth Series, 12 (1984), 157–67

Turner, Victor, 'Betwixt and Between: The Liminal Period in the *Rites de Passage*', in *Reader in Comparative Religion: An Anthropological Approach*, ed. by William A. Lessa and Evon Z. Vogt, 4th edn (New York, NY: Harper, 1979), pp. 234–43

——, *The Ritual Process: Structure and Anti-Structure* (New York, NY: Aldine de Gruyter, 1969)

Turner, Victor and Edith Turner, *Image and Pilgrimage in Christian Culture: Anthropological Perspectives* (Oxford: Blackwell, 1978)

Vincent, Nicholas, 'Some Pardoners' Tales: The Earliest English Indulgences', *Transactions of the Royal Historical Society*, 12 (2002), 23–58

Ward, Benedicta, *Miracles and the Medieval Mind: Theory, Record and Event 1000–1215* (Aldershot: Scolar, 1987)

Watkins, C. S., *History and the Supernatural in Medieval England*, Cambridge Studies in Medieval Life and Thought: Fourth Series, 66 (Cambridge: Cambridge University Press, 2007)

Weinstein, Donald and Rudolph M. Bell, *Saints and Society: The Two Worlds of Western Christianity, 1000–1700* (Chicago, IL: University of Chicago Press, 1982)

Whatley, E. Gordon, 'Late Old English Hagiography, ca. 950–1150', in *Hagiographies: histoire internationale de la littérature hagiographique latine et vernaculaire, en Occident, des origines à 1500*, ed. by G. Philippart and M. Goullet, 7 vols (Turnhout: Brepols, 1994–2018), II, 429–500

Wilson, Susan E., *The Life and Afterlife of John of Beverley: The Evolution of the Cult of an Anglo-Saxon Saint* (Aldershot: Ashgate, 2006)

Woodruff, Charles Eveleigh, 'The Financial Aspect of the Cult of St. Thomas of Canterbury', *Archaeologia Cantiana*, 44 (1932), 13–32

Yan, Yunxiang, 'Unbalanced Reciprocity: Asymmetrical Gift Giving and Social Hierarchy in Rural China', in *The Question of the Gift*, ed. by Mark Osteen (London: Routledge, 2002), pp. 67–84

Yarrow, Simon, *Saints and Their Communities: Miracle Stories in Twelfth Century England* (Oxford: Clarendon, 2006)

Index

Abbo 16, 25–6
Acca 47–8, 70, 73, 99, 112, 116
Aelred 18, 26
Alchmund 22, 47–8, 112
alternative sites of intercession 36–7, 71
animals: miraculous protection from 72, 75, 77, 100, 115; miraculous punishment involving 90, 102
Anselm 74–5, 77, 117
architecture 37–9, 48–9, 115–16
Arcoid 17–18, 19, 98, 104–5
Æthelburh 39–40, 49
Æthelthryth 67, 89, 90, 93–4, 98, 99
Æthelwold 15–16, 24, 45–7, 49, 79, 111
Augustine of Canterbury: beneficent miracles 36, 66–7, 69, 77–8, 112, 113, 116–17; punitive miracles 40–1, 90, 92, 99, 100, 102, 103
Augustine of Hippo 3

Babylas 44, 47–8
Bailey, Anne E. 42–3
Barking 17, 18, 36–7, 39–40, 49, 51
Becket, Thomas 4–5, 50, 115, 116
Bede 3, 4, 24, 27, 54, 71
Bege 88–90, 94, 99, 115, 117, 118
bells 1, 23, 45–6, 111–14, 123
Birinus 48–9
blindness, miraculous cures of 19, 22, 24, 37, 39, 44, 45, 47, 66–7, 70, 73, 76, 111, 112, 114–16; miraculous infliction with 90–4, 102, 103
Botulf 49
Bourdieu, Pierre 7, 128
brandea 44, 73
Brown, Peter 6–7, 43
Burton upon Trent 17, 88–9, 95–7, 111, 115

Bury St Edmunds 17, 38, 48, 50, 73, 75, 132–3, 136; miracles performed in 16, 24, 77, 88, 89, 91, 94, 101–3, 116, 117, 118
Byrhtferth 16, 25

calendars 23, 134–5
candles 36, 45–6, 51, 55, 80, 93; as offerings 1–2, 19, 72, 78, 89, 90, 100, 103, 114–15
canonisation 4–5, 18
Canterbury 17, 19, 20–1, 25, 37, 38, 48–9, 51, 52, 95, 113–14, 115 132–3; miracles performed in 22, 36, 40–1, 72, 74–5, 77–8, 92, 99, 100, 102, 103, 111, 112, 116–17
communality 7, 8, 56, 66, 114, 129
communitas 42–4
corporate thanksgiving 42, 111–14, 117
cult of the saints 2–7, 10, 19–25, 36–8, 66, 79, 118, 123–9; change in 23–4, 128–9; conflict in 20–2, 51–2, 95–6, 118–19, 127–9; contingency and 103, 124, 127–8; medieval critique of 103–05
Cuthbert 40, 50, 91–9, 112

deafness, miraculous cures of 116
death, miracles leading to 42, 87–9, 93–4, 100–1, 103
disability: miraculous cures of 24, 36–7, 39, 42, 46, 49, 55, 67, 69–71, 75–6, 110–11, 123; miraculous infliction with 40–1, 92–7, 102–3
doctors 69, 71, 80, 110
Dominic of Evesham 18, 25
dreams *see* visions
dumbness, miracles involving 1–2, 67, 87, 116

Index 153

Dunstan 15, 21, 25, 68; beneficent miracles 19, 35, 39, 70, 111, 112; punitive miracles 42; relics 72, 74
Durham 22, 38, 40, 91, 92, 134–5

Eade, John 43
Eadmer 17, 19, 21, 26; on miracles 3, 15, 25, 49
Eata 22, 47–8, 101–2
Ecgwine: beneficent miracles 1–2, 53, 55–6, 67, 72; punitive miracles 87–8, 92, 101, 117
Edith 89, 92, 94, 98–9, 103
Edmund the Martyr, king of East Anglia 16; beneficent miracles 22–3, 24, 37, 70, 116–17; punitive miracles 87–9, 91, 93–4, 101–3, 118; relics 49, 53, 52, 55, 73–4, 75
Edward the Confessor 38, 47, 50
Edward the Martyr 21, 49, 116
Egmond, Wolfert S. van 26
Ely 17, 20, 25, 51–2, 55, 89, 133, 136; miracles performed in 19, 67, 90, 93–4, 98, 99
Eormenhild 95
Erkenwald: beneficent miracles 19, 36–7, 69, 74, 78; punitive miracles 97–8, 100, 104–5; translation 39, 49, 51
Evesham 1–2, 18, 67, 87–8, 92, 117

fasting 69–70; examples of 45–6, 50, 54, 75, 87, 91, 103, 118
feast days: liturgy of 23–7, 113, 131–5; miracles on 39–40, 77, 88, 100–1, 104–5, 112
feretories *see* reliquaries; shrines
Finucane, Ronald 5, 6, 42
fire, miracles to extinguish 56, 77, 80
food and drink, miracles involving 100, 112
Frazer, James 73
Frithuberht 47–8

Geary, Patrick J. 27
Gennep, Arnold van 42–3
Geoffrey of Burton 3, 17, 20, 27, 66
Goscelin of Saint-Bertin 16–17, 21, 26, 27, 97–8; participating in saints' cults 19, 77
Graeber, David 7
Gregory of Tours 69
Gregory the Great 4, 37, 44–5, 73

Guibert of Nogent 105
Guthlac: miracles 88, 90, 91, 112; translation 48, 51, 124

Hadrian of Canterbury 70, 72
hagiography 5–6, 19–28, 43–4, 66, 125–6
Herman the Archdeacon 17, 19, 24, 26, 93
Hexham 18, 25, 26, 47–8; miracles performed in 22, 68, 70, 73, 91, 94, 101, 102, 112, 116
Hildelith 39, 49
humiliation of a saint 96–7
hymns 45–7, 76, 102, 111–4, 136

illness: miraculous cures of 18–19, 22–3, 49, 67, 70–6 110, 114, 117; miraculous infliction with 89, 95, 99, 102
imprisonment, miraculous freedom from 67–8, 76–7, 94
Indract 41
indulgences 41, 49–50
injury: miraculous cures of 69, 72, 76, 88–90, 92, 100; miraculous infliction with 86, 98, 100–2, 105, 116, 118
Ithamar 70, 72
Ivo: beneficent miracles 19, 37, 70, 72, 75, 77, 111; punitive miracles 89–90, 95, 97, 98, 100, 103, 105, 118

John of Beverley 36, 67, 94–5
Judoc 15, 25
Jurmin 49
Juthwara 71

Kenelm: beneficent miracles 37, 51–2, 110, 112; punitive miracles 87, 100, 104
Ketell, William 17
Koopmans, Rachel 7, 23

landscape 37
Lantfred 3, 15–16, 18–19, 25–6, 35–6, 110
Lapidge, Michael 136
Laudes Regiae 136
Laurence of Canterbury 49, 69, 113
legal system 41, 67–8, 76, 87–91, 93–7
litanies 55–6, 135–6
liturgy 15, 23, 27, 38–9, 113, 131–6
London 17–19, 39, 49, 50, 51; miracles performed in 53, 74, 78, 93, 97–8, 104–5, 115
Love, Rosalind 37

Martin of Tours 25, 45, 54, 69, 96–7, 113
Mass 4, 24, 55, 112, 131–3
material reciprocity 1–2, 98, 114–16
Mauss, Marcel 7, 118, 128
Mayr-Harting, Henry 43, 66
measuring and miracles 78, 128
medicine 70, 72, 88, 98, 99
Mellitus 49, 69
mementos of miracles 114–19
mental illness, miracles involving 40–1, 56, 68, 87, 89–90, 94
Mildburh 24, 72, 115
Mildrith: miracles 95, 98, 100, 111, 115, 117; translation 20–1, 37
miracle petitions 8, 75, 79, 101; failed 89, 103, 127; life crises and 41, 43, 68, 71, 79, 90, 117–19, 123–9; structure of 2, 65–8, 102, 105, 118–19, 127–9
miracles: distance miracles 75–9, 117; medieval definitions of 3–4; saints as agents of 66, 102–3, 119; unsolicited miracles 79–80; variety of 67–8, 101; witnesses to 16, 19, 21, 24–6, 39, 65–6; *see also* entries for categories of miracle; entries for locations; entries for saints
miracle stories 2–8, 15, 22–8, 36, 42, 66, 74–5, 117, 124–7; and pedagogy 27, 103–4

office 27, 46, 113, 131, 134
Osbern 17, 19, 25, 39, 112
Osbert of Clare 18, 20
Oswald of Worcester 49, 51, 55–6, 70, 75, 110
Oswine: miracles 36, 67, 70–1, 78, 100, 101, 102; translation 21–2
Osyth 50, 92, 97

penance 43, 50, 54, 67–8, 92–3
pilgrimage 2, 37, 41–3, 67–8, 79, 115–16
plague, miracles concerning 56, 93–4, 95–6, 98
possession: miracles of exorcism 68, 72, 74–5, 118; as punishment 88, 98, 101, 102
processions 24, 53–7, 88, 128–9, 135–6
property: land disputes 87–90, 103; lost property 68, 123; theft 91–2
prostration 68, 102; examples of 24, 47, 87–92, 96, 110, 112
psalms 39, 45–7, 52, 98, 112, 134; the seven penitential psalms 41, 48, 77, 87, 88, 91, 94, 96, 101–2

Ramsey 16–17, 25–6, 37, 51, 55; miracles performed in 19, 72, 75, 86–7, 89–90, 97, 98, 118
reciprocity 2, 6–7, 98, 114, 116–19
relics: contagious nature of 71, 73, 79; ownership of 19–25, 51–6, 92–4; secondary 38, 44, 70–5, 79, 92–4, 128; taken on tour 53; understanding of 4, 35–8, 41, 105, 125–6; use in miracles 87–8
reliquaries 37–9, 51, 53–7, 70, 73–5, 96–7; *see also* shrines; tombs
Ridyard, Susan J. 6–7
Robert of Shrewsbury 17–18
Rollason, David 6–7

Sahlins, Marshall 7
saints *see* entries for individual saints
Sallnow, Michael J. 43
sanctuary 40–1, 94–5
sea, miracles involving the 74, 77, 92
Seaxburh 23, 55, 98, 100
Sherborne 16–17, 41, 134; miracles performed in 36, 39, 71, 87–8, 100
shrines: activities at 22–3, 65–71, 90–3, 99–104, 114–15, 117–19, 125–9; description of 2, 7, 35–42, 79; physical interaction with 69–70; *see also* reliquaries; tombs
Sigal, Pierre-André 6, 42, 97
Swithun: beneficent miracles 18–19, 22, 24–5, 35–9, 41, 66–71, 75–80, 123–5; punitive miracles 86, 98, 100, 102–3; thanksgiving 110–11; translation 45–7

Te Deum Laudamus 1, 23, 46, 112–13, 117
Thanet 20–1, 37, 52, 98
thanksgiving *see* corporate thanksgiving; mementos of miracles; reciprocity; votives
Tilberht 47–8
tomb 4, 24–5, 36–41, 45–8, 71–4, 93–4; *see also* shrines
translation of relics 20–2, 44–53, 57, 92–4, 101–2, 123–5
Turner, Victor 7, 42–3

vigil 68–70; examples of 24, 39, 46, 53, 75, 77, 88, 90, 94, 99, 103, 111–14
visions 1–2, 22–3; examples of 41, 45, 49, 66–71, 74–9, 89, 92, 98–101, 111–12, 116
votives 38, 90, 92, 97, 114–19, 128

Wærburh 52
water: holy 37, 55, 102, 116; miraculous 71–5, 97–8, 105, 117, 128
weather, miracles involving the 49, 55–6, 77, 89, 91–2
weeping 68, 70, 88, 96–7, 112, 124
Wenefred 49, 72–3, 77
Wihtburh 37, 52, 55
William of Malmesbury 16, 18, 20, 21, 26
Winchester 15–16, 25, 35–9, 45–9, 77, 113, 124, 132–3; miracles performed in 41, 53, 66, 67, 70, 76, 78, 98, 103, 111, 114
Worcester 38, 49, 51–2; miracles performed in 56, 70, 75, 110, 135
Wulfhild 36, 39, 49
Wulfsige 39, 49, 71, 87–8, 100
Wulfstan II, bishop of Worcester 75, 101
Wulfstan the Cantor 16, 19, 26, 39, 45–9, 111–12

Yarrow, Simon 7, 65–6
Ywi 52